Economics, the Environment and Our Common Wealth

Dedicated to Betsy, Jamie and Tom

Economics, the Environment and Our Common Wealth

James K. Boyce

University of Massachusetts, USA

Edward Elgar

Cheltenham, UK • Northampton, MA, USA

Published by
Edward Elgar Publishing Limited
The Lypiatts
15 Lansdown Road
Cheltenham
Glos GL50 2JA
UK

Edward Elgar Publishing, Inc.
William Pratt House
9 Dewey Court
Northampton
Massachusetts 01060
USA

Reprinted 2014

A catalogue record for this book
is available from the British Library

Library of Congress Control Number: 2012941925

ISBN 978 1 78100 000 7 (cased)
      978 1 78254 020 5 (paperback)

Typeset by Servis Filmsetting Ltd, Stockport, Cheshire
Printed in Great Britain by Berforts Information Press Ltd

Contents

Figures

Tables

Acknowledgments

This book draws on a decade of writings since the publication of my book *The Political Economy of the Environment* in 2002. I have benefited greatly during this time from the knowledge and insights of the co-authors with whom I collaborated on earlier versions of several of these chapters: Manuel Pastor (Chapters 3 and 4), Robert Bullard, Alice Fothergill, Rachel Morello-Frosch and Beverly Wright (Chapter 3), Michael Ash, Grace Chang, Justin Scoggins and Jennifer Tran (Chapter 4), Jane d'Arista (Chapter 5), Matthew Riddle (Chapters 6 and 7) and Mark Brenner (Chapter 7).

I am grateful to Dorothy Andersen and the late Alfred Andersen for creating the Fair Sharing of the Common Heritage Award and to the Media Freedom Foundation and Project Censored for honoring me as its first recipient in 2011. Chapter 1, based on my acceptance speech, offers an ethical foundation for the remainder of the book.

Earlier versions of other chapters appeared in the following journals: Chapter 2 in *Research in Social Problems and Public Policy* (2008); Chapter 3 in *Race, Poverty and the Environment* (2006); Chapter 5 in *Challenge* (2002); Chapter 7 in *Energy Policy* (2007) and Chapter 9 in *Oxford Review of Economic Policy* (2004). I am grateful to the publishers for allowing me to publish revised versions of them here.

I am also grateful to Peter Barnes, Doris Ober, Richard Kirshman and the Mesa Refuge for their generous hospitality in Point Reyes Station, California, where this book was completed.

I thank my research assistants, Leila Davis and Alexis Doyle, for their help in preparing the manuscript; Alan Sturmer of Edward Elgar Publishing for his patience and support; and my wonderful colleagues at the Department of Economics and Political Economy Research Institute at the University of Massachusetts, Amherst, whose commitment to freedom of economic thought has made this my ideal intellectual home.

Finally, I want to thank the many people across the world whose daily struggles to defend our common right to a clean and safe environment are a source of constant inspiration.

Abbreviations

CASS	Chinese Academy of Social Sciences
CBO	Congressional Budget Office
CERT	Clean Energy Reinvestment Trust
CFCs	chlorofluorocarbons
CIMMYT	International Maize and Wheat Improvement Center
CLEAR Act	Carbon Limits and Energy for America's Renewal Act
CRA	Community Reinvestment Act
EFA	environmental finance authority
EKC	environmental Kutznets curve
EPA	(US) Environmental Protection Agency
EPCRA	Emergency Planning and Community Right-to-Know Act
FSC	Forest Stewardship Council
GDP	gross domestic product
GEF	Global Environment Facility
GNP	gross national product
IFI	international financial institution
IMF	International Monetary Fund
IPCC	Intergovernmental Panel on Climate Change
IRRI	International Rice Research Institute
NADB	North American Development Bank
NAFTA	North American Free Trade Agreement
NGO	non-governmental organization
NIOSH	National Institute for Occupational Safety and Health
NSSL	(US Department of Agriculture's) National Seed Storage Laboratory
OECD	Organization for Economic Cooperation and Development
OPEC	Organization of Petroleum Exporting Countries
PERI	Political Economy Research Institute
PIN	personal identification number
PPP	purchasing power parity
RFC	Reconstruction Finance Corporation
RSEI	Risk-Screening Environmental Indicators

S&Ls	savings and loan associations
SSB	(Chinese) State Statistics Bureau
TRI	Toxics Release Inventory
UNEP	United Nations Environment Programme

1. The environment as our common heritage

What does it mean to say that the environment is our 'common heritage'? On one level this is a simple statement of fact: when we are born, we come into a world that is not of our own making. The air we breathe, the water we drink, the natural resources on which our livelihoods depend, and the accumulated knowledge and information that underpin our ability to use these resources wisely – all these come to us as gifts of creation that have been passed on to us by preceding generations and enriched by their innovation and creativity.

Yet once we take seriously – as I do – the proposition that this common heritage belongs in common and equal measure to us all, we move beyond a positive statement of facts to a normative declaration of ethics. We move beyond an understanding of what *is* to an assertion of what *ought to be*.

To say that the environment belongs in common and equal measure to us all does not mean that we have inherited a free gift with no strings attached. For our common heritage carries with it a common responsibility: the responsibility to share the environment fairly among all who are alive today, and the responsibility to care for it wisely to ensure that our children, our grandchildren and the generations who follow will share fairly in our common heritage too.

Once we move onto the plane of morality, the proposition that the environment is our common heritage is no longer a simple matter. Indeed, the claim that the environment belongs in common and equal measure to us all may strike some as a utopian ideal – nice-sounding words but devoid of practical content.

Yet I believe that the fair sharing of our common environmental heritage is not only a real possibility, but also that it is in the process of becoming a reality here in the United States and across the world.

In making this claim, I do not wish to minimize the great environmental challenges that lie before us. From local landscapes burdened by toxic pollution and reckless resource extraction to the global threat of climate change, we can see the fruits of greed and short-sightedness, the results of the failure of our society and others to live up to the moral imperative summed up in the phrase 'fair sharing of the common heritage.'

But I am also mindful of the words of the late Raymond Williams, who wrote: 'To be truly radical is to make hope possible rather than despair convincing.' And I am conscious of the great steps forward that human-kind has made, and that through our struggles we continue to make, on the road to establishing that the environment is our common heritage both as a matter of moral principle and as a matter of law.

A CLEAN AND SAFE ENVIRONMENT AS A HUMAN RIGHT

Already today, the principle that the environment belongs in equal and common measure to all can be found enshrined in the most fundamental of legal documents: the constitutions of national governments and states.

For example, the Constitution of the Commonwealth of Massachusetts – the official name of my home state – says: 'The people shall have the right to clean air and water.' That's a direct quote.

The Constitution of the Republic of South Africa, adopted in 1994 fol-lowing the fall of the apartheid regime, states: 'Every person shall have the right to an environment which is not detrimental to his or her health or well-being.'

These constitutions – and many others at home and abroad – embrace the bedrock principle that access to a clean and safe environment is a human right.[1] It is not a privilege to be allocated on the basis of political power. It is not a commodity to be allocated on the basis of purchasing power. It is a right held in common and equal measure by all.

Of course, translating this lofty constitutional principle into on-the-ground practice is neither automatic nor simple. But the fact that the right to a clean and safe environment is embedded in constitutions around the world testifies to the great power of the common heritage ideal. And it helps to undergird and inspire efforts at home and abroad to translate this right into law and practice.

THE ENVIRONMENTAL JUSTICE MOVEMENT

The environmental justice movement is a prime example of such efforts. In combating disproportionate pollution burdens imposed upon low-income communities and people of color, the environmental justice movement today is claiming – or reclaiming – the right to a clean and safe environment.

An important tool for environmental justice activists, indeed for everyone who cares about the quality of the air they breathe and the water they drink, is right-to-know legislation such as the US Emergency Planning and Community Right to Know Act, passed in 1986 in the wake of the chemical disaster in Bhopal, India. The Act requires industrial polluters to disclose their releases of hundreds of toxic chemicals, and makes this information available to the public through the US Environmental Protection Agency's annual Toxics Release Inventory.[2] The simple fact that polluters know that the public has access to this information is sometimes enough to change their behavior – particularly when the right to know is coupled with communities actively voicing the demand for a clean and safe environment.

When communities stand up against polluters, they are sometimes accused of 'nimby-ism,' the not-in-my-back-yard philosophy that simply deflects pollution burdens onto other communities. The environmental justice movement has a clear and compelling reply to this charge: 'Not in anybody's back yard.'

But it would be utopian to imagine that we will be able prevent all pollution anytime soon. We can and must continue our efforts to reduce pollution, but we cannot expect to eliminate it altogether, at least not in our lifetimes.

What does the common heritage principle have to say, then, about the pollution that will not be prevented in the foreseeable future?

I believe there is a two-part answer to this question. First, pollution burdens should be distributed fairly, as advocated by the environmental justice movement, rather than concentrated in particular communities.

Second, polluters should pay for their use of the limited waste-absorptive capacities of our air and water. When polluters pay, they have an incentive to cut pollution above and beyond what is required by regulations. And in keeping with the principle that the environment belongs in common and equal measure to us all, the money the polluters pay should be distributed fairly to the public, as we are the ultimate owners of the air and water.

A COMMON HERITAGE CLIMATE POLICY

As an example of how this dimension of the common heritage principle could be translated into effective policy, consider the 'cap-and-dividend' climate bill that was introduced in the US Senate in December 2009 by Maria Cantwell (D-WA) and Susan Collins (R-ME), a bill that may be reintroduced when the country finally decides to tackle the problem of climate change.

The Cantwell-Collins Bill, officially called the Carbon Limits and

Energy for America's Renewal (CLEAR) Act, would put a ceiling (that is, a cap) on US carbon emissions from burning fossil fuels. To bring fossil fuels into the nation's economy, the oil and gas and coal companies will need to buy permits at monthly auctions.

Each permit will allow the firm to bring one ton of fossil carbon into the US economy, and ultimately into the atmosphere. Not one ton per year. One ton, period. Another ton will require another permit. In this way, buying a carbon permit is like putting money in a parking meter. Just as we pay to park an automobile on a city street, fossil fuel companies will pay to park carbon in the atmosphere. In both cases, the rationale is the same: there's a limited amount of parking space to be shared.

The total number of permits, fixed by the cap, will decline over time as the United States makes the transition to a clean energy economy. And as the permits become scarcer, their price will go up.

Most of the money from the permit auctions – 75 percent – will be returned directly to the American people in the form of equal per person 'dividends' paid out monthly via ATM withdrawals, electronic deposits into bank accounts or checks in the mail. The other 25 percent will be devoted to clean energy investments.

Unlike the cap-and-trade proposals that repeatedly have failed to pass the US Senate, the Cantwell-Collins Bill has no free giveaways of permits to polluters. Instead the polluters pay. And the permits are not tradable – any more than other sorts of permits, like parking permits or hunting permits, are tradable – so that unlike cap and trade, the bill does not create a new sandbox for Wall Street to play in.

If enacted into law, this cap-and-dividend policy will not only curb carbon emissions. It will also translate into very concrete practice – and into people's pocketbooks – the principle that the United States' share of the Earth's limited capacity to absorb carbon emissions belongs to all Americans in common and equal measure.[3]

CROP GENETIC DIVERSITY AS THE COMMON HERITAGE OF HUMANKIND

As a final example of how we can apply the common heritage principle to real-world challenges, I want to talk about seeds – specifically about rice, wheat, maize and the other crops on which we depend for our survival. These crops originated through what Charles Darwin called 'artificial selection,' as the earliest farmers saved and replanted seeds of those plants over successive generations that did best at providing palatable and nutritious food. In this way, they domesticated plants, breeding entirely new species that would never have come into existence without the guiding hand of human intervention.

This is perhaps the greatest example in history of what economists call 'investment in natural capital': human actions that positively enhance the ability of the environment to sustain our well-being in the long term.

Over the millennia, generations of farmers have bred hundreds of thousands of diverse crop varieties. This diversity is what enables plant breeders today to respond to outbreaks of new insect pests and crop diseases by finding resistant varieties.

Crop diversity is sustained in the field mainly by small farmers, most of them in the global South – maize farmers in southern and central Mexico; rice farmers in India, Bangladesh and Southeast Asia; potato farmers in the Andes; and so on. In so doing, these farmers provide an enormously valuable service to humankind, a service for which they currently receive no compensation.

In this case, the fair sharing of our common heritage does not only mean protecting crop diversity from a genetic version of the enclosure movement that privatized common agricultural lands in eighteenth-century Britain. It also means devising ways to reward small farmers, above all in the historic centers of crop genetic diversity in Latin America, Asia and Africa, for their vital contributions to long-term human food security.[4]

There is much in common between small-farmer movements around the world, many of which have banded together under the umbrella of the international alliance known as Via Campesina, and the environmental justice movement and efforts to forge a fair climate policy in the United States.

In these and other diverse arenas, these new environmentalists are upholding the moral principle that the environment, as our common heritage, should be shared fairly within the present generation and cared for responsibly on behalf of future generations.

This is why I believe that the common heritage principle is not a merely utopian aspiration. On the contrary, it is a powerful and living force in the world today. But we cannot be complacent. Although much has been achieved, much remains to be done.

As we join, each in our own way, in the common struggle to make this moral principle a practical reality, we can take heart both from the victories of those who came before us and from the knowledge that we have allies in this struggle across the globe.

We can take heart from the words penned by the nineteenth-century anti-slavery minister Theodore Parker, words repeated and made famous in more recent times by Dr Martin Luther King Jr: 'The arc of the moral universe is long, but it bends toward justice.'

We can take heart from the evidence all around us that history is on our side.

NOTES

1. For discussion, see Popovic (1996) and Meltz (1999).
2. The Right-to-Know Network has created a web-based interface that helps to put information from the Toxics Release Inventory into the hands of the public: see http://www.rtknet.org/db/tri (accessed 16 July 2012).
3. See Chapter 6 for a more extensive discussion of this policy. The text of the CLEAR Act is available on Senator Cantwell's website at http://www.cantwell.senate.gov/issues/CLEARAct.cfm (accessed 16 July 2012).
4. For a discussion of how to do this, see Chapter 8. See also Mann (2004).

REFERENCES

Mann, C. (2004), 'Diversity on the farm,' New York and Amherst, MA: Ford Foundation and Political Economy Research Institute.

Meltz, R. (1999), 'Right to a clean environment provisions in state constitutions, and arguments to a federal counterpart,' Washington, DC: Congressional Research Service.

Popovic, N. (1996), 'In pursuit of environmental human rights: commentary on the draft Declaration of Principles on Human Rights and the Environment,' *Columbia Human Rights Law Review*, **27**(487), 487–603.

2. Is inequality bad for the environment?

In the mid-1970s I lived in a rural village in northwestern Bangladesh, in one of the poorest parts of a poor country. Bangladesh had just had a famine in which some 200,000 people perished. The famine was caused not by an absolute shortage of rice, the staple food of the population, but rather by a combination of grain hoarding by merchants and government ineptitude and corruption. The village where I lived was located in the most famine-stricken district of the country.[1]

To the eyes of a young American, a striking feature of Bangladeshi village life – apart from the poverty of the people – was the virtual absence of negative environmental impacts from human activities. The villagers farmed rice and jute much as their ancestors had for centuries. Agrochemicals had only begun to appear on the scene, and village farmers used them sparingly if at all. Across the country, Bangladeshi farmers grew some 10,000 different varieties of rice adapted to microclimatic variations in rainfall, flood depths, temperature and soil type, making the country a storehouse for genetic diversity of humankind's most important food crop. Hundreds of fish species – more than in all Europe – lived in the country's rivers, ponds and rice paddies, supplying most of the animal protein in the Bangladeshi diet.

There was no trash-collection service in the village and no need for one, for the villagers produced little, if any, solid waste. Practically everything they consumed – food, cooking fuel, housing materials, herbal medicines – was harvested from their local environment. Crop residues and manures were returned to the earth or burned as fuel. Metal items were carefully recycled, tin containers fashioned into building supplies. Few villagers had ever seen plastic: local children amused themselves by repeatedly dropping a red plastic cup I had brought with me to the village, showing their friends that it did not break. Despite their poverty – in some ways, because of it – they did not harm the environment on which their livelihoods depended.

One time, while visiting Dhaka, Bangladesh's capital city, I stumbled upon what may have been the country's first environmental campaign. The government – a one-party state headed by a once-popular politician who recently had declared himself 'president for life' – had just announced a campaign of 'urban beautification.' Dhaka's sprawling slums, which had multiplied during the famine as starving people from the countryside migrated to the city in search of work or relief, were razed to the ground. Their inhabitants were brusquely herded onto trucks that deposited them outside town, far from the eyes and consciousness of the city's middle- and upper-class residents.

The human costs of this policy were vividly brought home to me by a scene I witnessed in front of Dhaka's general post office. An emaciated woman and her baby were sitting on a dirty cloth spread on the sidewalk. Passers-by occasionally dropped a coin. When I emerged from the post office a few minutes later, the woman was gone, perhaps trailing after a well-to-do stranger to plead for alms. Then a police truck drove by, its bed full of destitute people being relocated. Spying the baby, the truck pulled up and a policeman dismounted. He unceremoniously tossed her into the back of the truck, which lumbered off in search of more human cargo. I do not know whether they picked up the mother.

The irony was inescapable and terrible: in a land where they lived lightly on the earth, the poor themselves were regarded as pollution.

WHAT IS ENVIRONMENTAL HARM?

What does it mean to say something is 'bad for the environment' or 'good for the environment'? These value judgments rest, implicitly or explicitly, on ethical criteria by which we distinguish better from worse.

A criterion that has gained many adherents in the past two decades is 'sustainable development.' The World Commission on Environment and Development defined this in its 1987 manifesto, *Our Common Future* (known as the Brundtland Report, after Commission Chair Gro Brundtland), as development that 'meets the needs of the present without compromising the ability of future generations to meet their own needs.' By this criterion, 'environmental harm' means actions that compromise the ability of future generations to meet their needs. Conversely, 'environmental improvements' would refer to actions that enhance the ability of future generations to meet their needs.

The Brundtland criterion has the merits of affirming the importance of human well-being and our responsibility to future generations. But as Nobel Prize-winning economist Amartya Sen (2004) has remarked, 'Seeing people in terms of only their needs may give us a rather meagre view of humanity.' Sen suggests that the ethical basis for value judgments about the environment can be deepened by embracing a broader range of human values. For example, people may believe that we have a responsibility to safeguard the existence of other species (as an illustration, Sen mentions the spotted owl of the Pacific northwest) regardless of whether the species in question serves any practical human needs. In other words, people may value nature for intrinsic as well as instrumental reasons. If so, environmental quality can be seen as an end in itself, and not merely a means to other ends.

Sen also observes that people hold multiple values, and that these cannot be readily reduced to a summary measure such as overall fulfillment of human needs. For example, we may believe that future generations have the right to breathe clean air, and that infringement of this right cannot be adequately compensated by improvements in other dimensions of well-being. Not everything of value can be calibrated on a single scale.

This broader ethical framework – in which 'we think of human beings as agents, rather than merely as patients,' in Sen's words – implies a central role for citizenship in addressing environmental challenges. Freedom to make value judgments about environmental change, and rights to a clean and safe environment, are themselves important ethical objectives. This is not only a matter of moral vision, but also of practical politics. The extent to which people are able to act as citizens depends on how power is structured and distributed in society.

In this chapter, I use the term 'environmental harm' to mean impacts on the natural environment that reduce human well-being, with the latter understood to extend beyond needs to the wider canvas of values and rights. To say that actions are bad (or good) for the environment is to say that they are bad (or good) for humankind.

This ethical stance makes no pretense of impartiality: it is unabashedly human-centered. I do not regard *Homo sapiens* as just another species, whose well-being is of no greater consequence than that of any other. In many cases, what is good for other species is good for humans too. But not always. Sanitation and clean water-supply systems, for instance, improve human well-being by killing bacteria and other pathogens. I regard this as a good thing, an environmental improvement. The eradication of smallpox – the deliberate extinction of a virus species – counts as a good thing too. This stance does not imply a willful disregard for nature, nor indifference to the fates of other species. On the contrary, an environmental ethics grounded in human well-being recognizes that we are a part of nature, not apart from it.

THREE QUESTIONS

Whenever we analyse economic activities that generate environmental harm, we can pose three very basic questions:

- Who benefits from the economic activities that cause the harm? If no one benefits – or at least thinks they do – the activities would not occur.
- Who suffers environmental harm? If no one is hurt by these activities, they are not a problem – at least not in terms of human well-being.
- Why is the first group able to impose environmental harm on the second? That is, what allows some people to benefit at the expense of others?

The last of these questions is crucial to understanding the reasons for environmental harm. There are three possible answers to it.

One possibility is that those who are harmed belong to future generations, who are not here to defend themselves. In this case, the only remedy is to cultivate an ethic of intergenerational responsibility, one founded on a moral commitment to safeguard the well-being of our children and generations to come.

The second possibility is that those who are harmed lack information. They may know that their children are falling ill, for example, but not know what environmental circumstances are making them sick or who is responsible for them. In this case, the solution lies in greater access to information: environmental education in general and right-to-know laws in particular. In the United States, for example, the Toxics Release Inventory, which makes information on releases of toxic chemicals by industrial facilities, is available to the public.

The final possibility is that those who are harmed are alive today and well aware of the costs imposed on them, but lack the power to prevail in making social decisions about the environment. In this case, the solution lies in redistributing power, so that those who suffer environmental harm are better able to defend themselves – and the environment – from others who benefit from activities that cause the problem.

PURCHASING POWER AND POLITICAL POWER

Human beings are socially differentiated in terms of wealth and influence. Differences in wealth translate into differences in purchasing power. Differences in influence translate into differences in political power.

In this respect humans are different from other species. Consider, for example, pondweed, a plant species sometimes used by ecologists to illustrate the perils of exponential growth (see, for example, Brown 1978). Assume that the weed doubles in volume every day, and that in 30 days it will fill the pond completely, making further growth impossible and perhaps overwhelming ecological balances vital to the continued existence of the pondweed itself. When, the ecologist asks, is the pond half full? The answer, of course, is the 29th day. This parable is invoked to depict human pressure on the carrying capacity of planet Earth: metaphorically speaking, we are nearing the end of the month.

Each pondweed organism is pretty much like any other. But humans differ greatly from one another, both in their impacts on the environment and in their ability to shield themselves from these impacts. The pondweed analogy deflects attention from these differences, and from how they affect our interactions with nature.

To understand how inequalities among humans contribute to environmental harm, we need to look more closely at the two types of power: purchasing power and political power.

Purchasing Power

In a market economy, people vote on what to produce in proportion to the money they spend. Economists call this 'effective demand.' This differs from simple desire or need. A person can be hungry, and in that sense have demand for food, but she does not have effective demand – the ability to vote in the marketplace – unless hunger in her stomach is backed up by money in her pocket. The distribution of purchasing power determines how much of society's resources will be devoted to producing rice and beans, and how much to producing champagne and luxury automobiles.

Purchasing power plays a central role in describing what happens in markets. In cost-benefit analysis, it also plays a central role in prescribing what should happen if and when the government intervenes to correct 'market failures' that arise in cases of public goods, like highways, schools and national defense, and in cases of externalities, like pollution, that affect people who are not party to the market exchange between buyer and seller.

When the government promulgates regulations to curtail pollution, for example, it must confront the practical question: how much pollution is too much? It would be nice to live in a world with no pollution whatsoever, but, as economists are quick to point out, cutting pollution has costs as well as benefits. People need and want to eat, wear clothes, use medicines, move about and so on, and producing these goods and services often produces some pollution too. Faced with the choice between more goods and services and less pollution, and informed by the principle of diminishing returns (the more we have of anything, the less each additional increment is worth), the economist tells the government to aim for the 'optimal level of pollution,' defined as the point at which society's benefit from additional pollution reduction equals its cost in terms of forgone consumption of other goods and services.

The phrase 'optimal level of pollution' rankles many environmentalists, but it is hard to argue with the logical proposition that the costs and benefits of any course of action ought to be weighed against each other. The problem is how to measure all the relevant costs and benefits. The economist has a toolkit for this purpose: cost-benefit analysis. It translates all costs and benefits into a single unit of measurement, money. Economists have devised ingenious ways to translate non-market values – such as the value of cleaner air or the existence of the spotted owl – into monetary terms. Contingent valuation surveys, for example, are used to ask people how much they would be willing to spend for environmental quality – say, to protect an endangered species. Hedonic regression analysis, another popular technique, uses actual market data to infer implicit prices; for example, by analysing how housing prices vary with distance from an airport (controlling for other variables like the size of the house) in order to measure the cost of noise pollution.

The foundation for the valuation techniques of cost-benefit analysis is willingness to pay. The costs of environmental harms are measured by how much people are willing to pay to avoid them. This is how demand for goods and services is measured in the marketplace, so there is a certain consistency in using the same criterion to measure demand for environmental quality, and in using the results in making public policy. The willingness-to-pay criterion for valuation means, however, that the needs and desires of some people count more than the needs and desires of others – not necessarily because their desire for clean air or water is any stronger, but because they wield more purchasing power to back up their preferences.

Behind differences in willingness to pay lie differences in ability to pay. If my willingness to pay for gold mined near your community is high, and your community's ability (and hence willingness) to pay to protect its air and water from pollution by mining operations is low, then by the logic of the cost-benefit analyst I should get the gold and you should get the pollution. In this way, differences in purchasing power can affect not only decisions made by private parties in response to market signals, but also public-policy decisions made by governments.

Political Power

In practice, real-world political systems do not faithfully adhere to the prescriptions of cost-benefit analysts. Individuals, groups and classes differ from each other not only in their purchasing power but also in their political power. The latter includes differences in their ability to influence social decisions on environmental policies. As a result, costs and benefits may be weighted differently depending on who bears the costs and who gets the benefits. In effect, some costs and benefits may count more than others.

Political power takes various forms:

- decision power to prevail in contests to determine what decision-makers, both public and private, will or will not do;
- agenda power to keep questions off (or on) the table of the decision-makers;
- value power to shape others' preferences to coincide with one's own; and
- event power to alter the circumstances that others face – for example, by blowing smoke into the atmosphere – thus presenting them with a fait accompli.

Each of these forms of power can lead to decisions that diverge from the optimum prescribed by cost-benefit analysis.[2]

If political power were distributed equally across the population, and social decisions were based simply on cost-benefit calculations, then purchasing power would be the only dimension of human differentiation that matters for environmental decisions. Once we recognize, however, that political power in practice is unequally distributed, and that it tends to be correlated with purchasing power – that is, wealth and political influence generally go together – then both dimensions of social differentiation matter.

THE ENVIRONMENTAL IMPACT OF INEQUALITY: TWO HYPOTHESES

Two hypotheses can be advanced about the environmental impact of inequalities in the distribution of purchasing power and political power:

- First, environmental harm is not randomly distributed across the population, but instead reflects the distribution of wealth and power. The relatively wealthy and powerful tend to benefit disproportionately from the economic activities that generate environmental harm. The relatively poor and powerless tend to bear a disproportionate share of the environmental costs.
- Second, the total magnitude of environmental harm depends on the extent of inequality. Societies with wider inequalities of wealth

and power will tend to have more environmental harm. Conversely, societies with relatively modest degrees of economic and political disparities will tend to have less environmental harm.

Environmental Injustice

The first hypothesis operates on both the benefit side and the cost side of the coin. Benefits from economic activities that inflict environmental harm accrue to consumers insofar as the savings from cost externalization (for example, releasing toxic chemicals out the smokestack rather than spending money on pollution control) are passed to them in the form of lower prices. Benefits accrue to the owners of firms insofar as they are able to capture these savings in the form of higher profits. On the consumer side, the rich generally get a bigger share of the benefits, for the simple reason that they consume more than the poor. On the producer side, again they get a bigger share of the benefits, since they own more productive assets, including corporate stocks. For these reasons, no matter what the division of gains between consumers and firms, the rich reap the largest share. Even if the costs of environmental harm were equally shared by all – for example, if everyone breathes the same polluted air and drinks the same polluted water – this would skew the net benefits from environmentally harmful economic activities in favor of the wealthy.

In practice, many environmental costs are localized, rather than being uniformly distributed across space. This makes it possible for those who are relatively wealthy and powerful to distance themselves from environmental harm caused by economic activities (Princen 1997). Within a metropolitan area, for example, the wealthy can afford to live in neighborhoods with cleaner air and more environmental amenities. Furthermore, sometimes there are private substitutes for public environmental quality. In urban India, for instance, where public water supplies are often contaminated, the upper and middle classes can afford to consume bottled water. The poor cannot. In such cases, because access to private substitutes is based on ability to pay, again the rich are better able to avoid environmental harm.

A substantial literature on environmental justice in the United States has documented the fact that low-income people and communities of color (that is, communities with above-average percentages of non-white and non-Anglo residents) often bear disproportionate environmental harms – see, for example, Szasz and Meuser (1997), Bullard and Johnson (2000), Pastor (2003), Bullard (2008) and Mohai (2008). These findings are consistent with the first hypothesis. A number of these studies have found that race and ethnicity matter, even when controlling for income: communities with higher percentages of African-Americans, Latinos, Asian-Americans and Native Americans tend to face greater environmental hazards – see, for example, Bouwes et al. (2003) and Ash and Fetter (2004). This finding suggests that political power (which is correlated with race and ethnicity in the United States) has an impact on exposure to environmental harm, above and beyond whatever can be explained simply by differences in purchasing power.

Even in cases of environmental harm from which there is no escape – widely dispersed pollutants and global climate change are examples – those who are relatively poor and powerless tend to be most vulnerable. Living closest to the margin of survival, they have the least ability to withstand adversity. They have less ability to afford remedial measures, like health care. And they have less political clout to secure remedial actions from government authorities. Similar vulnerability disparities are revealed by natural disasters, as when Hurricane Katrina hit New Orleans in August 2005 (see Chapter 3).

More Inequality, More Harm?

The second hypothesis – that more inequality causes more environmental harm overall – may be less intuitively evident than the first. Inequalities of wealth and power could have two opposing effects. When the beneficiaries from environmentally harmful activities are more powerful than those who bear their costs, greater inequality can be expected to result in more environmental harm. On the other hand, when those who bear the costs are more powerful than the beneficiaries, we might expect the opposite: greater inequality yields less environmental harm.

Which scenario is more common? The second one certainly occurs, for example, when African tribespeople are expelled from their traditional hunting grounds on the grounds that their activities are environmentally harmful, in order to create protected areas for the enjoyment of affluent foreign tourists, a phenomenon that has been labeled 'coercive conservation.'[3] The slum clearance program in Bangladesh described in the opening paragraphs of this chapter is another example. But there are good reasons to believe that the first scenario is far more prevalent. If, as I have argued above, the benefits of environmentally harmful activities flow disproportionately to the relatively well-off by virtue of their higher consumption and capital ownership, and purchasing power is correlated with political power, it follows that the beneficiaries of these activities tend to be more powerful than those who bear net costs – in which case, wider inequalities can be expected to translate into greater environmental harm.

In a statistical test of the second hypothesis, Boyce et al. (1999) found that among the 50 US states, those with more equitable distributions of power (measured by voter participation, educational attainments, tax fairness and Medicaid access) tend to have stronger environmental policies and better environmental outcomes. Further evidence in support of this hypothesis comes from a study of the relationship between residential segregation and cancer risks from air pollution in the United States, which found that greater segregation along racial and ethnic lines is correlated with worse environmental and health outcomes for all groups, not only for people of color (Morello-Frosch and Jesdale 2006).

Similarly, cross-country studies at the international level have found that a more equitable distribution of power – measured by such variables as democracy, political and civil rights and adult literacy – is correlated with better environmental quality, even while controlling for other variables such as differences in per capita income.[4]

In sum, both theoretical reasoning and empirical evidence support the conclusion that inequality is bad for the environment. People are not like pondweed. How we treat the natural environment depends on how we treat each other.

ROOM FOR HOPE

There is another important way that humans differ from pondweed: we have brains. Indeed we are exceptional among all species in our ability to accumulate knowledge, pass it from one generation to the next and change our behavior accordingly. This includes knowledge about our interactions with the natural environment and with each other.

Respecting Nature's Limits

We can learn how to respect nature's limits, and thus how to limit environmental harm – if we choose to do so. We can learn about the growth rates of renewable natural resources, such as trees in forests and fish in the sea, and we can manage our own harvests of these resources to ensure sustainable yields. We can learn about nature's finite stocks of non-renewable resources, such as minerals and fossil fuels, and we can develop recycling and renewable alternatives to avert future shortages. We can learn about the limited capacity of air, land and water bodies to safely absorb and break down wastes, and we can limit the rates at which we discharge pollutants accordingly.

As an illustration, consider our response to the threat posed by chemicals that were depleting the Earth's protective ozone layer, exposing life on the planet to increasing levels of ultraviolet-B radiation. The danger was not recognized until the early 1970s, when scientists first hypothesized that chlorofluorocarbons (CFCs), man-made compounds used for a variety of purposes, including aerosol propellants and air conditioner coolants, were breaking down ozone molecules in the Earth's stratosphere. The harm was invisible but insidious. In a remarkable instance of international co-operation, by 1987 the nations of the world had agreed to curtail their CFC emissions via the Montreal Protocol (Haas 1992). No other species is capable of such conscious self-regulating behavior.

Of course, to say that we can modify our actions on the basis of knowledge about nature's limits does not mean that we necessarily will do so. But if we choose to act, we can. And, as the Montreal Protocol illustrates, sometimes we do. The question is, why do we act to protect the environment in some times and places, and not in others? The answer, I believe, is that whether and how we act (or fail to act) depends on the balance of power in the present generation between those who benefit by ignoring nature's limits and those who pay the price, and on whether we embrace an ethic of responsibility toward future generations.

Nor do I wish to imply that humans are omniscient, understanding fully the consequences of our actions. Had scientists been a few decades slower to grasp the environmental implications of CFC emissions, we might not have recognized the threat until it was too late. We need to understand not only nature's limits, but also the limits of our own knowledge. Given the uncertainties and unknowns about the environmental impacts of our actions, prudence demands that we adopt a 'precautionary' approach to environmental policy (for discussions, see Harremoës et al. 2002; Dorman 2005).

Investing in Nature's Wealth

Humans are not only capable of depleting nature's wealth; we can also increase it. If our value system is founded on long-term human well-being – if this is the basis on which we compare states of the world, and define what is good and bad for the environment – then we can improve the environment as well as harm it.

There are three ways that humans invest in nature's wealth:

- *Ecological restoration* repairs past harms. Examples include the reforestation of deforested landscapes; the replenishment of depleted fisheries; the cleanup of contaminated soils and water bodies; and the restoration of degraded wildlife habitat.[5]
- *Co-evolution* refers to human modifications that create an environment that is better able to support long-term human well-being.

One example is 'soil banking': farming practices that build deeper and more fertile soils, such as *terra preta do indio* ('dark earth of the Indians') in Amazonia (Mann 2002) and those of the *acequia* landscape mosaic in the upper Rio Grande bioregion of the south-western United States (Peña 2003).[6] Another example – arguably the most valuable investment in nature's wealth in human history – is the domestication of plants and animals that began some 10,000 years ago, and the subsequent evolution of genetic diversity in crops and livestock (see Chapter 8).

- *Environmental preventive health* refers to measures to reduce the prevalence of pathogens and disease-bearing insects. One example, already mentioned, is the eradication of the smallpox virus through an international effort that culminated in the mid-1970s. Another example is the modification of aquatic habitats to reduce mosquito populations, a form of investment that played a major role in eliminating malaria from Europe and North America (Kitron and Spielman 1989; Willott 2004).

In all three ways, human beings can and sometimes do improve the environment, from the standpoint of long-term human well-being. Humans are not necessarily a blight on the face of the planet, a cancer that ultimately will destroy its host. We have learned a great deal about how to respect nature's limits and invest in nature's wealth, and we have the capacity to learn more. In our dealings with nature, there is room for hope.

Making Social Change

The inequalities of power and wealth that generate environmental harm are not forces of nature. Political and economic disparities are social constructions, and as such they can be reconstructed.

To be sure, there is no certainty that social change will proceed inexorably toward more democratic distributions of political power and more egalitarian distributions of purchasing power. It is all too easy to find past and present examples of movements in the opposite direction. But to say that something is not inevitable is not to say that it is impossible.

In fact, an even stronger claim is possible: there is ample evidence that the overall trend in human history, notwithstanding periodic reversals, is toward more equality in our social arrangements. Only three centuries ago, monarchs and aristocracies ruled most of the world. A century and a half ago, slavery was still legal in much of the United States. The state of Massachusetts, the first in the country to mandate free primary education for all children, did so only in 1852; it was not until 1918 that all states had followed suit. The amendment to the US Constitution that granted women the right to vote was adopted less than a century ago. In much of Asia and Africa, colonial rule ended only two generations ago. It has been less than two decades since apartheid ended in South Africa. As Dr Martin Luther King reminded us, the moral arc of the universe bends toward justice.

There is room for hope in our dealings with each other too.

ONE WORLD, READY OR NOT

Both the prospects and the need for changes in our relationships with nature and each other are affected by changes in the scale at which human interactions occur. For much of human history, the implications of the fact that we share a single planet were hidden from view by spatial fragmentation. This slowly changed over time, especially with the development of agriculture, states and more effective means of transport beginning some ten millennia ago. The pace of change accelerated in the past few centuries, in the process nowadays dubbed 'globalization.' Today, the fact that we live in one world is not only a physical reality, but also an economic, cultural and political reality.

Uneven Globalization: Markets and Governance

Globalization has proceeded most rapidly in the economic arena. Around the world, production and consumption increasingly are being integrated into a single market. Indeed, for many the term 'globalization' has come to signify not only the process of economic integration, but also the subordination of more and more economic activity across the globe to the laws of the market. The extension of the market brings tangible benefits, as Adam Smith famously observed in *The Wealth of Nations*: responding to price signals, decentralized producers are guided by an 'invisible hand' to specialize in what they can make most cheaply, unleashing impressive productivity gains.

But the market also has important limitations:

- *Market failure*: One way to make goods cheaply is to push costs onto others – generating what economists call negative externalities. For example, firms that do not spend money on pollution control may enjoy a competitive advantage over firms that do. As markets extend their reach, the costs of such market failures can grow alongside the benefits of specialization.
- *Fairness*: The production and distribution of goods and services for

the market are driven by effective demand – that is, willingness to pay backed by ability to pay. An inequitable distribution of purchasing power leads to an inequitable distribution of resources.

- *Resilience*: The market pursues a logic of short-term optimization: lowest-cost producers using the 'best' technology can undersell rivals and ultimately drive them out of business. As a result, producers tend to converge on the same technology. Yet resilience – the ability to withstand shocks and adapt to changing circumstances – requires a range of alternative technological options (Rammel and van den Bergh 2003).
- *Moral capital*: Finally, by elevating a narrowly conceived 'self-interest' above all other values, markets may lead to depreciation of moral capital that is crucial to the functioning of society. In fact, widespread commitment to moral precepts is necessary for markets themselves to function, since respect for rights and contractual obligations typically rests not on self-interest but instead on accepted norms about what is the right thing to do (for discussion, see Basu 1983; Sen 1986; Bell 1996).

For all four reasons, the globalization of markets needs to be complemented by the globalization of governance. The latter includes not only formal international institutions and inter-governmental agreements but also informal governance by non-state institutions and networks. Many of the problems associated with globalization arise from the fact that it has been uneven: the development of global governance has lagged behind the development of global markets.[7]

NAFTA and the Environment: A Case Study in Uneven Globalization

The environmental consequences of uneven globalization can be illustrated by looking at the effects of the North American Free Trade Agreement (NAFTA), the free trade agreement among the United States, Mexico and Canada that came into effect in 1994. In the early 1990s, the debate over NAFTA split the US environmental movement. Some maintained that the trade agreement would promote 'harmonization upwards,' a continental convergence to higher environmental standards, by generating higher incomes and stronger demand for environmental protection in Mexico. Others contended that it would spark a 'race to the bottom,' as firms moved (or threatened to move) south of the US-Mexico border to take advantage of lax environmental regulations.

Both sides in the debate shared one premise: environmental practices in Mexico were evidently inferior to those in the United States and

Canada. This assumption helps to explain why few environmentalists voiced concern about what in the end may turn out to be NAFTA's most profound environmental impact: the erosion of Mexico's rich heritage of genetically diverse maize varieties by imports of cheap corn from the United States.

Maize ('corn' in US parlance) is the single most important crop in both countries.[8] On the eve of NAFTA, US maize was sold at roughly $110 per ton at the border, whereas Mexican growers were receiving $240 per ton for their crops. With the dismantling of trade barriers, the Mexican price is now converging to the lower US price, undermining the livelihoods of Mexican *campesinos*.[9]

By the measuring stick of market prices, US farmers are more efficient than Mexican growers. But this competitive edge results, in no small measure, from the neglect of market failures on both sides of the border, as well as from government subsidies and natural advantages such as more regular rainfall in the US corn belt (Boyce 1996; Wise 2010). US corn production relies on massive applications of pesticides, fertilizers and energy inputs, all of which generate substantial environmental harm. The resulting costs do not figure into the market price.

At the same time, the *campesino* farmers of southern and central Mexico today provide a great 'positive externality' to humankind by sustaining genetic diversity in one of the world's most important food crops. In their small plots, where corn was first domesticated some seven millennia ago, the maize plant continues to evolve via the process Darwin called 'artificial selection,' as farmers select seeds for the following year's crop from the plants that perform best in the face of changing conditions. Mexican farmers still grow thousands of varieties of maize. In the United States, by contrast, fewer than a dozen varieties now account for half of the country's total corn acreage.

As a result of its low diversity, the US corn crop has a high degree of genetic vulnerability – the eggs-in-one-basket syndrome – a problem dramatically revealed in 1970 when a new strain of leaf blight destroyed one-fifth of the nation's harvest. In the effort to stay ahead of the insects and plant diseases that evolve rapidly in genetically uniform fields, US plant breeders engage in a varietal relay race, constantly seeking to develop new resistant varieties. The average commercial lifespan of a corn variety in the United States is only seven years, after which new ones replace it (Duvick 1984, p. 164). In effect, modern agriculture substitutes diversity through time – the replacement of one variety by another – for diversity at any point in time. The raw material that plant breeders use in this relay race is the genetic diversity that has been bequeathed to us by generations of small farmers in Mexico and elsewhere.[10]

The irony is that under NAFTA, the success of US corn production in the marketplace is undermining the genetic base on which its own long-term viability depends. The globalization of the market is being accompanied by the globalization of market failure, and a loss of resilience. In the short term, the main people harmed by this process are the Mexican *campesinos*, who lack the political power to ensure that their investments in nature's wealth are rewarded. In the long term, those harmed are future generations around the world, whose food security is being undermined by the erosion of crop genetic diversity.

Remedying this environmental harm will require more than defensive actions by single individuals, communities or states, important though these may be. Ultimately this and other transnational environmental problems require building institutions that bridge the gap between the globalization of markets and the globalization of governance (see Chapter 9).

CONCLUDING REMARKS

In this chapter, I have explored some of the implications of recognizing that environmental harm is not a random by-product of economic activities, but instead a cost that is imposed on some and that benefits others. Rectifying the market failures and governance failures that lead to environmental harm requires repairing the disparities of wealth and power that enable these failures.

This does not mean that greater equality is a panacea for all environmental ills. A more democratic distribution of power and a more egalitarian distribution of wealth are not all that is needed to prevent environmental harm. To say that these are necessary does not imply that they are sufficient. Safeguarding the natural environment will also require us to cultivate an ethic of moral responsibility to others – particularly when the costs of environmental harm would primarily fall upon future generations.

We can have a healthy environment, and bequeath one to future generations, by respecting nature's limits and investing in nature's wealth. Achieving these goals does not only require rebalancing our relationships with nature. It will also require rebalancing our relationships with our fellow humans.

NOTES

*   This chapter is a revised version of an essay originally published in *Research in Social Problems and Public Policy* (2008), **15**, 267–88.

1. For accounts of the famine and its causes, see Sen (1981) and Ravallion (1987). For an account of the life in the village, see Hartmann and Boyce (1979, 1983).
2. For discussion, see Bartlett (1989) and Boyce (2002).
3. See, for example, Peluso (1993), Neumann (2001) and Mulder and Coppolillo (2005, pp. 31–7).
4. See, for example, Torras and Boyce (1998) and Barrett and Graddy (2000). For a review of these and other studies, see Boyce (2007).
5. For examples, see Narain and Agarwal (2007) on water harvesting in semi-arid zones of rural India, and Rahman and Minkin (2007) on the rehabilitation of inland fisheries in Bangladesh. A distinction is sometimes made between restoration and rehabilitation, with the former referring to returning an ecosystem to 'its historic trajectory' and the latter to 'the reparation of ecosystem processes, productivity and services' (Society for Ecological Restoration 2004). If humans are regarded as an alien species – if we are truly apart from nature, not a part of it – this distinction makes sense: one may imagine the 'historic trajectory' of ecosystems in the absence of any human impacts whatsoever. In my view, this is a peculiar view of history. In any event, proponents of this distinction have concluded that restoration 'probably encompasses a large majority of project work that has previously been identified as rehabilitation' (Society for Ecological Restoration 2004).
6. For more examples of soil banking, see Brookfield (2001, pp. 96–7).
7. See Chapter 9 and Young (1994).
8. Michael Pollan (2006, pp. 22–3) observes that once the cycling of corn through animals is counted, the average American today has more corn in his diet than the average Mexican.
9. For further discussion, see Chapters 8 and 9. So far, the sharp decline in Mexican corn production that was predicted by many as a result of NAFTA has not occurred, apparently because economic opportunities elsewhere in the Mexican economy have been so scarce (see Ackerman et al. 2003).
10. Samples of many Mexican maize varieties are stored in 'seed banks' at agricultural research institutes. But seed banks are insecure, being subject to the perennial hazards of inadequate funding, accidents and war. Moreover, having seeds in the bank is not the same as knowing about varietal properties such as pest resistance and climate sensitivity, information that is most readily obtained in the field. And seed banks can only conserve a static sample of genetic diversity; they cannot maintain the dynamic process of evolution that happens in the farmers' fields. For further discussion of the value of *in situ* (in-the-field) crop genetic diversity, see Chapter 8. See also Brush (2003) and Mann (2004).

REFERENCES

Ackerman, Frank, Timothy A. Wise, Kevin P. Gallagher, Luke Ney and Regina Flores (2003), 'Free trade, corn, and the environment: environmental impacts of US-Mexico corn trade under NAFTA,' Tufts University Global Development and Environment Institute working paper no. 03-06, Medford, MA.

Ash, Michael and T. Robert Fetter (2004), 'Who lives on the wrong side of the environmental tracks?' *Social Science Quarterly*, **85**(2), 441–62.

Barrett, Scott and Kathryn Graddy (2000), 'Freedom, growth, and the environment,' *Environment and Development Economics*, **5**, 433–56.

Bartlett, Randall (1989), *Economics and Power: An Inquiry into Human Relations and Markets*, Cambridge: Cambridge University Press.

Basu, Kaushik (1983), 'On why we do not try to walk off without paying after a taxi ride,' *Economic and Political Weekly*, **18**, 2011–12.

Bell, Daniel (1996), *The Cultural Contradictions of Capitalism*, 2nd edn, New York: Basic Books.

Bouwes, Nicolaas, Steven Hassur and Marc Shapiro (2003), 'Information for empowerment: the EPA's Risk-Screening Environmental Indicators Project,' in James K. Boyce and Barry G. Shelley (eds), *Natural Assets: Democratizing Environmental Ownership*, Washington, DC: Island Press, chapter 6.

Boyce, James K. (1996), 'Ecological distribution, agricultural trade liberalization, and *in situ* genetic diversity,' *Journal of Income Distribution*, **6**(2), 263–84.

Boyce, James K. (2002), *The Political Economy of the Environment*, Cheltenham, UK and Northampton, MA, USA: Edward Elgar Publishing.

Boyce, James K. (2007), 'Inequality and environmental protection,' in Jean-Marie Baland, Pranab Bardhan and Samuel Bowles (eds), *Inequality, Collective Action, and Environmental Sustainability*, Princeton, NJ: Princeton University Press, pp. 314–48.

Boyce, James K., Andrew R. Klemer, Paul H. Templet and Cleve E. Willis (1999), 'Power distribution, the environment, and public health: a state-level analysis,' *Ecological Economics*, **29**, 127–40, reprinted in Boyce (2002), chapter 6.

Brookfield, Harold (2001), *Exploring Agrodiversity*, New York: Columbia University Press.

Brown, Lester (1978), *The Twenty-ninth Day: Accommodating Human Needs and Numbers to the Earth's Resources*, New York: Norton.

Brush, Stephen B. (2003), 'The lighthouse and the potato: internalizing the value of crop genetic diversity,' in James K. Boyce and Barry G. Shelley (eds), *Natural Assets: Democratizing Environmental Ownership*, Washington, DC: Island Press, chapter 10.

Bullard, Robert D. (2008), 'Equity, unnatural man-made disasters, and race: why environmental justice matters,' in Robert C. Wilkinson and William R. Freudenburg (eds), *Equity and the Environment (Research in Social Problems and Public Policy)*, Vol. 15, Bingley, UK: Emerald Group Publishing, pp. 51–85.

Bullard, Robert D. and Glenn S. Johnson (2000), 'Environmental justice: grass-roots activism and its impact on public policy decision making,' *Journal of Social Issues*, **56**(3), 555–78.

Dorman, Peter (2005), 'Evolving knowledge and the precautionary principle,' *Ecological Economics*, **53**, 169–76.

Duvick, Daniel N. (1984), 'Genetic diversity in major farm crops on the farm and in reserve,' *Economic Botany*, **38**(2), 161–78.

Haas, Peter (1992), 'Banning chlorofluorocarbons: epistemic community efforts to protect stratospheric ozone,' *International Organization*, **46**(1), 187–224.

Harremoës, Poul, David Gee, Malcolm MacGarvin et al. (2002), *The Precautionary Principle in the 20th Century: Late Lessons from Early Warnings*, London: Earthscan, for the European Environment Agency.

Hartmann, Betsy and James K. Boyce (1979), *Needless Hunger: Voices from a Bangladesh Village*, San Francisco, CA: Institute for Food and Development Policy.

Hartmann, Betsy and James K. Boyce (1983), *A Quiet Violence: View from a Bangladesh Village*, London and San Francisco, CA: Zed Press and Institute for Food and Development Policy.

King, Martin Luther (1965), 'Staying awake through a great revolution,' commencement address at Oberlin College, June, Oberlin, OH.

Kitron, Uriel and Andrew Spielman (1989), 'Suppression of transmission of malaria through source reduction: antianopheline measures applied in Israel, the United States, and Italy,' *Reviews of Infectious Diseases*, **11**(3), 391–406.

Mann, Charles (2002), 'The real dirt on rainforest fertility,' *Science*, **297**(5583), 920–23.

Mann, Charles (2004), *Diversity on the Farm*, New York and Amherst, MA: Ford Foundation and Political Economy Research Institute.

Mohai, Paul (2008), 'Equity and the environmental justice debate,' in Robert C. Wilkinson and William R. Freudenburg (eds), *Equity and the Environment (Research in Social Problems and Public Policy)*, vol. 15, Bingley, UK: Emerald Group Publishing, pp. 21–49.

Morello-Frosch, Rachel A. and Bill Jesdale (2006), 'Separate and unequal: residential segregation and estimated cancer risks associated with ambient air toxics in US metropolitan areas,' *Environmental Health Perspectives*, **114**(3), 386–93.

Mulder, Monique B. and Peter Coppolillo (2005), *Conservation: Linking Ecology, Economics, and Culture*, Princeton, NJ: Princeton University Press.

Narain, Sunita and Anil Agarwal (2007), 'Harvesting the rain: fighting ecological poverty through participatory democracy,' in James K. Boyce, Sunita Narain and Elizabeth A. Stanton (eds), *Reclaiming Nature: Environmental Justice and Ecological Restoration*, London and New York: Anthem Press, chapter 3.

Neumann, Roderick P. (2001), 'Disciplining peasants in Tanzania: from state violence to self-surveillance in wildlife conservation,' in Michael Watts and Nancy Peluso (eds), *Violent Environments*, Ithaca, NY: Cornell University Press, chapter 13.

Pastor, Manuel (2003), 'Building social capital to protect natural capital: the quest for environmental justice,' in James K. Boyce and Barry G. Shelley (eds), *Natural Assets: Democratizing Environmental Ownership*, Washington, DC: Island Press, chapter 4.

Peluso, N. (1993), 'Coercing conservation: the politics of state resource control,' *Global Environmental Change*, **3**(2), 199–217.

Peña, Devon (2003), 'The watershed commonwealth of the Upper Rio Grande,' in James K. Boyce and Barry G. Shelley (eds), *Natural Assets: Democratizing Environmental Ownership*, Washington, DC: Island Press, chapter 9.

Pollan, Michael (2006), *Omnivore's Dilemma: A Natural History of Four Meals*, New York: Penguin Press.

Princen, Thomas (1997), 'The shading and distancing of commerce: when internalization is not enough,' *Ecological Economics*, **20**, 235–53, reprinted (2002) in Thomas Princen, Michael F. Maniates and Ken Conca (eds), *Confronting Consumption*, Cambridge, MA: MIT Press, chapter 5.

Rahman, Mokleshur and Stephen F. Minkin (2007), 'Net benefits: the ecological restoration of inland fisheries in Bangladesh,' in James K. Boyce, Sunita Narain and Elizabeth A. Stanton (eds), *Reclaiming Nature: Environmental Justice and Ecological Restoration*, London and New York: Anthem Press, chapter 4.

Rammel, Christian and Jeroen C.J.M. van den Bergh (2003), 'Evolutionary policies for sustainable development: adaptive flexibility and risk minimising,' *Ecological Economics*, **47**, 121–33.

Ravallion, Martin (1987), *Markets and Famines*, Oxford: Clarendon Press.

Sen, Amartya (1981), *Poverty and Famines: An Essay on Entitlements and Deprivation*, Oxford: Clarendon Press.

Sen, Amartya (1986), 'Adam Smith's prudence,' in Sanjaya Lall and Frances

Stewart (eds), *Theory and Reality in Development: Essays in Honour of Paul Streeten*, London: Macmillan, pp. 29–37.

Sen, Amartya (2004), 'Why we should preserve the spotted owl,' *London Review of Books*, **26**(3), 5 February.

Society for Ecological Restoration (2004), *The SER International Primer on Ecological Restoration*, Tucson, AZ: Society for Ecological Restoration International.

Szasz, Andrew and Michael Meuser (1997), 'Environmental inequalities: literature review and proposals for new directions in research and theory,' *Current Sociology*, **45**(3), 99–120.

Torras, Mariano and James K. Boyce (1998), 'Income, inequality, and pollution: a reassessment of the environmental Kuznets curve,' *Ecological Economics*, **25**, 147–60, reprinted in Boyce (2002), chapter 5.

Willott, Elizabeth (2004), 'Restoring nature, without mosquitoes?' *Restoration Ecology*, **12**(2), 147–53.

Wise, Timothy A. (2010), *Agricultural Dumping Under NAFTA: Estimating the Costs of US Agricultural Policies to Mexican Producers*, Washington, DC: Woodrow Wilson Center for International Scholars.

World Commission on Environment and Development (1987), *Our Common Future* (the Brundtland Report), New York: Oxford University Press.

Young, Oran (1994), *International Governance: Protecting the Environment in a Stateless Society*, Ithaca, NY: Cornell University Press.

3. In the wake of the storm: disasters and environmental justice
(with Manuel Pastor, Robert Bullard, Alice Fothergill, Rachel Morello-Frosch and Beverly Wright)

In late August 2005, Hurricane Katrina struck the Gulf coast, causing widespread devastation in Louisiana and Mississippi. The predominantly African-American city of New Orleans was especially hard hit, and in ensuing days extraordinary and deeply troubling footage of the storm's victims and survivors provoked an overdue national conversation about the racial and economic correlates of disaster vulnerability. This chapter, an earlier version of which was published in the journal *Race, Poverty and the Environment*, provides a synopsis of the six authors' longer report, *In the Wake of the Storm: Environment, Disaster, and Race After Katrina*, written in the wake of the storm and published in 2006 by the Russell Sage Foundation.

The southern United States has a long history of coping with weather-related disasters. It also has a legacy of institutionalized racism against African-Americans. Hurricane Katrina hit the region in a particularly vulnerable place: the storm pushed right up against an industrial corridor running from New Orleans to Baton Rouge, popularly known as 'Cancer Alley,' that is host to numerous petrochemical complexes as well as to poor African-American communities that have long complained of stark environmental disparities. The hurricane's most dramatic effects were felt in New Orleans itself, a city where black reliance on public transit was four times higher than that of whites, and where the public plans for evacuation in the event of a crisis were tragically deficient.

DISASTER VULNERABILITY AND ENVIRONMENTAL JUSTICE

How important for human well-being is racial inequality in environmental conditions? A Southern California study estimating lifetime cancer risk from air toxins shows, for example, that while risk declines as income rises, it is still around 50 percent higher at all income levels for African-Americans, Latinos and Asians (Morello-Frosch et al. 2001). And lead poisoning, commonly triggered by conditions in older housing, is five times more common among black children than white children (Kraft and Scheberle 2005).

The social dynamics that underlie the disproportionate environmental hazards faced by low-income communities and minorities also play out in the arenas of disaster prevention, mitigation and recovery. In a sense, environmental justice is about slow-motion disasters – and disasters reveal environmental injustice in a fast-forward mode. Both revolve around the axes of disparities of wealth and power.

Lack of wealth heightens the risks that individuals and communities face for three reasons. First, it translates into a lack of purchasing power to secure private alternatives to public provision of a clean and safe environment for all. Second, it translates into less ability to withstand shocks (such as health bills and property damage) that wealth would cushion. Third, it translates through the 'shadow prices' of cost-benefit analysis into public policies that place a lower priority on protecting 'less valuable' people and their assets. In the vicious circle of disaster vulnerability, those with less wealth face greater risks, and when disaster strikes their wealth is further sapped.

But risk is not just about money: even middle-class African-Americans, Latinos and Asians face elevated environmental risks. This reflects systematic differences in power and the legacy of racial discrimination. Power shows up in decisions by firms choosing where to site hazards and how much to invest in environmental protection: their choices are constrained not only by government regulations, but also by informal governance exercised by mobilized communities, civil society and the press. In both public and private arenas, power disparities drive outcome disparities – and the resulting patterns reflect race and ethnicity as well as wealth.

Land, Markets and Power

The power disparity explanation for environmental injustice suggests that low-income communities and people of color are systematically disadvantaged in the political decision-making process. This argument can incorporate other explanations: outcomes that seem to be based on rational land-use planning may be predetermined by political processes that already have designated disenfranchised communities as sacrifice zones.[1] Land-use decisions often build on accumulated disadvantage.

The interplay of land use, income and power means that certain variables used in statistical analysis of environmental injustice – such as zoning and household wealth – carry multiple meanings. To demonstrate convincingly that power shapes decisions on where to site hazardous facilities requires the inclusion of other variables that are directly and irrefutably connected to power.

The most important of these other variables is race.[2] Disparate patterns of environmental burdens by race, particularly when one has controlled for income and other variables involved in the land-use and market dynamics explanations for these disparities, point most clearly to the role of unequal influence and racial discrimination.

Racially disparate outcomes can result not only from the direct exercise of decision-making power but also from power disparities that are embedded in the nature of our urban form, such as housing segregation and racial steering in real estate markets; methods that informally exclude communities from participation in decision-making processes, including less provision of information on health risks; the past placement of hazards, which in turn justifies new ones as rational land use; and diverse other forms of 'institutionalized' or 'structural' racism (see Feagin and Feagin 1986; Institute on Race and Poverty 2002). It is precisely the racialized distribution of risk that has galvanized a movement for environmental equity rooted in civil rights law and activism.

Environmental justice and transportation justice are at the heart of emergency preparedness and emergency response. The former provides a guidepost as to who is most likely to be vulnerable to the disaster itself, and the latter provides information about who will need the most help when disaster strikes.

Not Just Hazards: Disaster Relief and Recovery

Unequal vulnerabilities before and during a disaster often continue to play out in the period after the disaster. Minorities and the poor often have greater difficulty in recovering from disasters due to less insurance, lower incomes, fewer savings, more unemployment, less access to communication channels and information and the intensification of existing poverty. For example, after Hurricane Andrew struck Florida and Louisiana in 1992, blacks and non-Cuban Hispanics were less likely than whites to receive adequate settlement amounts, and black neighborhoods turned out to be less likely to have had insurance with major companies, a fact that may have been connected to redlining policies by the companies.[3]

Racial, class and ethnic differences also show up in who receives disaster recovery assistance. Upper middle-class victims often are more likely to receive assistance than minorities and the poor because they know how to navigate the system, fill out the forms and work with the government bureaucracy (Aptekar 1990; Rovai 1994; Fothergill 2004). Poorer victims have more trouble making trips to the disaster assistance centers because of transportation, childcare and work difficulties (Dash et al. 1997). In addition, the traditional nuclear family model used by some relief programs can leave those poor and minority women who live in other types of households at a further disadvantage (Morrow 1996; Enarson 1998).

Housing is a significant issue for low-income and minority disaster victims in the recovery period. Post-disaster housing assistance tends to favor homeowners rather than renters. Of course, helping homeowners is important, and this help may be especially critical for black and Latino families who have much lower homeownership rates but tend to have more of their net worth tied up in home equity than do their white counterparts. But including renters more prominently in the relief mix is part of a more equitable approach.

Legal residency has been another critical issue in disaster recovery. Following disasters, many undocumented immigrants, unsure about Immigration and Naturalization Service policies, have avoided recovery assistance for fear of deportation (Subervi-Velez et al. 1992; Bolin and Stanford 1993). Muñiz (2006) offers anecdotal evidence that this was an issue in Katrina as well. She also shows how the assumption that Latino residents were undocumented rather than legal residents sometimes led the Federal Emergency Management Agency to fail to offer appropriate information about housing assistance to eligible individuals.

BEYOND KATRINA

Hurricane Katrina exposed for the entire nation the legacy of a discriminatory system and its consequences. Yet it also raised opportunities for civil rights, environmental, labor and environmental justice organizations to advocate for processes of relief, recovery and rebuilding that could address the socioeconomic and environmental inequalities that have plagued the region. Put simply, the aftermath of Katrina can become a time of important change for Americans – if we confront the contradictions between our democratic ideals and the injustices that Katrina laid bare.

Without good government, however, disaster can open the door to predators. In coastal Thailand, for example, land grabbers quickly arrived on the scene in the wake of the December 2004 tsunami to take advantage of the local residents' weakened circumstances (Montlake 2005). There is a distinct risk in New Orleans that asset transfers could turn the city into little more than a theme park for affluent tourists. Many in the low-income neighborhoods ravaged by the hurricane worry that federal, state and local officials will not prioritize their neighborhoods for clean up and reconstruction.

Part of the problem is a failure to learn positive as well as negative lessons from past experience. For example, the US Department of Housing and Urban Development responded to the 1994 Northridge earthquake in California by developing an effective program that quickly provided vouchers for permanent housing to the poorest victims and allowed these to be used anywhere in the state. This effort, curiously, was not duplicated in the Katrina case.

Hurricane Katrina opened a window on a dark side of America – the economic and environmental vulnerability of low-income communities and people of color. We can choose to close that window and shut out what it reveals, or we can use the new view to chart a healthier and more equitable future for us all.

NOTES

* This chapter is a revised version of an article originally published in *Race, Poverty and the Environment* (2006), **13**(1), 21–6.
1. For discussions of sacrifice zones in land-use planning, see Boone and Modarres (1999), Pulido (2000), Cole and Foster (2001) and Wright (2005).
2. Other power-related variables that have been explored in the literature include home ownership (which is not only an indicator of wealth but also highly associated with community engagement and political influence), voter turnout and recent immigration.
3. See Peacock and Girard (1997). For more on these issues, see Bolin and Bolton (1986), Hewitt (1997) and Bolin and Stanford (1998).

REFERENCES

Aptekar, L. (1990), 'A comparison of the bicoastal disasters of 1989,' *Behavior Science Research*, **24**(1–4), 73–104.
Bolin, R. and P. Bolton (1986), *Race, Religion, and Ethnicity in Disaster Recovery*, Boulder, CO: University of Colorado Institute of Behavioral Science.
Bolin, R. and L.M. Stanford (1993), 'Emergency sheltering and housing of earthquake victims: the case of Santa Cruz county,' in P. Bolton (ed.), *The Loma Prieta, California, Earthquake of October 17, 1989: Public Response*, Washington, DC: US Government Printing Office, pp. B43–50.

Bolin, R. and L.M. Stanford (1998), 'The Northridge earthquake: community-based approaches to unmet recovery needs,' *Disasters*, **22**(1), 21–38.

Boone, Christopher G. and A. Modarres (1999), 'Creating a toxic neighborhood in Los Angeles county: a historical examination of environmental inequity,' *Urban Affairs Review*, **35**(2), 163–87.

Cole, L. and S. Foster (2001), *From the Ground Up: Environmental Racism and the Rise of the Environmental Justice Movement*, New York: New York University Press.

Dash, N., W. Peacock and B. Morrow (1997), 'And the poor get poorer: a neglected black community,' in W. Peacock, B. Morrow and H. Gladwin (eds), *Hurricane Andrew: Ethnicity, Gender, and the Sociology of Disasters*, New York: Routledge, pp. 206–25.

Enarson, E. (1998), 'Through women's eyes: a gendered research agenda for disaster social science,' *Disasters*, **22**(2) 157–73.

Feagin, J. and C. Feagin (1986), *Discrimination American Style: Institutional Racism and Sexism*, 2nd edn, Malabar, FL: Kriege Publishing.

Fothergill, Alice (2004), *Heads Above Water: Gender, Class, and Family in the Grand Forks Flood*, Albany, NY: State University of New York Press.

Hewitt, K. (1997), *Regions of Risk: A Geographical Introduction to Disasters*, London: Addison Wesley Longman.

Institute on Race and Poverty (2002), *Racism and Metropolitan Dynamics: The Civil Rights Challenge of the 21st Century*, Minneapolis, MN: Institute on Race and Poverty.

Kraft, Michael E. and Denise Scheberle (2005), 'Environmental justice and the allocation of risk: the case of lead and public health,' *Policy Studies Journal*, **23**(1) 113–22.

Montlake, Simon (2005), 'In Thailand, a "land grab",' *Christian Science Monitor*, 8 April.

Morello-Frosch, Rachel A., Manuel Pastor and James L. Sadd (2001), 'Environmental justice and southern California's "Riskscape": the distribution of air toxics exposures and health risks among diverse communities,' *Urban Affairs Review*, **36**(4), 551–78.

Morrow, B. (1996), 'Hurricane Andrew through women's eyes: issues and recommendations,' *International Journal of Mass Emergencies and Disasters*, **14**(1), 5–22.

Muñiz, B. (2006), *In the Eye of the Storm: How the Government and Private Response to Hurricane Katrina Failed Latinos*, Washington, DC: National Council of La Raza.

Peacock, W. and C. Girard (1997), 'Ethnic and racial inequalities in hurricane damage and insurance settlements,' in W. Peacock, B. Morrow and H. Gladwin (eds), *Hurricane Andrew: Ethnicity, Gender, and the Sociology of Disasters*, New York: Routledge, pp. 171–90.

Pulido, L. (2000), 'Rethinking environmental racism: white privilege and urban development in southern California,' *Annals of the Association of American Geographers*, **90**(1), 12–40.

Rovai, E. (1994), 'The social geography of disaster recovery: differential community response to the north coast earthquakes,' in *Association of Pacific Coast Geographers: Yearbook 56*, Honolulu, HI: University of Hawaii Press.

Subervi-Velez, F., M. Denney, A. Ozuna and C. Quintero (1992), 'Communicating with California's Spanish-speaking populations: assessing the role of the

Spanish-language broadcast media and selected agencies in providing emergency services,' California Policy Seminar, University of California, Berkeley, CA.

Wright, Beverly (2005), 'Living and dying in Louisiana's cancer alley,' in Robert D. Bullard (ed.), *The Quest for Environmental Justice: Human Rights and the Politics of Pollution*, San Francisco, CA: Sierra Club Books, pp. 87–107.

4.   Justice in the air: tracking America's industrial toxics

(with Michael Ash, Grace Chang, Manuel Pastor, Justin Scoggins and Jennifer Tran)

On the long road to securing the right to a clean and safe environment, a historic milestone came when the US Congress passed the Emergency Planning and Community Right-to-Know Act in 1986. The law, passed in the aftermath of the Bhopal chemical disaster,[1] requires industrial facilities across the United States to disclose information on their annual releases of toxic chemicals into our air, water and lands.

The premise behind the law is simple: the public has the right to know what pollutants are in our environment and who put them there.

The data, available from the US Environmental Protection Agency (EPA) in the annual Toxics Release Inventory (TRI), are not always easily accessible or readily usable. You can track pollution to the plant that caused it, but not always to the company that is responsible. You can see the pounds of individual pollutants released at a plant, but it's hard to cumulate the overall health impact of the plant's multiple pollutants. And even if you can gauge the overall effect of a single facility, there is no easy way to determine what this means for a neighborhood burdened with pollution from many such sources.

This chapter tackles these issues by using a new dataset built upon the TRI. Among other things, we measure the extent to which toxic pollution released by industry disproportionately contaminates the air in neighborhoods where larger-than-average percentages of people of color and low-income families live. And we present a scorecard for companies that measures the extent to which their pollution is concentrated in these neighborhoods – the first time such a measure has been calculated and made available to the public.

This investigation builds upon the basic aims of the 1986 Right-to-Know legislation. The law's proponents expected that better access to information would not only increase public awareness, but also increase public demand for actions by firms and government officials to curb pollution. Information, they believed, is power. The right to know was intended as a means to the greater goal of securing our right to clean air and clean water.

The mere fact that companies are compelled to publicly disclose information about their releases of toxic pollutants has had a striking impact on their behavior (Konar and Cohen 1997). In the first ten years after the law went into effect, total emissions of the chemicals listed in the TRI fell by 44 percent (Tietenberg 1998). For the most part these reductions happened without new regulations: when companies knew that the public knew about their releases, they began to clean up their acts.

In the 1990s, the EPA took another major step to expand public information about toxic pollution. The agency launched the Risk-Screening Environmental Indicators (RSEI) project to assess the human health risks resulting from toxic chemical emissions at industrial sites. Building on the TRI data, the EPA added three additional sorts of information to assess the human health risks posed by toxic releases:

- fate and transport: how the chemical spreads from the point of release into the surrounding area;
- toxicity: how dangerous the chemical is, on a per pound basis; and
- population: how many people live in the affected areas.

This chapter uses this information to develop a measure of corporate environmental justice performance based on releases of toxic air pollutants. Along the way, we explain what the data mean, which states and metropolitan areas are most affected, and what companies and communities can do to improve their performance and the environment.

MAPPING INDUSTRIAL AIR POLLUTION

The building block for our analysis is the EPA's RSEI project. Facility-by-facility RSEI data on toxic releases are available on an EPA website, including each facility's 'RSEI score,' a measure of its total human health impact, and information about contributions of individual chemicals to the facility's total score.[2]

The EPA calculates the total chronic health risks (cancer and non-cancer) from toxic air pollution by applying inhalation toxicity weights to the TRI chemicals. Using a fate-and-transport model, EPA estimates exposure levels in each of more than 10,000 1 km-square grid cells around each facility. In the publicly available information, all of these impacts are

RSEI takes the toxic air release from each industrial source and uses wind and other information to determine where the releases go within a grid around each facility. RSEI attributes higher health impacts to grid cells exposed to higher-toxicity chemicals.

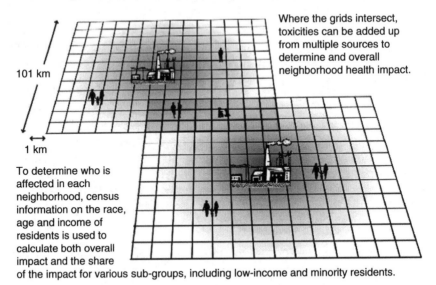

Where the grids intersect, toxicities can be added up from multiple sources to determine and overall neighborhood health impact.

101 km

1 km

To determine who is affected in each neighborhood, census information on the race, age and income of residents is used to calculate both overall impact and the share of the impact for various sub-groups, including low-income and minority residents.

Figure 4.1   The EPA's risk-screening environmental indicators

added up for each facility. Information is not provided for individual grid cells, as such a massive amount of data requires a great deal of storage space.

The geographic microdata for the individual grid cells have been made available to researchers, however. Using these finely disaggregated data, we can measure the cumulative impacts on any given locality from chemical releases by multiple facilities. The methodology is depicted in Figure 4.1. Using US Census data, we can then investigate the extent to which differences in community exposures to toxic air pollutants are correlated with differences in race, ethnicity and economic status.

One broad overall measure that we can calculate from these data is the toxicity-weighted exposure for residents in any given neighborhood, adding across all the toxic pollutants from all the industrial sources whose pollution reaches that neighborhood. We can then determine how many people live in those neighborhoods and calculate the toxic air pollution burden for the residents of a given city, metropolitan area or state. And because we have the data at the neighborhood level, we can then determine if there are higher or lower exposures in minority or low-income neighborhoods within these areas, calculating the share of the pollution burden borne by different population sub-groups.

Industrial facilities are not the only sources of air pollution, of course. In particular, mobile sources such as automobiles and trucks account for much of the nation's air pollution. Small-scale businesses such as dry cleaners and auto body shops are exempt from TRI reporting requirements, and so their emissions are not captured in the RSEI database. The chemicals in the TRI are toxic agents but do not include some bulk pollutants that also pose significant health and environmental risks, such as nitrogen oxides and carbon dioxide. A more complete picture of air pollution and the attendant health risks would encompass these other sources and pollutants too.

Here we focus on industrial air toxics for three reasons. First, the industrial releases we analyse do have significant local effects, and in some heavily impacted communities they account for the biggest share of air pollution exposure. Second, the RSEI data permit an exceptionally fine-grained mapping of the impacts of different industrial sectors on different communities. Third, with a bit of detective work on the ownership of facilities, the responsibility for this pollution can be traced directly to specific corporations.

WHO BREATHES AMERICA'S DIRTIEST AIR?

Figure 4.2 shows the state-by-state levels of exposure to toxic air pollution from industrial facilities, measured here as the toxicity-weighted exposure of the median resident. The states with the darkest shade – such as Ohio, Louisiana, and Tennessee – have the highest levels of exposure. Those with the lightest shade – such as Vermont and Wyoming – have the lowest. The variations reflect not only where industrial facilities are located, but also how strictly they are regulated, what pollutants they emit and how these emissions are dispersed by prevailing wind patterns.

Air pollution is unevenly distributed within states, as well as between them. A growing body of research has demonstrated that people of color and low-income communities often face the greatest environmental hazards (see, for example, Bullard 2000; Pastor 2007).

Toxic air pollution from industrial facilities is a case in point. Using the RSEI data, EPA researchers have found that nationwide, the most polluted locations have significantly higher-than-average percentages of blacks, Latinos and Asian-American residents (Bouwes et al. 2003).

This reflects differences within metropolitan areas as well as between them. Nationwide, blacks live disproportionately in cities with higher

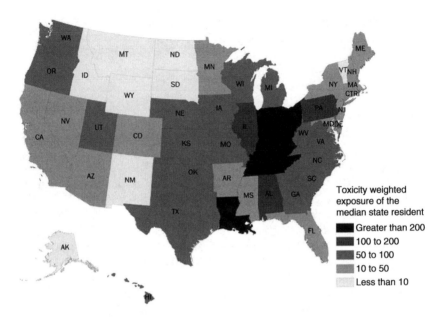

Toxicity weighted
exposure of the
median state resident

Greater than 200
100 to 200
50 to 100
10 to 50
Less than 10

Note: Alaska and Hawaii not to scale

Figure 4.2   Median exposure to industrial air toxics by state

industrial air pollution, while Latinos tend to live in less heavily polluted cities. Yet within any given metropolitan area, Latinos as well as blacks tend to live on the 'wrong side of the environmental tracks' (Ash and Fetter 2004).

The extent of racial, ethnic and class-related disparities in environmental quality varies across the country. Figures 4.3 and 4.4 depict these differences on a state-by-state basis. Figure 4.3 shows the differences between the share of racial and ethnic minorities in the total human health risk from industrial air toxics and their share in the state's population. The most dramatic disparity is in Tennessee, where the share of minorities in the health risk is 43 percent compared to their population share of 21 percent – a difference of 22 percentage points.

Figure 4.4 shows the same differences for low-income people. The most dramatic disparity in this case is in Illinois, where the share of low-income people in the health risk is 18 percent whereas their share in the state's population is 11 percent – a seven percentage point difference.

Tables 4.1 and 4.2 provide a more fine-grained look at these geographical variations. Here we examine metropolitan areas, focusing on those that

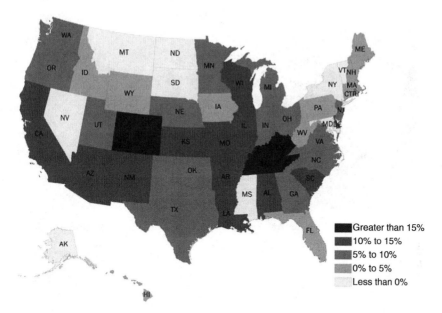

Greater than 15%
10% to 15%
5% to 10%
0% to 5%
Less than 0%

Note: Alaska and Hawaii not to scale

*Figure 4.3   Difference between minority share of health risk from
industrial air toxics and minority share of population by state*

have an above-average level of toxicity-weighted resident exposure and a
population large enough to rank among the nation's 100 biggest metropolitan communities.

Table 4.1 lists the ten metropolitan areas with the largest discrepancies
between the minority share of the health risk from industrial air toxics and
their share in the population. Topping the list is Birmingham, Alabama,
where minorities account for 65 percent of the health risk as compared
to 34 percent of the population – a discrepancy of 31 percentage points.
Baton Rouge, Louisiana, is not far behind, with Memphis, Chicago,
Harrisburg and others following in a tighter pack.

Table 4.2 presents comparable discrepancies for low-income households. Birmingham tops the list again: low-income people account for 24
percent of the health risk, compared to 13 percent of the population. Not
surprisingly, there is some overlap with Table 4.1: five metropolitan areas
appear on both lists. The fact that the overlap is not complete shows,
however, that income as well as race and ethnicity is an important locus of
environmental disparity.

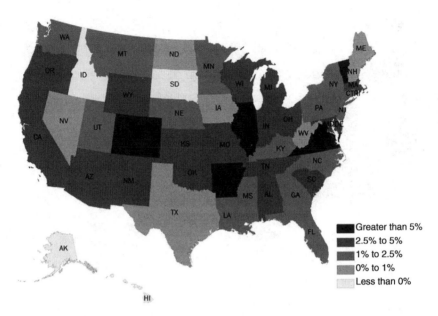

Note: Alaska and Hawaii not to scale

Figure 4.4   Difference between low-income share of health risk from industrial air toxics and low-income share of the population by state

Table 4.1   Disproportionate impacts on minorities: top ten metropolitan areas

Metropolitan area	Minority share of toxic score	Minority share of population	Minority discrepancy
Birmingham, AL	64.7	33.5	31.1
Baton Rouge, LA	63.6	36.1	27.5
Memphis, TN–AR–MS	70.6	48.1	22.5
Chicago, IL	61.2	42.0	19.2
Harrisburg–Lebanon–Carlisle, PA	32.2	13.5	18.7
Louisville, KY–IN	36.5	18.0	18.5
Gary, IN	50.0	32.1	17.9
San Diego, CA	62.7	45.1	17.6
Milwaukee–Waukesha, WI	43.0	25.5	17.5
Tacoma, WA	41.1	24.0	17.1

Table 4.2   Disproportionate impacts on low-income people: top ten metropolitan areas

Metropolitan area	Low-income share of toxic score	Low-income share of population	Low-income discrepancy
Birmingham, AL	23.8	13.1	10.7
Baton Rouge, LA	26.1	16.2	9.9
Youngstown–Warren, OH	21.3	11.5	9.8
Charleston–North Charleston, SC	23.0	14.0	9.0
Tacoma, WA	19.4	10.5	8.9
Gary, IN	19.0	10.8	8.2
Milwaukee–Waukesha, WI	18.3	10.6	7.7
Knoxville, TN	19.6	12.0	7.6
Columbus, OH	17.1	10.1	7.0
Detroit, MI	17.7	10.7	7.0

Just as income matters independently of race, so too does race matter independently of income. It is not the case that people of color simply happen to be poorer than whites and therefore live in industrial neighborhoods with lower property values. Multivariate studies that test statistically for effects of race and ethnicity, while holding income and other factors constant, have demonstrated that significant racial disparities in exposure persist across all bands of family income.[3]

If the first step to recovery is admitting that one has a problem, the United States must acknowledge that clean and safe air – which would seem to be a birthright of every person – today is not an equal opportunity affair.

TRACKING POLLUTERS

Where does toxic air pollution come from? Who owns the facilities – the refineries, power plants, factories and other industrial sources – that put these pollutants into our air?

The RSEI database provides information on emissions of toxic air pollutants from more than 16,000 industrial facilities nationwide. Combining this with information on the corporate ownership of these facilities, researchers at the Political Economy Research Institute (PERI) of the University of Massachusetts, Amherst, produce 'The Toxic 100,' a ranking of the top industrial air polluters in the United States.[4]

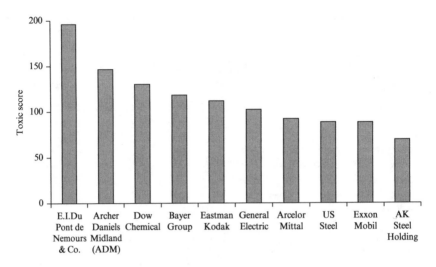

Figure 4.5   Top ten corporate air polluters in the Toxic 100

The top ten firms for 2005 are shown in Figure 4.5. The ranking is based on total human health impacts as estimated by the EPA's RSEI project, taking into account the pounds of chemicals released, their toxicity, the fate and transport of these releases in the environment and the number of people exposed. To derive these firm-level scores, we used the EPA's RSEI scores for each industrial facility that reports emissions in the TRI. The RSEI scores convey relative rankings: a score of 100 means that the human health impacts are ten times greater than a score of 10. Here we divide the firm's RSEI score, summed over all its facilities, by the total RSEI score for all firms nationwide to get a 'toxic share' that again conveys relative rankings, here expressed as the firm's share of the total impact of industrial toxic air pollution in the country. For ease of presentation, we set the total national score at 10,000 – thus, the top corporate toxic score of 196 means that the firm accounts for 1.96 percent of the national total of all health impacts from all air toxics emitted by all facilities in the RSEI database.

Topping the list is DuPont, the Delaware-based chemical company. The biggest single contributor to its score comes from chloroprene releases at a facility in Louisville, Kentucky. The National Institute for Occupational Safety and Health (NIOSH) reports that chloroprene, a chemical used in the production of synthetic rubber, can damage the eyes, skin, respiratory system and reproductive system.

Second on the list is Archer Daniels Midland (ADM), the Illinois-based agricultural processor. The biggest single contributor to its score comes from acrolein releases at its facility in Peoria, Illinois. According to the

Table 4.3   Top ten sectors by toxic score

Sector	Toxic score	Minority share	Low-income share
Steel Works, Blast Furnaces, Rolling and Finishing Mills	1054	24.1	17.2
Iron and Steel Foundries	939	41.3	16.6
Electric Services	736	40.3	17.9
Industrial Organic Chemicals	615	39.1	14.2
Plastics and Synthetic Materials	437	30.0	15.5
Motor Vehicles and Motor Vehicle Equipment	416	25.2	12.0
Industrial Inorganic Chemicals	401	33.1	15.8
Fabricated Structural Metal Products	393	33.7	15.3
Petroleum Refining	381	51.3	19.0
Fabricated Metal Products	371	54.4	16.3
Top Ten Total	5741	37.3	16.0
Total (all sectors)	10,000	34.8	15.3

NIOSH, acrolein – which was used as a chemical weapon during World War I – can damage the heart, eyes, skin and respiratory system.

Rounding out the top ten are Dow Chemical, Bayer Group, Eastman Kodak, General Electric, Arcelor Mittal, US Steel, ExxonMobil and AK Steel Holding. The EPA data indicate that between them, these ten companies alone accounted for more than 11 percent of the total human health risks from industrial air toxics in the United States in 2005.

These data also can be used to rank industrial sectors on the basis of their toxic air pollution. Table 4.3 lists the top ten sectors nationwide (again based on the 2005 data). Topping the list are two sectors in the primary metals industry. Taken together, these ten sectors accounted for more than 57 percent of the total human health risks from industrial air pollution nationwide. This reflects the phenomenon known as 'disproportionality': a small number of polluters often accounts for a large share of the pollution (Berry 2008). One implication of disproportionality, among both companies and sectors, is that remedial measures targeted to a small fraction of the nation's economy could go a long way toward cleaning up our air.

ENVIRONMENTAL JUSTICE: A NEW BENCHMARK FOR CORPORATE RESPONSIBILITY

Today there is growing interest in how companies compare in terms of their environmental performance. Investors, consumers and the public at large want to know which companies are operating in a socially responsible manner – and which are not.

A corporation's environmental performance has many dimensions, including pollution from the facilities it owns, the occupational health and safety of its workers and the impacts of its products once they are in the hands of consumers. Here we introduce a new dimension: whether the majority of a company's pollution affects neighborhoods largely populated by people of color or by families living in poverty. In other words, we make the connection between polluted neighborhoods and the polluters who are responsible for toxic air.

As shown above, environmental impacts can be quite uneven. In the case of toxic air pollution from industrial facilities, minorities and low-income communities in general suffer from unequal exposure. As in other dimensions of environmental performance, however, not all corporations are equally responsible or irresponsible. Some do better, some do worse.

Here we present two measures of corporate environmental justice performance. Both are based on the human health impacts from toxic air pollution released by facilities that corporations own: the first is a measure of unequal impacts on people of color, and the second is a measure of unequal impacts on people with incomes below the poverty line. Both are calculated using the same method we used for states and metropolitan areas: we compute the share of the total health hazard from toxic air pollution of a particular company that is borne by minorities or low-income people.[5]

Figure 4.6 shows the ten corporations from the Toxic 100 list that have the highest shares of racial and ethnic minorities in their toxic scores. In all of these cases, minorities bear more than half of the human health impact from the firm's toxic air releases. For example, minorities account for 69.1 percent of the impacts from facilities owned by ExxonMobil, although they comprise only 31.8 percent of the population nationwide. The corresponding figures for blacks – for whom the disparity is most pronounced – are 55.5 percent and 11.8 percent. Two of the top ten in terms of disparate impact – ExxonMobil and Arcelor Mittal – also rank in the top ten in terms of their total toxic score (see Figure 4.5).

Figure 4.6 also reports the distribution of human health impacts from the whole set of Toxic 100 firms, from other large publicly traded firms that do not make the Toxic 100 list and from all the other firms in the

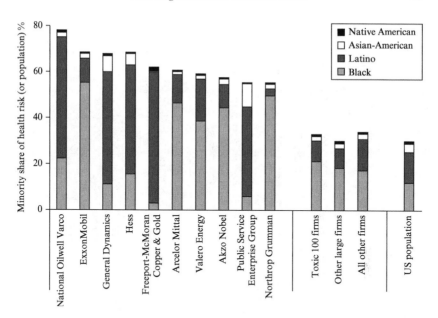

Figure 4.6   Minority share of health risk from industrial air toxics: top ten corporations

RSEI database. It is interesting to note that in all three groupings of firms, blacks are overrepresented compared to their share in the national population, whereas other minorities are generally underrepresented. Comparing the impacts of large publicly traded firms to those of other (smaller or not publicly traded) firms, we find that Latinos and Native Americans tend to be more heavily impacted by the latter.

Figure 4.7 provides a comparable ranking based on the share of people living below the poverty line. In all ten cases, poor people account for more than 20 percent of the human health impacts from the firms' toxic air releases, compared to 12.9 percent of the population nationwide. Again, there is considerable overlap with Figure 4.6: seven firms appear in both lists. Three of the firms – ExxonMobil, Arcelor Mittal and Archer Daniels Midland – also rank in the top ten in terms of their total toxic score (see Figure 4.5).

A corporation's environmental justice performance, as reported in these figures, reflects both the average share of minority or poverty groups in the human health impacts from all its facilities and where its dirtier-than-average facilities are located. To illustrate, Table 4.4 gives breakdowns for the top five facilities owned by ExxonMobil, ranked by their toxic scores, and for 50 other ExxonMobil facilities combined.

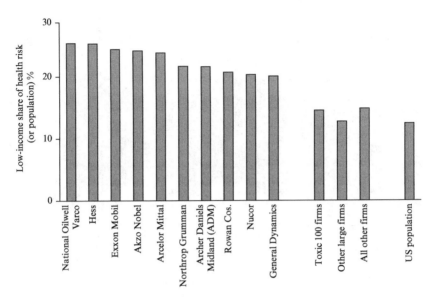

*Figure 4.7   Low-income share of health risk from industrial air toxics: top
ten corporations*

The top two facilities, both of them located in Baton Rouge, Louisiana,
clearly drive the exceptionally high share of blacks in the corporation's
environmental justice performance measure. It can also be seen that the
next two facilities – refineries located in Baytown, TX, and Torrance,
CA – have exceptionally high shares of Latinos and, in the latter case,
Asian-Americans.

In addition to comparing individual firms, we can compare the environmental justice performance of different industrial sectors. In Table 4.5,
we list the top ten sectors ranked by the minority share of health impacts
from their toxic air pollution emissions. Topping the list are the fabricated
metal products and petroleum-refining sectors, each of which accounts
for more that 3 percent of the total human health impact of toxic air pollution from industrial sources nationwide (as indicated by toxic scores
greater than 300). In both of these sectors, more than half of the health
impact from facilities is borne by racial and ethnic minorities. In Table 4.6,
we rank sectors by the share of low-income people in the health impact.
The beverages industry tops the list, a result that is primarily attributable to emissions from Archer Daniels Midland facilities in Illinois. The
petroleum-refining sector again places second.

Finally, it is important to note that corporate environmental justice

Table 4.4 Minority and low-income shares of health risk from industrial air toxics: ExxonMobil facilities

	Toxic score	Minority share	Black share	Latino share	Asian-American share	Native American share	Low-income share
Baton Rouge Refinery (LA)	42.7	78.0	75.3	1.1	1.0	0.1	31.1
Baton Rouge Chemical (LA)	17.0	73.1	70.0	1.2	1.1	0.1	29.1
Baytown Refinery (TX)	12.6	54.6	15.0	35.8	2.6	0.5	15.3
Torrance Refinery (CA)	4.6	69.9	10.8	40.9	15.5	0.7	15.1
Joliet Refinery (IL)	4.3	33.7	16.5	13.0	2.9	0.2	7.8
50 additional facilities	7.1	50.8	23.2	23.4	2.6	0.8	17.3
All facilities	88.3	69.1	55.5	10.4	2.2	0.3	25.4

Table 4.5   Top ten sectors by minority share of health risk from industrial air toxics

Sector	Toxic score	Minority share	Black share	Latino share	Asian-American share	Native American share
Fabricated Metal Products	371	54.4	45.8	5.6	1.7	0.3
Petroleum Refining	381	51.3	27.9	18.7	2.9	0.7
Asphalt Paving and Roofing Materials	37	48.9	22.0	23.2	2.1	0.4
Railroad Equipment	176	46.3	13.1	29.4	2.2	0.8
Agricultural Chemicals	68	45.2	16.0	26.7	1.5	0.5
Electrical Machinery and Equipment	89	43.0	34.5	5.3	1.8	0.3
Plastics Products	269	42.1	16.7	18.9	4.3	0.7
Metal Cans and Shipping Containers	61	41.8	15.1	20.9	4.1	0.6
Iron and Steel Foundries	939	41.3	17.0	19.9	2.3	0.8
Ship and Boat Building and Repairing	93	41.1	20.0	15.3	3.6	0.6
Total (all sectors)	10,000	34.8	18.1	12.6	2.2	0.6

Note: Top ten among sectors with a toxic score of 35 or greater.

performance often differs among firms within industrial sectors as well as across sectors. To illustrate these differences, Table 4.7 presents performance measures for the top firms in the petroleum-refining sector.[6] The share of minorities in total health impacts ranges from 24.5 percent in the case of Tesoro to 73.6 percent in the case of Pasadena Refining.

Table 4.6   Top ten sectors by low-income share of health risk from industrial air toxics

Sector	Toxic score	Low-income share
Beverages	123	24.8
Petroleum Refining	381	19.0
Electric Services	736	17.9
Agricultural Chemicals	68	17.9
Steel Works, Blast Furnaces, Rolling and Finishing Mills	1054	17.2
Wood Products	61	16.9
Iron and Steel Foundries	939	16.6
Paperboard Mills	41	16.6
Flat Glass	39	16.6
Coating, Engraving and Allied Services	196	16.5
Total (all sectors)	10,000	15.3

Note: Top ten among sectors with a toxic score of 35 or greater.

FROM THE RIGHT TO KNOW TO THE RIGHT TO CLEAN AIR

The right-to-know movement in the United States scored a landmark victory with the creation of the TRI. Building on this achievement, the US EPA launched the RSEI project to develop state-of-the-art information on not only the sources of industrial toxic emissions but also the geography of the resulting pollution exposure.

Meanwhile, in response to accumulating evidence indicating systematic patterns of disproportionate exposure to unsafe air and water among people of color and low-income communities, the environmental justice movement won its own landmark victory in 1994 when President Bill Clinton signed an Executive Order directing every federal agency to identify and rectify 'disproportionately high and adverse human health or environmental effects of its programs, policies, and activities on minority populations and low-income populations.'

Important as these accomplishments are, we have yet to achieve the goal of securing clean and safe air and water for all Americans.

There are four avenues along which we can work for further progress:

- *Defend and extend the right to know.* During the administration of President George W. Bush, the public's right to know about

Table 4.7 Minority and low-income shares of health risk from industrial air toxics: petroleum refining

	Facilities	Releases	Toxic score	Minority share	Black share	Latino share	Asian-American share	Native American share	Low-income share
Exxon Mobil	8	564	79.1	65.5	51.9	10.2	2.4	0.3	24.6
Conoco Phillips	17	790	62.1	34.8	19.6	10.6	2.3	0.9	15.4
Valero Energy	17	1031	57.2	59.8	38.6	18.3	1.8	0.5	19.7
BP	6	386	33.5	56.2	16.4	32.6	5.8	0.6	16.3
Citgo Petroleum Corp.	7	314	20.1	47.8	28.5	15.7	2.3	0.4	19.4
Pasadena Refining System Inc.	1	36	17.3	73.6	12.6	57.7	2.4	0.6	25.1
Sunoco	5	176	17.1	34.0	22.9	5.8	3.8	0.3	16.3
Tesoro	6	315	16.9	24.5	2.6	11.6	5.9	1.8	10.0
Suncor Energy	1	35	14.0	45.3	6.9	33.6	2.5	1.3	12.9
Motiva Enterprises L.L.C.	5	173	10.1	42.2	35.6	4.1	1.4	0.3	16.8
Hess	2	110	8.6	67.4	14.6	49.8	4.9	0.3	26.9
Sinclair Oil Corp.	3	171	8.5	35.3	18.2	6.8	1.1	5.3	20.3
Royal Dutch Shell	6	291	7.8	43.5	8.8	25.5	6.0	1.0	12.2
Marathon Oil	7	364	7.7	33.8	16.3	13.6	1.9	0.6	14.3
Chevron	7	432	3.8	66.2	17.4	31.9	13.3	0.6	18.9
All oil refining	163	6836	380.9	51.3	27.9	18.8	2.9	0.7	19.0
All firms	102,636	16,470	10,000	34.8	18.1	12.6	2.2	0.6	15.3
US population	–	–	–	31.8	11.8	13.7	3.7	0.7	12.9

environmental hazards was questioned. The administration proposed to raise the thresholds for reporting toxic emissions and to
shift TRI reporting to an every-other-year basis. Activists mobilized
to fend off most of these limits to the free flow of information. The
time is ripe for efforts to not only secure but also expand our right
to know.

One important step would be to strengthen enforcement of reporting requirements. Today there is little effort to verify the accuracy of
the information submitted by industrial facilities in their annual TRI
reports. It is possible that many releases are underreported, or even
go unreported. Environmental officials ought to be given adequate
resources to enforce compliance and assist firms in improving the
quality of the data. New efforts to collect data about greenhouse
gas emissions should include expanded coverage of 'co-pollutants' –
including the toxics that are the focus of this chapter – that can harm
the health of surrounding communities.

- *Link modeling and monitoring.* Air pollution monitoring – that is,
measurement of actual air pollution levels – would also improve the
quality of information on community-level exposures. The RSEI
model is a state-of-the-art tool for mapping exposure to pollutants
from industrial sources, but models can only produce estimates.
Partly because of inadequate funding, the US government has failed
to make use of its own RSEI project as a guide to help target air
monitoring to locations with the greatest risk of exposure to toxic
hazards. Indeed, it fell to the newspaper *USA Today* to undertake
the first such effort. Working with researchers at the University of
Massachusetts Political Economy Research Institute and at Johns
Hopkins University, reporters identified the schools across the
United States where the RSEI model predicted the greatest risks,
and then sent teams with monitoring equipment to conduct meas-
urements of pollutants at those sites. The results were published in
December 2008, along with a website providing details on schools
nationwide.[7] In response, Senator Barbara Boxer, Chair of the
Senate Environment and Public Works Committee, pledged to 'do
what I have to do' to make sure that the government monitors the
air quality in schools across the nation. 'If *USA Today* can do this,'
she declared, 'certainly the EPA can do this.'

- *Adopt a cumulative impacts approach to pollution standards.* Most of
the toxic air pollution reported in the TRI is not illegal: the emissions are within the existing legal limits, if any limits have been
established. But the same community can be affected by releases
of pollutants from many facilities. One of the great merits of the

RSEI model is that it permits assessment of cumulative exposures from multiple pollution sources. At a minimum, the resulting health impacts can be expected to be additive as hazard piles upon hazard; at worst, they may be multiplicative due to interactions among toxic pollutants. The cumulative nature of these impacts should be taken into account by federal and state environmental protection agencies. Environmental justice activists have raised awareness of this issue, since the communities with the greatest cumulative burdens often have the largest numbers of minorities and low-income families. If government agencies truly are to rectify 'disproportionately high and adverse human health or environmental effects,' they must frame regulatory standards that take account of cumulative impacts.

- *Encourage community, shareholder and consumer activism.* As reductions in pollution in response to the TRI have demonstrated, corporations can be spurred to protect human health and safety not only by government standards but also by public opinion, community mobilization and shareholder involvement. Where environmental harms may ultimately lead to financial liabilities for cleanup or compensation, a reasonable case can be made that improved performance is a fiduciary responsibility as well as a moral imperative. The corporate environmental justice scorecard presented here can be a new tool to promote informal regulation and encourage corporate responsibility. For example, the New York-based Interfaith Center on Corporate Responsibility assists community-based organizations across the United States that are fighting for a healthier environment by educating them about shareholder democracy and by supporting corporate dialogues and shareholder campaigns. Such efforts can be backed with systematic data on corporate performance, including 'in-class' comparisons with other firms in the same industry, along with specific information on affected communities.

All four avenues – defending and extending the right to know, linking modeling and monitoring, extending pollution standards to assess cumulative impacts and encouraging community, shareholder and consumer activism – can help to protect our right to clean air and reduce environmental disparities. By reinforcing each other, these can create a virtuous circle in which the whole is more than the sum of its parts.

In 2006, former US Vice President Al Gore challenged the nation to address the threat of climate change by presenting Americans with 'an inconvenient truth' – that our collective actions and inaction threaten the planet and the well-being of our children and grandchildren. Equally inconvenient is the truth that America's history of racial inequality has been stamped not only on our labor and housing markets, but also on the very air we breathe.

But history is not destiny. We can develop smarter environmental policies that strengthen communities most affected by pollution. We can shoulder our responsibilities as citizens, communities and corporations. In so doing, we can secure a future in which the right to clean air is truly shared by all.

NOTES

1. The Act was passed in response to the public demand for information on toxic hazards following a massive industrial disaster in Bhopal, India, where early one morning in December 1984 a cloud of methyl isocyanate escaped from an insecticide-manufacturing plant owned by an American chemical company, Union Carbide. In the poor neighborhoods near the factory, the release killed at least 2000 people and injured many thousands more. The disaster sparked an international outcry and raised concerns in the United States about the risks to the public at home, concerns that intensified in ensuing months when the US Environmental Protection Agency disclosed that there had been more than two dozen leaks of the same chemical in the past five years at another Union Carbide plant near Charleston, WV.
2. The data are available, along with more details about the RSEI, at http://www.epa.gov/oppt/rsei/ (accessed 16 July 2012).
3. See, for example, Bouwes et al. (2003), Pastor et al. (2005), Rinquist (2005) and Mohai and Saha (2006).
4. The Toxic 100 data reported here are based on 2005 emissions data for the nation's largest publicly traded companies – those that appear on the Fortune 500, Fortune Global 500, S&P 500 or Forbes Global 2000 lists. These are not only the biggest firms in terms of annual revenue, but also may be the most responsive to demands from shareholders and the public for improved performance in safeguarding public health. The Toxic 100 website (http://www.peri.umass.edu/toxic100/, accessed 16 July 2012) presents these and updated data, and provides details on the chemicals and facilities that account for each company's total toxic score.
5. For details, see Ash and Boyce (2011).
6. Because diversified corporations own facilities operating in a number of different industrial sectors, we restrict our inter-firm comparison here only to facilities in the petroleum-refining sector.
7. *USA Today*, 'The smokestack effect: toxic air and America's schools,' available at http://content.usatoday.com/news/nation/environment/smokestack/index (accessed 16 July 2012).

REFERENCES

Ash, Michael and James K. Boyce (2011), 'Measuring corporate environmental justice performance,' *Corporate Social Responsibility and Environmental Management*, **18**(2), 61–79.

Ash, Michael and T. Robert Fetter (2004), 'Who lives on the wrong side of the environmental tracks?' *Social Science Quarterly*, **85**(2), 441–62.

Berry, Lisa M. (2008), 'Inequality in the creation of environmental harm,' in Robert C. Wilkinson and William R. Freudenburg (eds), *Equity and the Environment*, Amsterdam: Elsevier, pp. 239–65.

Bouwes, Nicolaas, Steven Hassur and Marc Shapiro (2003), 'Information for empowerment: the EPA's Risk-Screening Environmental Indicators Project,' in James K. Boyce and Barry G. Shelley (eds), *Natural Assets: Democratizing Environmental Ownership*, Washington, DC: Island Press, chapter 6.

Bullard, Robert (2000), *Dumping in Dixie: Race, Class, and Environmental Quality*, 3rd edn, Boulder, CO: Westview.

Konar, Shameek and Mark A. Cohen (1997), 'Information as regulation: the effect of community right to know laws on toxic emissions,' *Journal of Environmental Economics and Management*, **32**, 109–24.

Mohai, Paul and Robin Saha (2006), 'Reassessing race and socioeconomic disparities in environmental justice research,' *Demography*, **43**(2), 383–9.

Pastor, Manuel (2007), 'Environmental justice: reflections from the United States,' in James K. Boyce, Sunita Narain and Elizabeth A. Stanton (eds), *Reclaiming Nature: Environmental Justice and Ecological Restoration*, London: Anthem Press, pp. 351–78.

Pastor, Manuel, James Sadd and Rachel Morello-Frosh (2005), 'The air is always cleaner on the other side: race, space, and air toxics exposures in California,' *Journal of Urban Affairs*, **27**(2),127–48.

Rinquist, Evan J. (2005), 'Assessing evidence of environmental inequities,' *Journal of Policy Analysis and Management*, **24**(2), 223–47.

Tietenberg, Tom (1998), 'Disclosure strategies for pollution control,' *Environmental and Resource Economics*, **11**(3–4), 587–602.

5. Where credit is due

(with Jane D'Arista)

Public policies for credit allocation are intended to alter the patterns of lending that would result if financial decisions were guided solely by the 'free play' of market forces. These policies include both lending by public-sector institutions, often at below-market rates, and the use of regulations and incentives to influence the behavior of private-sector lenders.

The primary rationale for these interventions is to redress market failures caused by public goods and externalities, including those related to economies of scale and long-term time horizons. Another important set of market failures are those that result in socially undesirable environmental degradation, but credit allocation rarely has been targeted to redressing market failures of this type.

This chapter explores the potential for using credit allocation as a tool to advance environmental goals. First, we discuss the need for public policies to advance environmental goals domestically and internationally. We then describe some of the most important techniques for credit allocation that are used in the US economy. Finally, we explore several ways in which credit allocation could be harnessed for environmental goals, both domestically and internationally.

ENVIRONMENTAL GOALS AND PUBLIC POLICY

Environmental degradation threatens the well-being of current and future generations worldwide. It takes two broad forms: first, the depletion of natural sources of wealth, such as soils, forests, minerals and biodiversity; and second, the abuse of environmental sinks via the discharge of wastes into water bodies, the air and the global atmosphere.

Environmental Degradation as Market Failure

In mainstream economic theory, socially undesirable environmental degradation occurs because not all of the costs and benefits of market activities flow to the buyers and sellers who engage in the production, exchange and consumption of a good or a service. Some costs and benefits accrue to third parties who are not involved in the market transaction. These 'externalities' lead to inefficient outcomes. External benefits (or positive externalities) are underproduced, because those who generate them are not compensated for doing so. External costs (or negative externalities) are overproduced, because they are not borne by those who generate them.

Environmental sources and sinks are subject to both types of externalities – positive and negative. A few examples will illustrate:

- Open-access natural resources such as ocean fisheries are subject to chronic overuse, resulting in harvests well below the biological potential, and in some cases leading to the extinction of commercially valuable species. In the absence of incentives to do so, individuals do not take account of the external costs their own extraction activities impose on others.[1]

- The many thousands of varieties of the world's food crops constitute perhaps the single most important form of biodiversity from the standpoint of the well-being of future generations of humankind. The conservation and ongoing evolution of this crop genetic diversity is an enormously valuable service provided by peasant farmers worldwide, particularly in such historic centers of diversity as south-central Mexico and Guatemala in the case of maize, or eastern India and Bangladesh in the case of rice. Yet in the absence of incentives to continue providing this external benefit, peasants are today abandoning the cultivation of diverse crop varieties, switching to fewer 'modern varieties' or to non-agricultural pursuits.[2]

- Air and water pollution have numerous adverse effects, including impacts on human health, forests and crops, wildlife, and materials such as buildings and statues damaged by acid rain. The polluter shares, at most, a minor fraction of these consequences; most of the effects of discharging wastes into environmental sinks fall on others in the form of external costs.

- Carbon is stored ('sequestered') in trees and other plants, thereby removing some carbon dioxide from the air and helping to counter global warming. Since farmers and forest owners receive no compensation for providing this external benefit, they have no incentive to factor it into their land-use decisions.

The first two cases exemplify negative and positive externalities, respectively, with respect to environmental sources. The second two are examples

Type of environmental resource	Type of externality	
	Negative	Positive
Source	Fisheries depletion; deforestation	Conservation and evolution of crop genetic diversity
Sink	Pollution of air and water	Carbon sequestration

Figure 5.1   Examples of negative and positive externalities

of negative and positive externalities with respect to environmental sinks (Figure 5.1). In each case, markets alone fail to provide adequate incentives for environmental management.

Of course, governments can fail too. In theory, market failures can be corrected by a variety of government interventions designed to induce or compel private actors to 'do the right thing' – for example, to take environmental externalities into account in their decision-making. But in practice there is no guarantee that the government itself will do the right thing. The willingness and ability of governments to advance the public interest is filtered through the political process, and so the government's de facto definition of the public interest reflects the distribution of power in the society. International evidence suggests that countries with a more egalitarian distribution of power – as exhibited by the distribution of income, the extent of political rights and civil liberties and the rate of adult literacy – tend to have better environmental quality.[3]

Policy Instruments

There are three broad classes of policy instruments by which governments can seek to advance environmental goals: 'command-and-control' regulations, the creation of market-based incentives and credit allocation. To date, the first two classes of instruments have received far more attention than the third.

Regulations alter the rules of the game by requiring producers or consumers to act in ways designed to safeguard the environment. Emission standards, which limit the amount of pollution that factories or motor vehicles can release into the air, are one example. Mandated pollution-control technologies, such as scrubbers in smokestacks or catalytic converters in motor vehicle engines, are another. Historically, regulation has been the most important avenue by which governments have moved to protect the environment.

Market-based incentives operate not by regulating quantities, but by creating new prices. This is done through pollution taxes or marketable emission permits, both of which effectively put a price tag on emissions and then let firms and individuals decide how much to emit. This class of instruments has been advocated in recent decades by many economists, on the grounds that market-based incentives can secure a given level of pollution reduction at a lower total cost than command-and-control regulations, by allowing polluters who can cut emissions more cheaply to cut them more than those for whom pollution control is relatively expensive. The best-known example of putting this theory into practice in the United States is the sulfur dioxide emission-permit trading scheme introduced in the 1990 Clean Air Act amendments.

Credit allocation has rarely been included in the environmental policy toolkit, in part because government responsibilities for finance and environmental protection are housed in different bureaucratic boxes. Indeed, it can be plausibly argued that in many instances credit allocation has exacerbated environmental degradation around the world by subsidizing everything from the construction of coal-burning power plants and aluminum mining to tropical deforestation and the nuclear power industry.[4] Yet, in principle, the purpose of credit allocation – whether via public-sector lending or interventions in private-sector financial markets – is to promote the internalization of externalities. In the past, the externalities targeted by credit allocation have mainly been those associated with public infrastructure, scale economies and financial stability. But there is no reason that environmental externalities – both positive and negative – could not also be addressed with credit allocation policies.

The International Policy Arena

These environmental policy instruments can be applied internationally as well as domestically. There is, of course, no international government to enact command-and-control regulations or to establish and manage market-based incentive systems, but both sorts of instruments can be adopted at the international level via negotiated inter-governmental agreements, such as the 1987 Montreal Protocol for phasing out the production and use of CFCs to protect the ozone layer, or the 1997 Kyoto agreement to limit carbon emissions. Such agreements are, however, both time-consuming and difficult – as the failure of the US Senate to ratify the Kyoto agreement illustrates – making these instruments most readily suited to domestic environmental policy.

Credit allocation may offer greater scope for advancing environmental goals at the international level, at least in the short run, since there are already established institutions to govern international finance. The World Bank and International Monetary Fund (IMF), regional development banks and bilateral aid and export-promotion agencies already provide international public-sector credit at below-market rates, and help to shape the regulation and incentive regime for international private-sector credit via negotiated agreements and conditionalities.

CREDIT ALLOCATION: PAST OBJECTIVES AND TECHNIQUES

Governments have used a wide variety of techniques to allocate credit in support of economic and social objectives. Direct allocation of public funds using tax revenues or government borrowing is perhaps the most basic form of credit allocation, and is often used to finance projects that private lenders shun because the risk is high or the private return low. But in Western market economies, concerns about the degree of state control and the tax burden have often constrained the use of public funds for lending. As an alternative, governments in these economies have relied heavily on credit allocation techniques that channel private savings to particular borrowers or sectors, using market-based institutions and instruments. These strategies, which allow policy-makers to target diverse priority objectives, are deeply embedded in existing fiscal, monetary and regulatory policy frameworks in developed market economies and in many developing countries as well.

Past and Current Objectives

Strategies for channeling credit to particular sectors and borrowers have been developed to stabilize economies, aid priority borrowers and pursue distributional goals. To stabilize the economy, governments can use quantity controls as a tool of monetary policy, setting overall limits on lending by private institutions and relaxing or tightening those limits as needed. Credit controls that promote institutional soundness can also contribute to macroeconomic stability. The use of credit controls in the United States, for example, reflects a long-standing awareness that overlending can lead to market failure. The National Bank Act of 1865 required that banks limit loans to individual borrowers to 10 percent of their capital. The Securities and Exchange Act of 1934 authorized the Federal Reserve to impose margin requirements, limiting the percentage of the value of corporate stocks that can be borrowed to purchase them. More recently, capital requirements for banks have been used to provide market discipline and curb overlending.

In the last two decades of the twentieth century, the view that regulation should be used to stabilize credit expansion and contraction fell out of favor. In the United States and other major industrial countries, central banks adopted open market operations as the primary monetary policy tool for stabilization purposes. But this can result in unequal effects on different borrowing sectors that are themselves destabilizing.[5]

Moreover, institutional factors may lead to persistent allocative distortions. In countries dominated by large financial institutions and institutional investors, for example, large corporate borrowers typically have preferential access to bank loans and to markets for both short-term and long-term securities. In the United States, strategies to counter this bias, so as to ensure a more balanced flow of credit across the economy, include providing interest rate subsidies for loans, support for special-purpose agencies and institutions, and regulatory requirements that channel funds to small businesses, homeowners and consumers.

After the deregulation in the last decades of the twentieth century, the most important of the remaining US regulatory requirements is the Community Reinvestment Act (CRA). Its objective is to ensure that a substantial share of funds that originate as deposits in a given community are re-lent there to meet local credit needs, including those of low- and moderate-income neighborhoods. A major strength of the CRA is that it provides opportunities to members of the community to voice concerns about the lending policies of depository institutions. Its major weakness is that it applies only to depository institutions and not to other financial sectors.

The divergent preferences of market participants create another obstacle to ensuring a balanced flow of credit. Creditors prefer short-term commitments; borrowers prefer longer maturities to free up a larger share of income to meet other obligations. Although private financial intermediation can solve this problem for some borrowers and lenders, not all borrowers have access to the long-term funding they need. In the United

States, it has been government, not the market, that has taken the lead in expanding access to long-term credit for a larger number of borrowers. In the 1930s, for example, the Reconstruction Finance Corporation (RFC) and its subsidiaries introduced medium-term credits in lending to businesses, extending the then traditional commercial bank loan with a 90-day maturity to loans with maturities of up to five years. Similarly, the Federal National Mortgage Association – an RFC subsidiary now known as Fannie Mae – introduced the long-term, self-amortizing mortgage to replace the medium-term balloon mortgages that led to widespread defaults and bank failures in the 1930s (Patman 1969).

Promoting wider access to credit at reasonable cost has been a priority objective of US policy since the early decades of the twentieth century. This resulted in institutional structures, tax credits and regulatory requirements that seek to address inequities in the way markets allocate credit – in particular, credit to lower-income homebuyers and consumers (D'Arista 1994).

Credit allocation techniques also have been widely used in industrial countries in the post-World War II era to direct credit to priority sectors of the economy, including agriculture, housing, exports, industrial and regional development, transportation and tourism.

Institutional Strategies

The United States began using government-sponsored agencies to allocate credit when Congress established the Farm Credit System in the 1920s. A more ambitious effort was undertaken in the 1930s with the establishment of the RFC. Used first to recapitalize weak but solvent banks, the RFC evolved into a major lender to small businesses, homeowners and state and local governments, and it subsequently funded and operated agencies engaged in the war effort.

The largest government-sponsored enterprise now in existence, Fannie Mae, began its operations under the RFC umbrella, as noted above. Fannie Mae survived the RFC's dissolution in 1954, and went on to become the largest single borrower and lender in US financial markets in the 1990s (Federal Reserve System 2000).

Fannie Mae and other government-sponsored enterprises (GSEs) dedicated to housing finance – the Federal Home Loan Mortgage Corporation (Freddie Mac) and the Federal Home Loan Bank Board – can raise funds at a lower cost than the private institutions they support by virtue of their quasi-governmental status and (limited) authority to borrow from the US Treasury. Their support for private lenders became necessary in the 1970s as inflation and rising nominal interest rates eroded another major allocative strategy also created in the 1930s: the system of private savings and loan associations (S&Ls) that could lend only for housing (D'Arista 1994).

Variations of these US combinations of government-sponsored agencies and private lending for housing have been developed in other countries as well, such as the United Kingdom and Sweden (Dymski and Isenberg 1998). In addition, almost all industrial countries have government-sponsored export-import banks that use tools such as tax preferences, insurance and interest rate subsidies to increase the flow of credit to sectors engaged in this priority activity.

Like the domestic agencies sponsored by national governments, the World Bank and the various regional development banks are able to borrow at below-market rates to lend to preferred borrowers because of their support from member governments. Thus, they represent institutional strategies for allocating credit at the international level.

Quantity Controls

In the United States, reserve requirements are used in conjunction with open-market operations to control bank lending and influence the overall supply of credit. While many other countries have recently adopted open-market operations as their primary policy tool, they previously relied on directives or guidelines that set limits on the amount of credit that banks could extend within a given time period. The United States generally has not used that form of control, although it did so to limit banks' foreign lending in the period 1965–74 as part of the effort to reduce balance-of-payments deficits (Brimmer 1975). But other central banks have a long history of using quantity controls both for restrictive purposes and to expand credit to preferred sectors. Their allocative strategies were implemented by waiving limits on loans to designated borrowers and by providing incentives to channel a larger share of credit to those borrowers.

Another strategy is the use of supplemental or asset-based reserve requirements. This technique requires institutions to hold non-interest-bearing reserves against loans in addition to (or instead of) deposits (see Pollin 1993; Palley 2000). An institution can lower or eliminate the required reserves by lending to preferred sectors. If the institution does not lend to the preferred sectors, it is in effect making an interest-free loan to the government or central bank. For example, Sweden used this strategy in the 1960s to maintain an even flow of credit to housing across the business cycle. All financial institutions – not just banks – were subject to the supplemental reserve requirement (US House of Representatives 1972).

Quantity controls can take a variety of other forms too. In addition to margin requirements for stock purchases, the amount required for down payments on homes and consumer goods and the terms of loans may be regulated, with modifications from time to time so as to discourage or encourage new borrowing. Some countries use quantity controls to limit new issues of equities and bonds, and most have used blanket controls during wartime or other emergency periods. The US Credit Control Act, for example, which dates from World War I, was reactivated in 1980 to brake inflation and stem the fall in the value of the US dollar.

Price Adjustments

Credit allocation can also be implemented through policies that lower the cost of credit to preferred sectors. This method is generally regarded as a tool of fiscal rather than monetary policy, and hence is administered by treasury departments or ministries of finance rather than by central banks. It includes such techniques as lowering or waiving taxes on loans (or taxes on the interest on loans) to preferred sectors, subsidizing interest payments on loans and guaranteeing and insuring loans made by private lenders. These techniques have been used heavily in the United States to reduce the cost of credit for state and local governments, corporate and small businesses, farms, ship builders, home buyers, veterans, students and other preferred borrowers. Because these market-based strategies generally do not involve the direct allocation of public funds, the loss of revenue is termed a 'tax expenditure' and is often viewed as relatively costless. The potential cost of loan guarantees and other contingent liabilities associated with these programs can be considerable, however, in the event of a deep or prolonged recession.

POLICY OPTIONS

Many projects that advance environmental goals require long-term or concessional finance. In some cases – for example, the development of alternative or renewable sources of energy – there are substantial lags before the projects will generate cash flows large enough to repay principal and interest. In other cases, such as loans to small farmers whose agriculture helps to preserve crop genetic diversity, cash flows may never be large enough to service loans on purely commercial terms. To date, there have been few efforts to use credit allocation to correct for the market's failure to finance these and other environmental investments. In national and international credit markets, only governments, top-rated corporations and priority sectors already supported by credit allocation techniques are able to borrow at long maturities and concessional rates (BIS 2000).

In the United States, one such priority sector has been private single-family mortgages. By 2000, these accounted for one-third of total outstanding credit to private non-financial borrowers, and the debt of GSEs and federally related mortgage pools (over $4 trillion) accounted for 15 percent of the outstanding debt of all sectors – government, private and financial (Federal Reserve System 2000). While this is a rousing testament to the efficacy of credit allocation, it could be argued that the focus on single-family houses contributed to environmental degradation by promoting suburban sprawl and increased reliance on the automobile as opposed to public transportation. As recognition of the importance of environmental problems grows, it is appropriate to question the wisdom of continuing to make single-family housing the top priority for credit allocation while at the same time ignoring the needs of our 'house in common,' the environment.

Here we explore three policy alternatives that would build on traditional credit allocation techniques, redirecting them to serve environmental objectives. The first would operate at the national level, by providing long-term funding for environmental projects. The second and third would reallocate funding through existing international financial institutions to support environmental projects and policies.

Creating a US Environmental Finance Authority

The energy crisis in the 1970s prompted a series of discussions about the need to allocate credit for the production of non-oil energy (Federal Reserve Bank of Boston 1973; US House of Representatives 1975). Former Federal Reserve Board Governor Sherman J. Maisel (1973) proposed an environmental finance authority, modeled on Fannie Mae and the Federal Home Loan Bank Board, to support loans originated by private lenders to develop alternative energy strategies. As reasonable as this proposal appeared to many at the time, and as prescient as it seems in retrospect, it was lost in the growing ascendancy of free-market ideology that shunned government intrusion in private market decisions (BIS 1995).

In 1994, a new development bank whose mandate includes environmental objectives was created in conjunction with the passage of the North America Free Trade Agreement. This entity, the North American Development Bank (NADB), is authorized to fund development on both sides of the US-Mexican border, and it has a specific mandate to finance environmental infrastructure on the Mexican side, although its initial performance was disappointing.[6] Many environmental projects require a national focus, however, because of both their scope and the scale of financing required.

A more appropriate model for an US environmental finance authority (EFA) would be an agency with a national mandate to focus expertise in financing a targeted set of projects and concerns. The EFA could begin operations as a wholly public entity, whose stock is owned by the federal government rather than by private investors. Like other GSEs, it could be given limited authority to borrow from the Treasury as well as authority to expand its funding by issuing its own securities. The Treasury contribution could be regarded as capital, with the EFA's total borrowing (and lending) restricted to a multiple of this amount. In addition to this capital requirement, strong disclosure and transparency requirements would help to guard against excessive and high-risk lending, problems that eventually surfaced in the case of Fannie Mae. To ensure that funding is adequate to meet the needs of this new entity, one could tap yet another credit allocation technique: imposing a small supplementary reserve requirement on all US financial institutions that can be satisfied by investing in the obligations of the EFA as well as by providing direct funding for environmental projects.

Public ownership would require that overall policy guidelines be set by Congress, a process that would generate meaningful debate on environmental issues. The EFA would allow for a mix of financing options to implement existing objectives, support new research and respond to emerging problems. Such a mix might include loans, grants, interest rate subsidies, tax credits, and guarantees for loans and securities originated by private lenders. The EFA could pool and securitize its own loans, tapping private investors both for its initial funding and to redistribute its portfolio. For example, the EFA could pool and securitize long-term loans to states and municipalities to clean up brownfields, to purchase land or conservation easements, and to fund water and sewerage projects, significantly increasing the number and effectiveness of these efforts. Similar techniques – perhaps with the addition of interest rate subsidies and tax credits – could be used to promote such activities as *in situ* conservation of crop genetic diversity, sustainable forestry and renewable energy projects.

The history of lending by GSEs to other priority sectors supports the view that the government needs to assume a leadership role to make adequate and innovative funding available for environmental objectives. It can be hoped that other countries also would establish EFAs with similar objectives. But unilateral action by the United States alone could make a very substantial contribution to improving not only the nation's environment but also the global environment.

International Financial Institution Lending Operations

The World Bank and the regional development banks – the Inter-American Development Bank, the Asian Development Bank, the African Development Bank and the European Bank for Reconstruction and Development – were created to allocate credit internationally, based on explicit recognition that private credit markets cannot provide an adequate channel for financing investments that yield long-term payoffs and social returns not fully appropriable by the private investor.

Minimally, one might hope that these international financial institutions (IFIs) would not allocate credit for projects that exacerbate serious environmental problems. Yet in practice, even by this modest standard, the IFIs have often fallen short. All too often their lending has subsidized investment in fossil fuel-based power generation, tropical deforestation, pesticide-intensive agriculture and other environmentally destructive activities. The result is a double subsidy: a financial subsidy in the form of publicly backed credit at below-market rates, on top of the 'pollution subsidy' (Templet 1995) that is present whenever firms save money by passing the costs of pollution onto others rather than internalizing the costs of pollution control.

One example is the unconscionable bias of World Bank energy-sector lending in favor of fossil fuels. In the six years following the 1992 Earth Summit, the Bank spent 25 times more on fossil fuel energy projects than it did on renewable energy projects (Institute for Policy Studies 1998). The Bank invested a small fraction of its funds – with disproportionate publicity – in renewable energy projects, including a $100 million loan to China (Friends of the Earth-US et al. 2000). Through the Global Environmental Facility (GEF), implemented jointly with the United Nations, the Bank also helped to establish a global equity fund called the Renewable Energy and Energy Efficiency Fund, and a Solar Development Group that seeks to stimulate the market for photovoltaic technology in developing countries (World Bank 2000b). These efforts were dwarfed, however, by more than $15 billion in World Bank lending for oil, gas and coal projects.

A more ambitious – but not unreasonable – hope would be that IFI credit allocation would not only do no harm, but also actually do some good by positively advancing environmental goals. For example, if the majority of the energy-sector lending by the World Bank and the regional development banks were redirected into solar, wind and other renewable energy investments, this would do much to foster the technological innovations and scale economies needed to reorient global energy development toward a sustainable path. Yet a proposal to earmark even 20 percent of its lending for clean and renewable energy was cut from the final version of the World Bank's 1999 Energy and Environment Strategy (Friends of the Earth-US et al. 2000).

A further avenue by which the IFIs could positively advance environmental aims would be to support the establishment of national EFAs, along the lines suggested above, in borrower countries. These could provide a vehicle to support a variety of environmentally beneficial investments, including small-scale activities in agriculture, forestry and other sectors.

Green Conditionality

International credit allocation can also advance environmental goals by impacting domestic environmental policies. Access to international credit on favorable terms invariably requires borrowers to accept certain conditions set by the creditors. Historically, these conditions have ranged from favorable treatment for foreign investors, to the adoption of neoliberal economic reforms, to (in rarer cases) more vigorous efforts to reduce poverty. By framing conditions to require borrowers to adopt domestic policies to address environmental goals, international allocation of publicly backed credit could alter the constraints and incentives facing domestic policy-makers, much as domestic policy-makers themselves can alter the constraints and incentives facing private-sector creditors.

The typical conditions attached to loans from the IFIs and bilateral aid agencies – macroeconomic stabilization, structural adjustment and trade liberalization – at best have had mixed impacts on the environment (Reed 1996). In a candid internal review of its forestry strategy, for example, the World Bank (2000a, p. 13) observed: 'The Bank does not require environmental impact assessment of structural adjustment loans . . . Yet policies associated with economic crisis and adjustment – such as devaluations, export incentives, and removal of price controls – tend to boost production of tradable goods, including agricultural and forestry products. In doing so, and without mitigatory measures, they encourage forest conversion. Further, constrained fiscal situations may lead to reduced public spending on environmental protection and weaken the capacity of forest ministries to enforce laws and regulations.'

In the 1990s, 'second-generation' conditionalities – seeking to advance new objectives such as good governance, democratization and the protection of human rights – began to be implemented by some donors. In a similar fashion, green conditionality could be used to advance environmental goals. Just as national-level credit allocation includes not only public-sector lending but also policies that shape the rules and incentives for private lenders, so international credit allocation can help to shape the rules and incentives for national governments. International lenders could encourage borrower governments to deploy a range of policy instruments – regulations, market-based incentives and domestic credit allocation – to protect the environment.

This can be done either through *ex ante* conditionality – providing credit to borrowers who agree to implement policy reforms – or through *ex post* conditionality (or 'selectivity'), preferentially channeling credit to governments that have good environmental records and hoping that the demonstration effect will induce others to follow suit. In either case, two preconditions must be met if environmental conditionality is to be effective. First, there must be a domestic constituency for the environmental policies within the borrower country. Conditionality can help to strengthen the hand of those seeking environmental policy reforms, but only if there is already a hand to be strengthened. Second, there must be a credible commitment to sound environmental policies by the creditor institutions and the creditor countries themselves.

It is not enough for conditions to be attached to a loan: words on paper must be matched by actions on the ground. This has not always been the case. In the Brazilian Amazon, for example, the World Bank conditioned loans for road construction and infrastructure development on various environmental safeguards, including the creation of biological reserves and the restriction of agriculture to suitable soils, but these conditions were then not met (Repetto and Gillis 1988, p. 34).

In a review of instances in which the World Bank used conditionality in an effort to bring about reforms in forestry policy, Seymour and Dubash (2000, p. 2) report that the Bank was able 'to catalyze key forest policy changes' when, as in Papua New Guinea, it allied with progressive reformers in the government to oppose the vested interests, including foreign companies, who profited from rapacious logging. The authors conclude, however, that such 'limited successes are counterbalanced by significant failures and omissions,' which they attribute in part to wavering commitment within the Bank itself.

The credibility and legitimacy of green conditionality will be seriously undermined as long as the creditor nations fail to put their own environmental houses in order. In sheer quantitative terms, domestic policies within the advanced industrialized countries are the single most important avenue to address global environmental degradation, and will remain so as long as these countries account for the bulk of the world's production and consumption. The countries whose average incomes place them in the richest one-fifth of the world's population account for more than two-thirds of world income, while the countries whose average incomes place them in the poorest fifth account for only 1 percent (United Nations

Development Programme 1992, p. 36). Whether the amount of environmental degradation generated by a dollar's worth of economic activity is higher in the poor countries than in the rich countries is an open question, but if we assume that the degradation per dollar is roughly comparable in both sets of countries, then the richest account for approximately 70 times more environmental damage than the poorest. Put differently, the amount of environmental degradation driven by the activities of the poorest countries could equal that driven by the richest only if their degradation per dollar was 70 times higher – a thoroughly implausible figure.[7]

In this context of extreme international income inequality, the domestic policies of the richest countries therefore will continue to have enormous weight in worldwide environmental quality. Developing countries naturally, and justifiably, are reluctant to shift to renewable energy sources or to adopt other policies to safeguard the global environment as long as economic activities in the creditor countries continue to drive the lion's share of global environmental degradation.

SUMMARY AND CONCLUSIONS

The allocation of credit is nowhere left entirely to private capital markets, for good reasons. Financial markets work well when investments generate cash flows over fairly short-term time horizons. Investments that yield long-term returns, and investments that yield significant benefits to others but only small cash flows to the investor, are chronically underfunded by private capital markets.

For these reasons, national governments and international institutions play important roles in allocating credit throughout the world. They do so not only by lending public monies, but also by shaping the regulatory and incentive structures facing private lenders. To date, however, this policy instrument has not been systematically used on behalf of environmental goals.

The main instruments of environmental policy have instead been regulations and, more recently, the creation of market-based incentives designed to internalize environmental impacts in private decision-making. Important and useful as these real-sector policies are, they could be strengthened by the use of complementary financial-sector policies. Credit allocation can serve as a third leg in the stool on which environmental policy sits.

We have offered several examples of how this could be done. We are well aware that there is no guarantee that interventions by governments or international institutions necessarily will advance public well-being.

History provides ample evidence that they can do the opposite, benefiting politically powerful individuals and groups at the expense of the society at large. Credit allocation and environmental protection are not immune to this risk. Yet at the same time, these tasks cannot safely be left to private markets. The best way to ensure that public policies for both credit allocation and environmental protection genuinely serve the public interest is to ground them in decision-making processes that are transparent, accountable and democratic.

NOTES

* This chapter is a revised version of an article originally published in *Challenge* (2002), **45**(3), 58–82.
1. Following Hardin (1968), this phenomenon is often called the 'tragedy of the commons.' More accurately, it should be called the 'tragedy of open access,' to distinguish it from the formal and informal common-property management institutions that have sustainably managed natural resources in many parts of the world. On the contrast between open-access and common-property fisheries, see Tierney (2000); on common property more generally, see Ostrom (1990).
2. For discussion of this genetic erosion, see Boyce (1996), Brush (2003) and Chapter 8.
3. See Torras and Boyce (1998). Similarly, in a study of the 50 US states, Boyce et al. (1999) find that states with a more equitable distribution of power – as measured by an index based on voter participation, tax fairness, Medicaid access and educational attainment – tend to have stronger environmental policies and better environmental quality.
4. See, for example, Rich (1994) on the environmental impacts of World Bank lending; Cohn (1997) on the role of the US government in the development of the nuclear power industry; and Rich (2000) on the environmental impacts of US and European export credit agencies.
5. For discussion, see Maisel (1973), US House of Representatives (1975), Pollin (1993) and Palley (2000).
6. NADB lending was limited to a narrow range of sectors (water, wastewater and sewerage). Moreover, the commercial terms imposed on borrowers (15-year maturities and 25–27 percent interest rates) were inappropriate, and the geographic limits (100 km on either side of the border) inhibited the bank's ability to fund needed projects (Alden 2000).
7. If we adjust national income for international differences in purchasing power, this narrows to 16 timers, still an implausible ratio (see Chapter 9).

REFERENCES

Alden, Edward (2000), 'Fox looks to bank to close crossborder income gap,' *Financial Times*, 22 August.
BIS (Bank for International Settlements) (1995), *Annual Report*, Basle, Switzerland: BIS.
BIS (Bank for International Settlements) (2000), *International Banking and Financial Market Developments*, Basle, Switzerland: BIS.
Boyce, James K. (1996), 'Ecological distribution, agricultural trade liberalization, and in situ genetic diversity,' *Journal of Income Distribution*, **6**, 263–84.

Boyce, James K., Andrew R. Klemer, Paul H. Templet and Cleve E. Willis (1999), 'Power distribution, the environment, and public health: a state-level analysis,' *Ecological Economics*, **29**, 127–40, reprinted in James K. Boyce (2002), *The Political Economy of the Environment*, Cheltenham, UK and Northampton, MA, USA: Edward Elgar Publishing, chapter 6.

Brimmer, Andrew (1975), statement before the Subcommittee on Domestic Monetary Policy of the US House Committee on Banking, Currency and Housing on H.R. 212, An Act to Lower Interest Rates and Allocate Credit, 5 February, Washington, DC.

Brush, Stephen (2003), 'The lighthouse and the potato: internalizing the value of crop genetic diversity,' in James K. Boyce and Barry Shelley (eds), *Natural Assets: Democratizing Environmental Ownership*, Washington, DC: Island Press, chapter 10.

Cohn, Steven M. (1997), *Too Cheap to Meter: An Economic and Philosophical Analysis of the Nuclear Dream*, Albany, NY: State University of New York Press.

D'Arista, Jane (1994), *The Evolution of US Finance: Volume II*, Armonk, NY: M.E. Sharpe.

Dymski, Gary and Dorene Isenberg (1998), 'Housing finance in the age of globalization: from social housing to life-cycle risk,' in Dean Baker, Gerald Epstein and Robert Pollin (eds), *Globalization and Progressive Economic Policy*, Cambridge: Cambridge University Press, pp. 219–39

Federal Reserve Bank of Boston (1973), *Credit Allocation Techniques and Monetary Policy*, proceedings of a conference held in September at Melvin Village, NH,

Federal Reserve System (FRS) (2000), *Flow of Funds Accounts of the United States*, Washington, DC: FRS.

Friends of the Earth-US, Institute for Policy Studies and Center for International Environmental Law (2000), 'Hot dividends: the World Bank's investments in climate changing fossil fuels,' Prague 2000 Issue Briefings, August.

Hardin, Garret (1968), 'The tragedy of the commons,' *Science*, **168**, 1243–8.

Institute for Policy Studies (1998), *The World Bank and the G-7: Still Changing the Earth's Climate for Business, 1997–1998*, December, Washington, DC: Institute for Policy Studies, Sustainable Energy and Economy Network.

Maisel, Sherman J. (1973), 'Improving our system of credit allocation,' in Federal Reserve Bank of Boston (ed.), *Credit Allocation Techniques and Monetary Policy*, proceedings of a conference held in September at Melvin Village, NH, pp. 15–30.

Ostrom, Elinor (1990), *Governing the Commons: The Evolution of Institutions for Collective Action*, Cambridge: Cambridge University Press.

Palley, Thomas (2000), *Stabilizing Finance: The Case for Asset-based Reserve Requirements*, report in the Financial Markets and Society Series, Philomont, VA: Financial Markets Center.

Patman, Wright (1969), 'The RFC model should be used in today's economy,' *Congressional Record*, 4 August.

Pollin, Robert (1993), 'Public credit allocation through the Federal Reserve: why it is needed; how it should be done,' in Gary A. Dymski, Gerald Epstein and Robert Pollin (eds), *Transforming the US Financial System*, Economic Policy Institute, Armonk, NY: M.E. Sharpe, pp. 321–54.

Reed, David (ed.) (1996), *Structural Adjustment, the Environment, and Sustainable Development*, London: Earthscan.

Repetto, Robert and Malcolm Gillis (eds) (1988), *Public Policies and the Misuse of Forest Resources*, Cambridge: Cambridge University Press.

Rich, Bruce (1994), *Mortgaging the Earth: The World Bank, Environmental Impoverishment, and the Crisis of Development*, Boston, MA: Beacon Press.

Rich, Bruce (2000), 'Trading in global negligence: the need for reform of export credit agencies,' paper presented at the Workshop on the Environmental Dimensions of Global Financial Architecture, New America Foundation, 20 June, Washington, DC.

Seymour, Frances and Navroz Dubash (2000), *The Right Conditions: The World Bank, Structural Adjustment, and Forest Policy Reform*, Washington, DC: World Resources Institute.

Templet, Paul (1995), 'Grazing the commons: externalities, subsidies, and economic development,' *Ecological Economics*, **12**, 141–59.

Tierney, John (2000), 'A tale of two fisheries: as New Englanders overfish their way to ruin, Australians have profited by becoming conservationists,' *New York Times Magazine*, 27 August, pp. 38–43.

Torras, Mariano and James K. Boyce (1998), 'Income, inequality, and pollution: a reassessment of the environmental Kuznets curve,' *Ecological Economics*, **25**, 147–60, reprinted in Boyce (2002), chapter 5.

United Nations Development Programme (1992), *Human Development Report 1992*, New York: Oxford University Press.

US House of Representatives (1972), *Foreign Experience with Monetary Policies to Promote Economic and Social Priority Programs*, staff report of the Committee on Banking and Currency, Washington, DC: Government Printing Office.

US House of Representatives (1975), hearings before the Subcommittee on Domestic Monetary Policy of the Committee on Banking, Currency and Housing on H.R. 212, An Act to Lower Interest Rates and Allocate Credit, 4–6 February, Washington, DC.

World Bank (2000a), *A Review of the World Bank's 1991 Forest Strategy and its Implementation. Volume I: Main Report*, 13 January, Washington, DC: World Bank, Operations Evaluation Department.

World Bank (2000b), 'Implementation of the World Bank's GEF Program,' *Environment Matters: Annual Review 2000*, Washington, DC: World Bank, pp. 56–7.

6. Cap and dividend: carbon revenue as common wealth

(with Matthew E. Riddle)

This chapter explores the economics of a cap-and-dividend strategy for reducing emissions of carbon dioxide – the principal greenhouse gas – in the United States. It does so by analysing the Carbon Limits and Energy for America's Renewal (CLEAR) Act, a bill introduced by Senators Maria Cantwell (D-WA) and Susan Collins (R-ME) in December 2009, that would have capped the nation's carbon emissions, auctioned the permits by which the cap is implemented and recycled most of the revenue directly to the American people in the form of equal dividends paid to every woman, man and child.

After the American Clean Energy and Security Act – the bill that was backed by the Democratic leadership – failed to clear the Senate in the summer of 2010, climate policy slipped off the nation's political agenda. But climate change will not go away. When Congress musters the political will to tackle the issue again, the CLEAR Act or something like it could re-emerge.

The CLEAR Act aims to safeguard the Earth's climate while at the same time protecting the economic security of American families. The Act seeks to protect the climate by capping the use of fossil fuels. The cap would tighten over time, reducing US carbon emissions to only 20 percent of current levels by 2050. At the same time, the Act seeks to protect family incomes by recycling three-quarters of the revenues from the sale of carbon permits directly to the public, and by devoting the remaining one-quarter to job-creating investments in the clean energy transition.

The principle behind the dividends is that the American people own the country's share of the Earth's scarce carbon absorptive capacity in equal and common measure. The dividend provisions of the CLEAR Act thus are not only about protecting families from the impact of higher fossil fuel prices. They are also about ensuring a democratic distribution of the novel property rights that will be created by capping carbon emissions.

In this chapter, we first sketch the basic features of the CLEAR Act. We then estimate its impacts on household incomes, state by state and across income brackets, taking into account the net impacts of higher fuel prices and revenue recycling. Finally, we estimate the job creation that would result if the investment funds were allocated across the states based on differences in their carbon emissions from electricity consumption, unemployment and population.

CLEAR BASICS

The CLEAR Act is a '100-75-25-0' climate policy:

- 100 percent of the permits to bring fossil carbon into the US economy will be auctioned – there are no permit giveaways. The bill strictly limits the buying and selling of permits to prevent carbon market speculation and profiteering.
- 75 percent of the auction revenue is returned directly to the public in the form of equal dividends per person. These 'energy security dividends' are paid monthly to every man, woman and child lawfully residing in the United States.
- 25 percent of the auction revenue is deposited into a Clean Energy Reinvestment Trust (CERT) Fund to be used for investments in energy efficiency, clean energy, adaptation to climate change and assistance to sectors that face economic dislocation during the transition from the fossil-fueled economy.
- Zero 'offsets' are allowed. Polluters cannot avoid buying permits or curbing their use of fossil fuels by paying someone else in the United States or elsewhere to clean up after them.

Equal Treatment Across Firms and Households

The Act provides equal treatment for firms in the fossil fuel industry, regardless of whether the fuel is coal, oil or natural gas. Firms are required to buy permits, called 'carbon shares,' one for each ton of fossil carbon that they bring into the nation's economy. At the mine heads, pipelines and ports where the fuels enter the economy, the firms surrender one permit for each ton of carbon. Another ton requires another permit. The total number of permits is set by the cap, which decreases year by year. Because all permits are auctioned – with no free giveaways to favored industries – the result is a level playing field: every atom of fossil carbon is treated equally.

The Act provides equal treatment for consumers, too. All US residents receive the same monthly dividend, regardless of their income and regardless of where they live. These dividends insulate family purchasing power, or real incomes, from the impact of higher energy prices that result from the cap. Households that consume below-average amounts of fossil fuels (and things produced and distributed using them) will come out ahead in pocketbook terms: their dividends will exceed what they pay in higher prices. Households that consume large quantities of fossil fuels will pay more than they get back. All households have an incentive to economize on the use of fossil fuels, in response to the price signal resulting from the cap. For any given household, the net impact of the policy on real income depends on its consumption decisions.

How will Dividends be Paid?

The most efficient way to pay the monthly climate policy dividends to the public is via electronic funds transfer (EFT). ETF is now the most widely used method by which federal and state agencies distribute recurrent payments to individuals. The US Treasury's Financial Management Service currently disburses almost one billion payments annually on behalf of the Social Security Administration, the Department of Veterans Affairs and other federal agencies, and more than 80 percent of these are disbursed electronically.

The two main EFT methods are direct deposit into bank accounts and Electronic Benefit Transfer cards. The first requires that the recipient have a bank account. The second transfers funds through an industry-standard magnetic-stripe debit card that is protected by a personal identification number (PIN). Paper checks are sent to the minority of recipients who prefer non-electronic transfers. Because paper checks are more costly than EFT, the Treasury Department launched its 'Go Direct' campaign that has persuaded millions of recipients to switch from paper checks to EFT. The costs of electronic transfers amount to pennies each – a tiny fraction of the payments themselves.

Region-specific Allocations of Investment

While equal treatment across firms and households is a central feature of the bill, the CLEAR Act recognizes that weaning the economy from fossil fuels poses special challenges for carbon-intensive regions and states. For this reason, the bill specifies that the CERT Fund will provide targeted, region-specific assistance to workers, communities, industries and small businesses that experience hardship during the nation's transition to a clean energy economy.

Other uses of the CERT Fund include investments in the reduction of emissions of greenhouse gases other than carbon dioxide; biological carbon sequestration, at home and abroad; and energy efficiency and clean energy research and development.[1] Subject to the Act's guidelines on eligible uses, decisions on how to allocate CERT funds among alternative investments are left to the Congressional appropriations process.

Carbon Revenue: Follow the Money

The amount of money that will be raised annually by carbon permit auctions, and redistributed via dividends to the public and CERT Fund investments, is likely to be quite substantial. In 2020, the reference year for which we present estimates in this chapter, the cap would limit carbon dioxide emissions to 5.4 billion tons. If we assume a permit price of $25 per ton – which is within the 'collar' of minimum and maximum prices mandated in the bill[2] – this translates into annual permit revenue of $135 billion.

These billions do not materialize out of thin air. The counterpart to the total value of the permits is the higher cost to consumers, as firms pass through the cost of carbon permits to end-users of fossil fuels.[3] Although higher fuel prices are a cost to consumers, they are not a cost to the US economy as a whole. Instead they are a transfer. Unlike the situation when fuel prices rise for other reasons – such as Organization of Petroleum Exporting Countries' (OPEC) supply caps or rising world demand – the extra dollars paid as a result of a cap-and-permit policy are recycled within the national economy. The economic pie remains intact. What changes is how the pie is sliced – and this depends on who gets the money.

THE CLEAR DIVIDEND: IMPACT ON HOUSEHOLD INCOMES

The CLEAR Act specifies that carbon permits will be auctioned to fossil fuel firms, rather than distributed free of charge. Firms will pass through the costs of the permits to consumers via higher prices. In other words, the money that the firms receive from consumers by virtue of higher prices equals what they pay for the permits.[4] The CLEAR Act specifies that 75 percent of the carbon permit revenue will be recycled directly to the public in monthly dividends.

The net impact of this transfer on household incomes is the difference between what the household receives as dividends and what it pays as a result of higher fossil fuel prices. When its dividends exceed what it pays, the household experiences a net financial benefit as a result of the policy.

When what it pays exceeds its dividends, the household experiences a net financial cost. Here we describe how net benefits vary across states and income brackets.

Net Impacts Across the States

Table 6.1 shows state-by-state net impacts on median households – households whose per capita income puts them exactly in the middle of the state's income distribution. The dividend per person, shown in the first column, is the same in every state: in 2020, at a permit price of $25 per ton, it comes to $297 per person. What the household pays as a result of higher fossil fuel prices differs across states, however, because consumption patterns vary due, among other reasons, to differences in median incomes, home heating and cooling needs and the carbon intensity of the state's electricity supply.[5] As a result, net impacts vary across the states too.

Interstate differences in the impact of higher fossil fuel prices ('carbon price impacts') are shown in the second column of Table 6.1. Nationwide, the annual cost to the median household is $234 per person. Differences across the states are fairly small: in the lowest-cost state (Oregon), the annual carbon price impact is $40 less; in the highest-cost state (Indiana), it is $58 more. The range is narrow because total carbon use per capita is fairly similar across the country; so when all fossil carbon is treated equally, carbon price impacts are similar too. Many of the factors that contribute to differences in carbon use across states have offsetting effects. For example, states that use more energy for home heating generally use less for air conditioning. Similarly, states that have more coal-intensive electricity tend to have lower median incomes, and hence lower consumption, which leads to lower carbon price impacts.

It is important to recognize that interstate differences in the impact of higher fossil fuel prices will occur under any policy to cap carbon emissions. Interstate differences in net impacts will depend on who gets the money. The most striking feature of the results shown in Table 6.1 is that the net impact of CLEAR on the median household is positive in every state.[6] Nationwide, the average net benefit works out to $63 per person, or $252 for a family of four.

Net Impacts Across the Income Spectrum

Table 6.2 presents a more fine-grained picture: it shows how net benefits vary across the income-distribution spectrum in each state. In the lower-income deciles (a decile is 10 percent of the population), the

Table 6.1   *Net impact of carbon dividends on median households ($ per capita, 2020)*

State	Dividend	Carbon price impact	Net benefit
Alabama	297	236	61
Alaska	297	244	54
Arizona	297	213	85
Arkansas	297	226	71
California	297	205	93
Colorado	297	270	27
Connecticut	297	248	49
Delaware	297	282	15
DC	297	282	15
Florida	297	221	76
Georgia	297	263	34
Hawaii	297	250	47
Idaho	297	201	96
Illinois	297	254	43
Indiana	297	292	5
Iowa	297	270	28
Kansas	297	270	27
Kentucky	297	262	36
Louisiana	297	234	63
Maine	297	212	85
Maryland	297	270	27
Massachusetts	297	253	44
Michigan	297	263	34
Minnesota	297	277	20
Mississippi	297	215	82
Missouri	297	270	28
Montana	297	223	74
Nebraska	297	255	43
Nevada	297	239	58
New Hampshire	297	236	61
New Jersey	297	250	47
New Mexico	297	225	72
New York	297	206	92
North Carolina	297	249	48
North Dakota	297	270	27
Ohio	297	274	23
Oklahoma	297	235	62
Oregon	297	194	103
Pennsylvania	297	233	65
Rhode Island	297	226	72
South Carolina	297	217	81

Table 6.1   (continued)

State	Dividend	Carbon price impact	Net benefit
South Dakota	297	226	71
Tennessee	297	243	54
Texas	297	248	49
Utah	297	259	38
Vermont	297	197	100
Virginia	297	275	22
Washington	297	198	99
West Virginia	297	245	52
Wisconsin	297	281	16
Wyoming	297	268	29
US average	297	234	63

net impact is invariably positive, reflecting the fact that low-income households consume less than the average amount of carbon. In the top deciles, the net impact is negative, reflecting their above-average levels of consumption.

Two conclusions from Table 6.2 stand out. First, the middle class is 'made whole' by the CLEAR dividends. Approximately 70 percent of the US population comes out ahead from the policy, including not only lower-income families but also the middle class. 'Come out ahead' here means a net benefit in simple pocketbook terms, not counting the policy's main benefits in the form of reduced dependence on fossil fuels and protection from climate change.

Second, interstate differences are quite small compared to differences across the income spectrum. Across the income classes, the average net benefit nationwide ranges from +$190 per person in the bottom decile to −$208 in the top decile. Across the states, by contrast, the net benefit to the median family (see Table 6.1) is always positive, and lies within a much narrower range: +$5 to +$103.

Some opponents of a cap-and-dividend policy have exaggerated regional differences in impacts by confusing interstate differences with differences across the income spectrum. For example, the chief executive of one of the nation's largest coal-based electric utilities claimed in 2010 that the policy would take money from 'mom in the Midwest and dividend it to Paris Hilton.'[7] This assertion stands reality on its head. If 'mom in the Midwest' lives in a median-income household in the 12-state Midwestern region (defined by the US Census Bureau as Illinois, Indiana, Iowa, Kansas, Michigan, Minnesota, Missouri, Nebraska, North Dakota, Ohio,

*Table 6.2   Net impact of CLEAR Act by state and income decile
            ($ per capita, 2020)*

State	Decile									
	1	2	3	4	5	6	7	8	9	10
Alabama	189	152	125	100	75	47	15	−24	−82	−207
Alaska	173	137	112	89	66	41	13	−22	−72	−177
Arizona	199	166	142	119	97	72	43	7	−45	−160
Arkansas	191	156	130	107	83	58	28	−8	−61	−173
California	213	179	154	130	106	79	48	9	−50	−179
Colorado	164	123	94	68	41	12	−21	−62	−123	−254
Connecticut	189	149	119	92	64	34	−2	−47	−115	−270
Delaware	153	112	83	56	29	1	−32	−73	−132	−258
District of Columbia	184	137	102	68	33	−5	−50	−109	−197	−405
Florida	198	163	137	113	89	62	31	−9	−67	−197
Georgia	172	132	102	75	48	19	−15	−57	−119	−250
Hawaii	173	136	109	85	60	34	3	−36	−92	−212
Idaho	202	170	148	127	107	84	59	27	−19	−116
Illinois	179	139	110	84	57	29	−4	−46	−106	−237
Indiana	146	104	73	46	19	−9	−42	−82	−139	−259
Iowa	159	119	91	66	41	14	−16	−54	−107	−218
Kansas	163	122	93	67	41	13	−19	−59	−116	−235
Kentucky	173	133	104	77	50	21	−12	−54	−114	−241
Louisiana	191	154	127	102	76	49	17	−23	−81	−206
Maine	197	164	140	118	96	73	46	12	−36	−141
Maryland	164	123	94	68	41	13	−20	−62	−122	−253
Massachusetts	181	141	112	86	59	29	−5	−48	−111	−253
Michigan	169	129	100	74	48	20	−13	−53	−111	−234
Minnesota	158	117	87	61	34	6	−27	−67	−125	−248
Mississippi	201	167	142	118	95	69	40	3	−51	−166
Missouri	166	125	95	69	42	13	−20	−61	−119	−244
Montana	189	155	130	108	86	62	34	0	−49	−153
Nebraska	170	132	104	80	55	29	−1	−37	−90	−200
Nevada	182	145	119	95	71	45	15	−23	−78	−196
New Hampshire	180	145	119	96	73	48	20	−16	−67	−177
New Jersey	182	143	114	88	61	32	−2	−45	−109	−252
New Mexico	191	157	131	108	85	59	30	−7	−60	−174
New York	213	179	153	129	105	78	46	4	−58	−200
North Carolina	179	141	113	87	62	34	3	−37	−94	−216
North Dakota	160	120	92	66	41	13	−17	−55	−109	−221
Ohio	162	121	91	64	37	8	−24	−65	−124	−248
Oklahoma	187	150	123	99	75	48	18	−19	−73	−188
Oregon	210	179	156	135	114	91	65	31	−18	−124

Table 6.2   (continued)

State	Decile									
	1	2	3	4	5	6	7	8	9	10
Pennsylvania	188	152	125	101	77	51	21	−17	−72	−192
Rhode Island	194	158	132	109	84	58	28	−10	−66	−187
South Carolina	198	164	139	116	93	68	39	3	−49	−162
South Dakota	189	154	129	106	83	59	31	−4	−53	−157
Tennessee	184	146	119	93	67	40	8	−32	−90	−215
Texas	184	145	116	90	63	34	1	−41	−101	−231
Utah	161	124	98	74	50	25	−3	−38	−89	−192
Vermont	205	174	152	131	111	89	64	32	−15	−114
Virginia	164	122	92	64	36	7	−28	−71	−134	−269
Washington	209	177	154	132	110	87	60	25	−26	−136
West Virginia	182	144	117	91	66	38	7	−32	−89	−208
Wisconsin	151	110	81	55	29	2	−29	−67	−122	−236
Wyoming	160	121	93	67	42	15	−16	−54	−109	−224
US average	190	154	126	102	76	49	18	−22	−81	−208

Note: Each decile equals 10 percent of the population, ranked by per capita income (decile 1 = lowest; decile 10 = highest).

South Dakota and Wisconsin), her family receives an annual net benefit of $28 per person (see Table 6.1). If 'Paris Hilton' is meant to connote someone in the top 10 percent of the income spectrum in California, she pays an annual net cost of $179 (see Table 6.2); and if she is meant to connote someone at the very top of the income spectrum – say, in the top 0.1 percent – her net cost, due to her disproportionately high carbon consumption, would be far greater. The accurate way to characterize differences in net impacts would be to say that cap and dividend 'takes money' from elite consumers with outsized carbon footprints and dividends it to everyone equally.

These results have political implications as well as economic significance. The fact that the cap-and-dividend policy protects the real incomes of the middle class and yields net benefits for most families can help ensure that a policy like the CLEAR Act will receive durable support from the public – support that must be sustained over several decades in order to make the clean energy transition. And the fact that interstate differences are relatively small means that the policy has the potential to attract support across the country, from the public in 'red' states, 'blue' states and swing states in between.

THE CERT FUND: INVESTMENT AND JOB CREATION ACROSS THE STATES

Although interstate differences in CLEAR's impacts on consumers are relatively small, there are reasons to be concerned about the dislocations that any policy to reduce the use of fossil fuels will cause on the production side of the economy, particularly in states where coal mining and industries reliant on coal-fired electricity are important sources of jobs and incomes.

The CLEAR Act addresses this concern by specifying that the CERT Fund shall be used, among other things, to carry out programs, provide incentives and make loans and grants 'to provide targeted and region-specific transition assistance to workers, communities, industries and small businesses' in states that experience 'the greatest economic dislocations due to efforts to reduce carbon emissions and address climate change.'

The CERT Fund, as noted above, is the vehicle for allocating the 25 percent of total carbon revenue that is not recycled directly to the public as monthly dividends. The Act provides guidelines for eligible uses of the CERT Fund, but it does not micro-manage its allocation, leaving this to legislative priorities that may change over time.

Interstate Allocation of CERT Investment: An Illustration

Here we provide an example of how CERT resources could be used to address interstate differences in economic impacts of climate legislation on production sectors. In our calculations, we assume that 85 percent of CERT funding will flow back to the states in one way or another – either through federal agencies such as the Department of Energy's Weatherization Assistance Program or through block grants to state governments.[8]

The interstate allocation of the CERT funds presented here is based on three variables: (1) the state's share of total US carbon emissions associated with the consumption of electricity; (2) the state's share of total US unemployment; and (3) the state's share of the total US population.

Our allocation formula puts 25 percent of the weight on carbon emissions, 25 percent on unemployment and 50 percent on population (for details and data, see Boyce and Riddle 2011). Table 6.3 shows the resulting allocation of the CERT Fund by state, again for 2020 with a permit price of $25 per ton. The total amount of money invested in the states is roughly $28.8 billion, or $84 per person. States with larger populations receive more dollars, but the amount per person varies across the states because

Table 6.3   Interstate allocations of CERT investments plus dividends ($ per capita, 2020)

State	CERT investment	Dividend	Total state receipts
Alabama	96	297	393
Alaska	73	297	371
Arizona	76	297	373
Arkansas	84	297	381
California	78	297	375
Colorado	81	297	379
Connecticut	72	297	369
Delaware	94	297	391
DC	109	297	406
Florida	89	297	386
Georgia	88	297	386
Hawaii	75	297	373
Idaho	79	297	376
Illinois	83	297	380
Indiana	108	297	405
Iowa	93	297	391
Kansas	91	297	388
Kentucky	119	297	416
Louisiana	89	297	387
Maine	72	297	369
Maryland	80	297	377
Massachusetts	77	297	374
Michigan	93	297	390
Minnesota	86	297	383
Mississippi	87	297	384
Missouri	95	297	392
Montana	84	297	382
Nebraska	84	297	381
Nevada	93	297	390
New Hampshire	67	297	364
New Jersey	76	297	373
New Mexico	84	297	381
New York	70	297	367
North Carolina	87	297	384
North Dakota	103	297	400
Ohio	97	297	394
Oklahoma	89	297	387
Oregon	73	297	371
Pennsylvania	80	297	377
Rhode Island	83	297	381
South Carolina	88	297	386

Table 6.3   (continued)

State	CERT investment	Dividend	Total state receipts
South Dakota	74	297	371
Tennessee	91	297	389
Texas	85	297	382
Utah	80	297	377
Vermont	60	297	357
Virginia	81	297	378
Washington	68	297	365
West Virginia	99	297	397
Wisconsin	89	297	386
Wyoming	134	297	431
US average	84	297	381

we include unemployment and carbon emissions from electricity in our allocation formula. The resulting CERT allocations range from $60 to $134 per capita, and hence total revenue recycling (dividends plus CERT funds) ranges from $357 in Vermont to $431 in Wyoming.

Comparing the distribution of CERT funds under this formula to the net benefits from dividends to consumers, reported in Table 6.1, we find that states with lower net benefits to consumers generally receive higher allocations from the CERT Fund. Four of the ten locations with the lowest net benefits to consumers (Indiana, Delaware, Ohio and the District of Columbia) would be among the top ten recipients of CERT funds per capita. At the other end of the spectrum, five of the ten states with the largest net benefits to consumers (Oregon, Vermont, Washington, New York and Maine) are among the bottom ten recipients of CERT funds per capita. In no case does a state rank in the top ten or bottom ten in both respects. This balancing effect is not coincidental, since the carbon intensity of the state economy affects both net impacts on consumers and the allocation of the CERT Fund.

In other words, in allocating investments from the CERT Fund, Congress can further promote interstate equity under the CLEAR Act in two ways: by addressing the impacts of the carbon cap on the production side of the economy and, at the same time, channeling greater investment to states that receive smaller net benefits on the consumer side.

Figure 6.1 depicts the interstate differences in the economic impacts of the CLEAR Act. To put these variations in perspective, we also show interstate differences in federal defense expenditures per person in 2008. Compared to defense spending (indeed, compared to most government

CLEAR Act: dividends plus CERT investments

The CLEAR Act would devote 25 percent of carbon revenues to the CERT Fund. Targeting CERT funds to states with more carbon-intensive electricity and higher unemployment would create modest variations across states in total returns (dividends plus CERT investments). The amount received per person in 2020 would vary from $357 in Vermont to $431 in Wyoming.

Federal defense expenditures

All federal policies have disparate economic impacts across the states. The interstate differences are typically much larger than those of the CLEAR Act. Defense expenditures, for example, varied in 2008 from $106 per person in Idaho to $5014 per person in Virginia.

Source: Authors' calculations (upper map); National Priorities Project (lower map).

Figure 6.1 Interstate differences in net impact of the CLEAR Act compared to defense expenditure ($ per capita)

Table 6.4   Employment impacts of spending on fossil fuels, energy efficiency and renewable energy

Sector	Job creation (no. of jobs per $ million)
Fossil fuels	
Oil and natural gas	3.7
Coal	4.9
Energy efficiency	
Building retrofits	11.9
Mass transit/freight rail	15.9
Smart grid	8.9
Renewables	
Wind	9.5
Solar	9.8
Biomass	12.4

Source: Pollin et al. (2009, Table 4).

spending), the CLEAR Act would have strikingly equal economic impacts across the states.

Job Creation Impacts

The CLEAR Act will foster job creation in two ways. First, the shift of private expenditure from fossil fuels to greater spending on energy efficiency and renewable energy will boost jobs. Second, public investments from the CERT Fund will create jobs. The distribution of these jobs across the states can be influenced by Congressional decisions on the allocation of CERT expenditures.

The market price signals created by the cap on carbon emissions will lead to a reorientation of household and business expenditures away from fossil fuels, and boost private spending on energy efficiency and renewable energy. There will be job losses in the fossil fuel sector, and job gains in other sectors such as construction, mass transportation, wind power, solar power and alternative liquid fuels. Spending on energy efficiency and renewables generates considerably more jobs per dollar than spending on fossil fuels (Table 6.4), in part because they are more labor-intensive and in part because they have higher domestic content. So the net effect of this private expenditure shifting will be job creation.

Job growth resulting from private expenditure shifting may surpass the jobs created by public investment from the CERT Fund. Here we focus

on public investments, however, since this is the main avenue by which
Congress can shape the interstate distribution of job creation resulting
from the CLEAR Act. To estimate how many jobs CERT Fund investments would create in each state, under the investment allocation formula
described above, we translate public expenditures into jobs using the
methodology developed by our colleagues Robert Pollin, James Heintz
and Heidi Garrett-Peltier in their 2009 study, *The Economic Benefits of
Investing in Clean Energy*. This study used input-output data at the state
level from the US Department of Commerce to estimate the number of
jobs per dollar of spending on energy efficiency (building retrofits, smart
grid, public transportation and co-generation) and renewable energy
(on-grid renewable electricity, off-grid renewables and alternative motor
fuels). Our estimates include the jobs created in these industries and in the
other industries that supply intermediate goods (such as steel and building
supplies) to them.[9]

The results are presented in Table 6.5. The data again refer to 2020, with
a permit price of $25 per ton of carbon dioxide. We estimate that CERT
Fund investments would create roughly 360,000 jobs nationwide. The
interstate differences in job creation shown in the table roughly mirror the
interstate allocation of CERT dollars.[10]

CONCLUSIONS

The CLEAR Act would put a cap on the use of fossil fuels so as to reduce
emissions of carbon dioxide, the most important greenhouse gas. Any
policy that limits the use of fossil fuels will raise their price, impacting real
family incomes. But the net impact on family incomes depends on who
gets the money that is paid by consumers as a result of higher fuel prices.
The CLEAR Act recycles 75 percent of this money to the public in the
form of equal monthly dividends, and devotes the remaining 25 percent to
clean energy investments.

The dividends are the same for all, but the net impact on family
incomes (dividends minus the impact of carbon prices) will vary among
households, depending on the amount of fossil fuels they consume
directly and indirectly. Families who consume more will have lower
net benefits. Families who consume less will have higher net benefits.
Regardless of their consumption level, all will have an incentive to limit
their use of fossil fuels in response to the market price signals resulting
from the cap.

Because high-income households generally consume more fossil fuels
(and more of just about everything) than low-income and middle-income

Table 6.5   *CERT Fund investment and job creation by state*
              ($ per capita, 2020, with permit price of $25 per ton)

State	CERT investment ($ million)	Jobs created
Alabama	501	7012
Alaska	57	667
Arizona	559	6873
Arkansas	270	3888
California	3189	33,683
Colorado	454	5705
Connecticut	280	3160
Delaware	93	1067
DC	73	767
Florida	1828	23,807
Georgia	967	13,080
Hawaii	108	1377
Idaho	135	1828
Illinois	1193	14,182
Indiana	770	10,177
Iowa	312	4178
Kansas	285	3808
Kentucky	571	8081
Louisiana	447	5962
Maine	106	1583
Maryland	508	6012
Massachusetts	565	6574
Michigan	1029	13,012
Minnesota	504	6462
Mississippi	284	4143
Missouri	631	8585
Montana	91	1294
Nebraska	168	2246
Nevada	273	2959
New Hampshire	99	1312
New Jersey	736	8354
New Mexico	187	2647
New York	1515	17,355
North Carolina	909	11,996
North Dakota	74	1011
Ohio	1244	16,715
Oklahoma	367	5436
Oregon	312	4151
Pennsylvania	1120	14,435
Rhode Island	97	1148
South Carolina	449	6168

Table 6.5 (continued)

State	CERT investment ($ million)	Jobs created
South Dakota	67	979
Tennessee	639	9167
Texas	2346	29,479
Utah	248	3283
Vermont	42	619
Virginia	707	9414
Washington	505	6161
West Virginia	201	2913
Wisconsin	560	7319
Wyoming	81	1057
US total	28,757	363,287

households, they will tend to pay more as a result of higher fuel prices than they receive as dividends. These income-related differences in net impacts also apply at the level of interstate comparisons: all else equal, states with lower per capita incomes will receive higher net benefits from dividends under the CLEAR Act than states with higher per capita incomes.

Of course, all else is not equal: states differ not only in average incomes, but also in other ways that affect net impacts, such as the carbon intensity of their electricity supplies. At any given income level, families in states that get most of their electricity from coal-fired plants will face bigger price increases than families in states that get most of their electricity from less carbon-intensive sources. To some extent, this effect is offset by the fact that more coal-intensive states tend to have lower incomes.

Analysing the economic impacts of the CLEAR Act across the states, we find that interstate differences in impacts on household incomes are much smaller than differences across the income spectrum, and vastly smaller than the differences in other federal programs, such as defense spending. Indeed, the dividends paid to individuals under the CLEAR Act deliver positive net benefits to the majority of households in every state.

Interstate differences would be further reduced by directing more investments under the CERT Fund to states with higher unemployment and/or greater potential economic dislocations from the shift away from dependence on fossil fuels. An advantage of this approach to public invest-ment allocation is that it focuses attention on the production side of the economy, where interstate differences are likely to be more significant, rather than on the consumption side, where they are small. Our estimates indicate that investments from the CERT Fund will create roughly 360,000 jobs nationwide. The economic and political implications of how this employment creation is distributed across the states may turn out to be more important than relatively minor interstate differences in the impacts of the cap-and-dividend policy on consumers.

NOTES

1. For a complete list of eligible uses, see Section 6(c) of the CLEAR Act, available at http://www.cantwell.senate.gov/issues/CLEARAct.cfm (accessed 16 July 2012).
2. The minimum and maximum permit prices set by the bill for the year 2012 are $7 and $21, respectively. The bill specifies that the real (inflation-adjusted) minimum price will rise by 6.5 percent per year and the real maximum price by 5.5 percent per year. Therefore, in 2020, the price collar (in 2012 dollars) will be $11.58–$32.23.
3. Household consumption – both direct expenditures on fossil fuels and indirect expenditures on goods and services produced and distributed using them – accounts for roughly 66 percent of US carbon emissions. The remainder comes from local, state and federal government expenditure, non-profit institutions and exports (Boyce and Riddle 2008, table 1).
4. Most economic analysts assume that firms will pass 100 percent of the permit cost onto consumers. For an analysis of how alternative assumptions on the percentage pass-through would affect estimated impacts on households, see Boyce and Riddle (2007).
5. For details on the methods of calculating net benefits, see Riddle and Boyce (2007). For a more detailed discussion of the reasons for interstate differences, see Boyce and Riddle (2009).
6. This reflects the fact that US household incomes are skewed (in the strict statistical sense of that term) toward upper-income groups: hence the mean (average) is greater than the median (middle). The impact of higher fossil fuel prices is proportional to consumption, so this too is skewed to the top of the distribution. Because the median household is below average in terms of its income and consumption, it pays less than the average into the total carbon-revenue pool. An additional boost to household net benefits comes from the fact that, as noted above, household share of total carbon revenue (75 percent) is somewhat greater than household share of the nation's total carbon consumption (66 percent).
7. Michael Morris, president and CEO of American Electric Power, quoted in Juliet Eilperin and Steven Mufson, 'Senators to propose abandoning cap-and-trade,' *The Washington Post,* 27 February 2010, p. A1.
8. We assume that the remaining 15 percent is devoted to international climate change mitigation and adaptation. The economic benefits from these uses are not included in our analysis.
9. We assume that CERT Funds are allocated across different types of energy efficiency and renewable energy investments in the same proportions assumed in the Pollin et al. (2009) study. We do not count induced employment effects from the consumption multiplier (that is, jobs created when workers in these industries spend their earnings to buy goods and services), because CERT Fund investments recycle carbon permit revenues rather than creating additional demand as in an economic stimulus program.
10. The number of jobs per dollar varies somewhat across the states for two reasons. First, the input-output data from the Commerce Department show some interstate differences in the ratio of jobs per dollar in any given sector. Second, some of the job creation in the supply of intermediate goods spills across state borders (we allocate the

out-of-state portion of this indirect job creation across states in proportion to the relative size of the state economies).

REFERENCES

Boyce, James K. and Matthew E. Riddle (2007), 'Cap and dividend: how to curb global warming while protecting the incomes of American families,' Political Economy Research Institute working paper no. 150, Amherst, MA.

Boyce, James K. and Matthew E. Riddle (2008), 'Keeping the government whole: the impact of a cap-and-dividend policy for curbing global warming on government revenue and expenditure,' Political Economy Research Institute working paper no. 188, Amherst, MA.

Boyce, James K. and Matthew E. Riddle (2009), *Cap and Dividend: A State-by-State Analysis*, Amherst, MA and Portland, OR: Political Economy Research Institute and Economics for Equity and Environment.

Boyce, James K. and Matthew E. Riddle (2011), *CLEAR Economics: State-level Impacts of the Carbon Limits and Energy for America's Renewal Act on Family Incomes and Jobs*, July, Amherst, MA: Political Economy Research Institute.

Pollin, Robert, James Heintz and Heidi Garrett-Peltier (2009), *The Economic Benefits of Investing in Clean Energy*, Amherst, MA and Washington, DC: Political Economy Research Institute and Center for American Progress.

7. A Chinese sky trust
(with Mark Brenner and Matthew E. Riddle)

This chapter examines the scope for addressing two problems in the Chinese economy with one policy. The problems are rising fossil fuel consumption and rising income inequality. The policy is a 'sky trust': a cap-and-dividend system of carbon charges in which the revenues are recycled to the public on an equal per capita basis.

The choice of China as a setting for this analysis is motivated by three considerations. First, China's rising use of fossil fuels is widely seen as jeopardizing both the sustainability of the country's rapid economic growth and the prospects for redressing global climate change. Second, China's rising income inequality, particularly urban-rural inequality, is a source of concern from the standpoints of both human development and potential social unrest. Third, as a developing country, China's pattern of fossil fuel use is likely to differ from that in the industrialized countries where most prior studies of the distributional impacts of carbon charges have been undertaken.

CHINA AND THE GLOBAL CARBON ECONOMY

China is the world's largest emitter of carbon dioxide (CO_2), the most important 'greenhouse gas' implicated in global climate change. In 2009, China's CO_2 releases from fossil fuel combustion amounted to 2.1 billion metric tons of carbon (tC), or 25.4 percent of worldwide emissions; the United States, the world's second largest consumer of fossil fuels, emitted 1.5 billion tC, or 17.9 percent of the total (Figure 7.1).[1]

In per capita terms, China's carbon emissions are less than one-third of those in the United States (Figure 7.2). In recent years, however, the absolute volume of China's emissions has risen substantially, propelled by the country's rapid economic growth. Roughly 70 percent of the country's total energy supply comes from coal. China's fossil fuel consumption has grown at less than half the rate of the country's gross domestic product (GDP), with a relatively small income elasticity of fossil fuel consumption

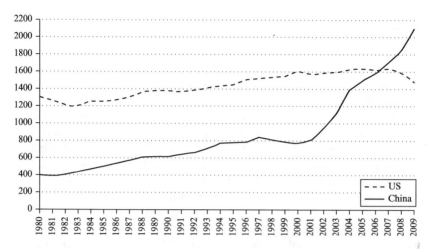

Source: US Energy Information Administration, *International Energy Statistics*, http://
www.eia.gov/cfapps/ipdbproject/IEDIndex3.cfm?tid=90&pid=44&aid=8 (accessed 21
February 2012).

Figure 7.1   *Annual carbon emissions from the consumption of energy,
China and the United States, 1980–2009 (million metric tons
of carbon)*

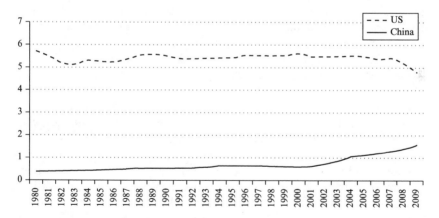

Source: US Energy Information Administration, *International Energy Statistics*, http://
www.eia.gov/cfapps/ipdbproject/IEDIndex3.cfm?tid=90&pid=44&aid=8 (accessed 21
February 2012).

Figure 7.2   *Annual carbon emissions per capita from the consumption of
energy, China and the United States, 1980–2009 (metric tons
of carbon per capita)*

(0.4) compared to other low-income economies.[2] Even so, extrapolation from current trends implies that China's carbon emissions will continue to rise sharply in the coming decade.

A comprehensive picture of China's role in the global carbon economy would include other sources of CO_2 releases, notably from the burning of wood and other biomass resources, as well as the reabsorption of CO_2 by terrestrial and marine plant life. Apart from the additional data needed for such an analysis, this would require grappling with the thorny question of how the carbon reabsorptive capacity of the biosphere – including that of the oceans, which accounts for about half the total – ought to be allocated across countries.[3] Here we avoid these complications by focusing solely on CO_2 emissions from the burning of fossil fuels.

As a developing country, China was not subject to the mandatory emission-reduction targets specified in the 1997 Kyoto Protocol. No international agreement limiting the carbon emissions of developing countries is imminent. Even in the absence of such an agreement, however, it is possible that China at some point will choose to act unilaterally to curb its use of fossil fuels. Several considerations could bring this about. First, China is not well endowed with fossil fuel resources; as a result, the country is now importing coal from Australia, in addition to being the world's fastest-growing importer of oil.[4] Second, China may be more vulnerable to climate change than are the industrialized countries, due to the much higher share of agriculture, an especially climate-sensitive sector, in its GDP.[5] Third, the health and environmental benefits of reduced use of fossil fuels (or slower growth in their use) by virtue of lower emissions of pollutants with localized effects – sulfur dioxide, nitrogen oxides and particulates – would reduce, or perhaps even offset, the net social cost of emission reductions.[6] Fourth, China faces mounting international pressure on this issue.[7] Finally, China has already introduced a system of pollution charges to curb sulfur dioxide emissions, a precedent that may lower the administrative and institutional barriers to the introduction of carbon charges.

To assess the prospects for measures to limit fossil fuel consumption in China, and the potential economic and social effects of such measures, it is important to assess the likely distributional impacts of such policies. Income inequality in China has grown rapidly in recent years, with the Gini coefficient rising from 0.382 in 1988 to 0.452 in 1995 (Khan and Riskin 2001). Rural-urban disparities are a major component of this inequality, with the average income per capita in urban areas (5706 yuan or US$683 in 1995) being 2.5 times higher than that in rural China (2307 yuan or US$276).[8] Accordingly, 17 percent of the rural population was classified as living in poverty in 1995, compared to only 4 percent of the urban population.[9]

To a substantial extent, carbon emissions are driven by household expenditure.[10] Yet to the best of our knowledge, prior studies of China's carbon economy have not disaggregated across households on the basis of income and the rural-urban divide. This chapter is an attempt to address this lacuna.

DISTRIBUTIONAL INCIDENCE OF CARBON CHARGES

One way to reduce carbon emissions is to establish a system of carbon charges that curtails demand for fossil fuels by raising their price.[11] The distributional incidence of carbon charges is important in assessing both their welfare effects and the political economy of their introduction. Two questions arise. First, how will higher prices for fossil fuels (and for goods and services whose production uses fossil fuels) affect different households? Second, how will the revenues generated by carbon charges be used and the resulting benefits distributed? We begin by reviewing the available evidence on the first question; we then consider the second.

Several European countries have introduced carbon charges, starting with Finland in 1990 and followed by Norway, Sweden, Denmark, the Netherlands and Italy (Baranzini et al. 2000). A European Union-wide carbon tax was proposed, but not implemented, in the 1990s (Smulders and Vollebergh 2001). Studies in these and other industrialized countries generally have concluded that carbon charges are regressive − taking a bigger slice in percentage terms from low-income households than from high-income households, mainly because the poor devote a higher fraction of their expenditure to necessities, including fuels − or in some cases, distributionally neutral or mixed.

For example, a simulation analysis by Symons et al. (1994) found that a carbon tax in the United Kingdom would be 'severely regressive.' In Canada, according to Hamilton and Cameron (1994), a carbon tax would be 'moderately regressive.' Cornwell and Creedy (1996) likewise found that a carbon tax in Australia would be regressive. Symons et al. (2000) reported regressive effects in Germany, France and Spain, a mixed effect in the United Kingdom and a neutral effect in Italy. Klinge Jacobsen et al. (2003) and Wier et al. (2005) find that Denmark's carbon taxes are regressive, and Brännlund and Nordström (2004) report that increases in carbon taxes in Sweden would be regressive. Summarizing the results of studies from various Organization for Economic Cooperation and Development (OECD) countries, Cramton and Kerr (1999, p. 261) conclude: 'The weak regressivity of carbon regulation appears to hold across countries and modeling techniques.'[12]

In assessing distributional impacts, studies have often stratified households on the basis of expenditure rather than income, on the grounds that expenditure provides a better proxy for lifetime income and is less subject to transitory shocks. If distributional incidence instead is calculated on an income basis, carbon charges look even more regressive, because expenditure-to-income ratios generally decline as household incomes rise (for discussion, see Metcalf 1999).

The methodologies used in these studies have ranged from relatively simple computations based on the shares of energy products in household expenditure to computable general equilibrium models. Most studies assume that carbon charges are fully shifted forward to consumers, altering the relative prices of goods and services in proportion to their carbon content. The regressive incidence of carbon charges thus reflects the fact that the expenditure patterns of low-income households tend to be more carbon-intensive than those of high-income households.[13]

Whether these findings can be generalized to the developing countries of Asia, Africa and Latin America is an open question. Patterns of household expenditure and energy use in developing countries differ from those in industrialized countries. For example, ownership and use of automobiles is less prevalent in developing countries, and more concentrated in high-income households. Less fuel is used for home heating in tropical and subtropical climates. And biofuels, such as wood and crop residues, are widely used for cooking, particularly in poor rural households.[14] Given these differences, it is not evident that higher prices for fossil fuels would have a regressive impact in developing countries. It has been speculated that 'the net effect of adding a carbon tax in developing countries may well be proportional to income, or even progressive' (OECD 1995, p. 25).

A handful of empirical studies have investigated the distributional impact of carbon charges in developing countries, with mixed results. Shah and Larsen (1992) found that with full forward shifting to consumers, a carbon tax in Pakistan would be regressive (but that with only partial shifting it could be progressive). In a study of Iran, Jensen and Tarr (2002) similarly report that the withdrawal of subsidies on domestic energy products would have a regressive effect, although if this were accompanied by lump-sum redistribution of the savings the net effect would be progressive. On the other hand, in studies of Ghana and Madagascar, respectively, Younger (1996) and Younger et al. (1999) conclude that taxes on petroleum products other than kerosene are progressive.[15]

THE 'SKY TRUST' OPTION FOR LUMP-SUM REVENUE RECYCLING

The net distributional effect of a carbon-charge system depends not only on the impacts of price changes on households, but also on the uses of the revenues generated by the charges. If carbon-charge revenues flow to government as a carbon tax, and are used to increase public expenditure and/ or reduce other taxes, the net effect depends on the incidence of these policies. In this chapter we consider an alternative revenue-recycling option: lump-sum redistribution to all households on an equal per capita basis. Such a system has been dubbed a 'sky trust' (Barnes 2001) or a 'cap-and-dividend' policy (see Chapter 6).[16]

A sky trust would be an autonomous institution established by government action but operating outside the government budget, akin to social security trust funds. It would receive the revenues from carbon charges, and redistribute them to households after a small deduction for administrative costs. Revenues would be most easily and inexpensively collected 'upstream': at the coal mines, oil refineries, natural gas facilities and ports where fossil fuels first enter the economy.[17]

The sky trust option has three attractive features. First, it asserts the principle of common ownership of nature's wealth: rights to benefit from the carbon-absorptive capacities of the biosphere are allocated equally to all. Second, it yields a progressive redistribution of income, the scale of which depends on the level of the carbon charges and on how the carbon intensity of household expenditure varies with income. Third, unlike tax shifting and increased public expenditure, the distributional outcome of the sky trust does not depend on the willingness and ability of government to do 'the right thing' – however defined – with present and future carbon revenues; in other words, once it is established, the sky trust is insulated from the vagaries of fiscal politics.[18]

Several studies have analysed the distributional impact of a hypothetical sky trust in the United States. Recognizing that 'the amount of wealth that a US carbon trading policy would redistribute could reach into the tens or hundreds of billions of dollars,' the US Congressional Budget Office (CBO) compared two methods of allocating carbon emission allowances – selling them (that is, carbon charges), or giving them away to fossil fuel producers and importers free of charge – and two methods of revenue recycling: reducing corporate taxes or rebating an identical lump-sum to each household.[19] The only scenario that was found to have a progressive distributional effect was the combination of allowance sales with lump-sum redistribution: in this case, the regressive effect of price increases (arising from an inverse relation between income and the share of income spent on carbon-intensive goods) was outweighed by the progressive effect of equal payments. With a carbon charge of $100 per ton, the CBO estimated that after-tax incomes in the lowest quintile of the income distribution would rise by 1.8 percent, while those of the top quintile would decrease by 0.9 percent. In an extension of the CBO analysis, Dinan and Rogers (2002) reported even stronger redistributive impacts: a 3.5 percent rise in incomes for the lowest quintile, coupled with a 1.6 percent decline for the top quintile.[20]

Both these studies assumed that carbon charges are distortionary, creating 'deadweight losses' by reducing fossil fuel consumption (and also, in the Dinan and Rogers study, by lowering real returns to labor and capital and thereby reducing factor supplies). For example, when consumers curtail fuel consumption in response to higher prices, they suffer welfare losses in the form of 'the discomfort associated with keeping their house cooler in the winter or the loss in satisfaction that would result from canceling a vacation because of high gasoline prices' (US Congressional Budget Office 2003, p. 3). By placing a monetary value on the forgone consumer surplus and distributing these losses across households, the studies diminish the sky trust's positive effect on incomes of low-income households, and augment its negative effect on those of high-income households. It can be argued, however, that the true distortion is the subsidy currently implicit in the failure to charge for use of the limited carbon absorptive capacities of the biosphere. If so, appropriately calibrated carbon charges would remove a distortion rather than creating one.

Neither study attempts to estimate the welfare gains that would result from reductions in carbon emissions via mitigation of climate change and associated reductions in emissions of other pollutants. Yet these gains are the prime rationale for introducing carbon charges. A comprehensive analysis of the distributional impacts of carbon charges would allocate them across households too. In the absence of this accounting, the incorporation of 'deadweight losses' from carbon charges gives a misleading picture of net welfare effects: in effect, this procedure counts the cost of correcting for the welfare losses from excessive carbon emissions, without counting the benefits. In this chapter, we adopt the simpler – and, in our view, more appropriate – procedure of estimating the distributional impacts of the carbon charges and revenue recycling alone, without attempting to incorporate other welfare effects.

Barnes and Breslow (2003) followed this procedure in a third analysis of the distributional impact of a US sky trust, using a higher carbon price of $191 per ton. They found that the bottom decile would receive a net benefit equal to 5.1 percent of income, while the top decile would bear a net loss of 0.9 percent, and that seven deciles would see net gains. That is, the majority of the population would receive more in rebates than they paid as a result of higher fuel prices. Insofar as public policy follows the principle of majority rule, this result suggests that the establishment of a sky trust would be politically feasible.

Subsequent studies of the distributional impacts of a cap-and-dividend policy in the United States by Boyce and Riddle (2007, 2008, 2009), including the impacts of the CLEAR Act proposed in 2009 by Senators Maria Cantwell and Susan Collins (see Chapter 6), found that if 75 percent of carbon revenue were recycled to the public and the remaining 25 percent retained for other uses, the majority of households still would gain positive net benefits in purely pocketbook terms – not counting the benefits of climate change mitigation and reduced air pollution – with low- and middle-income households coming out ahead.

METHODOLOGY

In order to examine the distributional implications of a carbon charge in China, this study draws on a nationally representative household income and expenditure survey conducted for the year 1995. The survey was designed and overseen by scholars at the Chinese Academy of Social Sciences (CASS), and provided the first publicly available, nationally representative household data from China in the reform era. Households in the CASS sample are drawn from the Chinese State Statistical Bureau's (SSB) annual income and expenditure survey, and SSB enumerators administered the CASS questionnaires.[21]

Household Expenditure Patterns

Table 7.1 provides an overview of the expenditure patterns for households by expenditure decile (each of which represents 10 percent of the population). In the all-China data presented in the top panel, three features stand out:

- First, the top two deciles account for more than half of all household expenditures.
- Second, in the lowest decile, food expenditures comprise more than three-quarters of total household spending, an indication of severe poverty. This share falls to less than 40 percent for the highest decile. A corollary is that the share of non-food items rises as we move up the expenditure distribution.
- Finally, we see that carbon-intensive categories of household spending – items such as fuel, electricity and transportation – account

Table 7.1 Breakdown of household expenditures in China

Per capita expenditure decile	Per capita expenditure (yuan)	Share of total expenditure (%)	Food (%)	Industrial goods (%)	Housing (%)	Household fuels and electricity (%)	Transport and communication (%)	Other[a] (%)
All households								
1	591	2.3	77.4	11.2	1.1	1.4	0.9	8.0
2	840	3.3	76.2	11.0	1.3	1.2	1.5	8.7
3	1022	4.0	76.6	10.6	1.6	1.2	1.3	8.6
4	1218	4.8	74.8	10.7	2.5	1.2	1.5	9.5
5	1451	5.7	73.2	10.8	2.6	1.1	1.4	11.0
6	1771	6.9	70.0	11.5	3.3	1.4	1.7	12.0
7	2258	8.8	63.6	14.0	4.5	1.8	1.8	14.2
8	3097	12.1	55.2	16.3	6.2	2.6	2.1	17.5
9	4414	17.3	48.2	19.9	7.0	2.7	2.5	19.7
10	8866	34.7	38.7	24.7	9.0	2.3	2.5	22.8
All	2553	100.0	65.4	14.1	3.9	1.7	1.7	13.2
Rural households								
1	542	3.5	77.0	11.4	0.9	1.5	0.9	8.2
2	756	4.9	77.4	11.0	1.2	1.3	1.2	8.0
3	894	5.8	76.6	10.6	1.4	1.1	1.5	8.8
4	1021	6.6	76.1	10.8	1.6	1.2	1.4	8.9
5	1161	7.5	75.6	10.6	2.5	1.1	1.5	8.7
6	1315	8.5	74.9	10.5	2.3	0.9	1.4	9.9

7	1505	9.7	73.2	10.5	2.8	1.0	1.6	11.1
8	1760	11.4	71.5	10.9	3.3	1.1	1.9	11.3
9	2154	13.9	67.2	12.0	4.2	1.0	2.3	13.2
10	4353	28.2	56.5	12.7	9.4	1.0	4.7	15.7
All	1546	100.0	72.6	11.1	3.0	1.1	1.8	10.4

Urban households

1	1657	3.3	60.2	16.5	3.8	4.0	0.7	14.8
2	2437	4.9	55.9	18.3	4.9	3.7	0.9	16.3
3	2973	5.9	53.6	19.1	5.5	3.4	1.1	17.3
4	3438	6.9	51.4	18.7	5.5	3.5	1.5	19.3
5	3907	7.8	49.5	20.1	6.4	3.2	1.6	19.4
6	4468	8.9	47.4	21.6	5.9	3.0	1.6	20.5
7	5151	10.3	46.1	21.4	6.4	3.0	1.8	21.3
8	6046	12.1	42.0	22.8	7.2	2.7	2.0	23.4
9	7506	15.0	39.9	24.0	8.3	2.5	1.8	23.5
10	12,530	25.0	31.4	31.0	8.4	1.9	2.1	25.1
All	5013	100.0	47.7	21.4	6.2	3.1	1.5	20.1

Note: [a] Other categories include education, medical expenditures and miscellaneous expenses.

Source: Authors' calculations from 1995 CASS survey data.

for a small share of average household expenditures, but that this share rises with household expenditure. This pattern is the opposite of what is typically found in the industrialized countries of Europe and North America, as discussed above.

Separate results for rural and urban China (presented in the two lower panels of Table 7.1) are broadly similar, the main difference being that the share of spending on fuels and electricity tends to fall as we move up the expenditure distribution. The opposite finding at the all-China level is clearly driven by rural-urban differences.

Measuring Household Carbon Usage

We measure carbon usage at the household level in two steps. First, we separate household spending into six categories: (1) food, including the value of self-produced agricultural products; (2) industrial goods, including clothing, daily use consumption goods and durable goods; (3) housing, specifically new construction and repair costs; (4) household fuels and electricity; (5) transportation and communication; and (6) other expenditures, including education, medical expenditures and other miscellaneous spending.

Second, we apply a carbon-loading factor to each of these six expenditure categories, in order to estimate the carbon usage embodied in these different types of household consumption. We derive the loading factors by matching the six expenditure categories from the survey data to corresponding categories in the Chinese system of national accounts.[22] This provides us with a metric to evaluate the distributional implications of a carbon charge.

The Carbon Charge

To assess the distributional implications of a carbon charge and sky trust revenue-recycling scheme in China, we assume a charge of 300 yuan per tC. This is squarely within the range of hypothetical carbon charges used in prior research on China. For example, Zhang (1998) evaluates the degree to which a carbon charge would reduce CO_2 emissions in China under two scenarios: a charge of 205 yuan per tC and another set at 400 yuan per tC. Zhang estimates that the first scenario would lead to a 20 percent reduction in projected carbon emissions over 20 years, while under the second scenario emissions would fall by 30 percent. In a study of the impact of a carbon charge on emissions in Shanghai, Gielen and Chen (2001) use a charge of 100 yuan per tCO_2 (equivalent to 367 yuan per tC);

they estimate that this would result in an 11 percent reduction in carbon emissions over ten years, along with a substantial shift in types of abatement technology deployed.

The charge of 300 yuan per tC is also comparable with existing carbon charges in other countries. For example, five European countries had coal taxes in place in 1999, ranging from $14 per tCO_2 in Finland to $67 per tCO_2 in Denmark; this range is equivalent to 103 yuan per tC to 491 yuan per tC.[23]

For simplicity, we calculate the distributional impact of carbon charges on the basis of the 1995 consumption patterns, without estimating changes in demand in response to higher fossil fuel prices.[24] Equivalently, we could use a higher carbon charge coupled with commensurately lower demand. For example, a 400 yuan per tC charge that reduced carbon demand to 75 percent of the 1995 level would yield the same results.

In calculating the distributional impact of recycling carbon revenues through a sky trust, we deduct 1 percent from total revenues to cover administrative costs. We regard this as a conservative assumption (that is, a high-end estimate of the administrative costs). As noted above, administrative costs would be minimized by revenue collection at the mine heads, refineries and ports where fossil fuels enter the Chinese economy.

RESULTS

Our main results are presented in Tables 7.2 and 7.3. Table 7.2 shows the distributional incidence of a carbon charge on its own, without taking into account the use of the proceeds. Table 7.3 shows the effect of a sky trust, with the carbon revenue recycled to the Chinese people on an equal per capita basis. The incidence of the charge on each household is calculated by multiplying per capita carbon consumption by 300 yuan per tC. The charge/expenditure column is the average of the charge incidence to expenditure ratios for each person in the decile.[25]

Distributional Effects of Carbon Charges

Table 7.2 shows that in China, even without an egalitarian redistribution of the revenues, the overall effect of the carbon charge would be progressive. The lowest decile pays 2.1 percent of their total expenditures into the charge, whereas the highest decile pays 3.2 percent. This reflects the fact that the mix of products that relatively rich people in China buy is, on average, more carbon-intensive than what relatively poor people buy. This contrasts with results from studies in other countries that have found

Table 7.2   Distributional incidence of a Chinese carbon charge

All households			
Per capita expenditure decile	Per capita expenditure (yuan)	Per capita carbon charge[a] (yuan)	Carbon charge/ expenditure[b] (%)
1	591	12	2.1
2	840	17	2.0
3	1022	20	2.0
4	1218	24	1.9
5	1451	28	1.9
6	1771	37	2.1
7	2258	54	2.4
8	3097	87	2.8
9	4414	136	3.1
10	8866	282	3.2
Rural households			
1	542	11	2.1
2	756	15	2.0
3	894	17	1.9
4	1021	20	2.0
5	1161	22	1.9
6	1315	24	1.8
7	1505	28	1.9
8	1760	34	2.0
9	2154	43	2.0
10	4353	86	2.1
Urban households			
1	1657	55	3.3
2	2437	80	3.3
3	2973	96	3.2
4	3438	112	3.3
5	3907	126	3.2
6	4468	146	3.3
7	5151	168	3.3
8	6046	195	3.2
9	7506	244	3.3
10	12,530	440	3.5

Notes:
[a] Calculated from expenditure breakdown reported in Table 7.1.
[b] Average charge/expenditure ratio for each household in the decile (see note 25).

Table 7.3   *Distributional incidence of a Chinese sky trust*

Per capita expenditure decile	Per capita expenditure (yuan)	Household size	Net benefit per capita[a] (yuan)	charge	dividend	net benefit
All households						
1	591	5.3	57	2.1	12.4	10.3
2	840	4.9	52	2.0	8.2	6.3
3	1022	4.8	49	2.0	6.8	4.8
4	1218	4.8	45	1.9	5.7	3.7
5	1451	4.6	41	1.9	4.8	2.8
6	1771	4.5	32	2.1	3.9	1.8
7	2258	4.1	15	2.4	3.1	0.7
8	3097	3.7	−18	2.8	2.2	−0.6
9	4414	3.4	−67	3.1	1.6	−1.5
10	8866	3.2	−213	3.2	0.9	−2.3
Rural households						
1	542	5.4	58	2.1	13.4	11.3
2	756	5.0	54	2.0	9.1	7.2
3	894	4.9	52	1.9	7.7	5.8
4	1021	4.8	49	2.0	6.8	4.8
5	1161	4.8	47	1.9	5.9	4.0
6	1315	4.7	45	1.8	5.2	3.4
7	1505	4.7	41	1.9	4.6	2.7
8	1760	4.6	34	2.0	3.9	2.0
9	2154	4.3	26	2.0	3.2	1.2
10	4353	4.1	−17	2.1	2.0	0.0
Urban households						
1	1657	3.9	14	3.3	4.5	1.2
2	2437	3.6	−11	3.3	2.8	−0.4
3	2973	3.5	−27	3.2	2.3	−0.9
4	3438	3.4	−43	3.3	2.0	−1.3
5	3907	3.4	−57	3.2	1.8	−1.5
6	4468	3.3	−77	3.3	1.5	−1.7
7	5151	3.2	−99	3.3	1.3	−1.9
8	6046	3.2	−127	3.2	1.1	−2.1
9	7506	3.1	−175	3.3	0.9	−2.3
10	12,530	3.0	−371	3.5	0.6	−2.9

Note: [a] Based on a carbon tax of 300 yuan per tC, which yields a dividend of 69 yuan per person.

a carbon charge to be either regressive or neutral. Our results for China call into question the generality of this conclusion.

A closer look at what lies behind this progressive incidence is useful. The breakdown into urban and rural areas shows that the incidence of the charge in urban areas is higher than in rural areas. As we saw in Table 7.1, urban areas have more carbon-intensive expenditure patterns, spending significantly more than rural households on household energy and industrial goods, the two most carbon-intensive sectors in China. The rural population, in contrast, devotes a larger share of its expenditure to food, which is much less carbon-intensive. The result is that households in urban areas would pay an average of 3.3 percent of their expenditure into the sky trust, while households in rural areas would pay 2.0 percent. Since the average income in urban areas is considerably higher than in rural areas, this difference makes the overall incidence of the charge progressive.[26]

A similar pattern may exist in other developing countries – particularly where rural areas are relatively poor, consume few industrial products and obtain much of their direct energy use from firewood and other biomass that would not be subject to carbon charges. In other words, in contrast to the typical pattern found in industrial countries, carbon charges may turn out to be progressive in many developing countries.

Distributional Effects of a Chinese Sky Trust

Table 7.3 shows the incidence of the sky trust, in which the money from the carbon charge is redistributed to households on an equal per capita basis. The size of the dividend payout, which comes to 69 yuan per person, is found simply by dividing the total revenue by the number of people in China (after deducting 1 percent for administrative costs). The net benefit is the payout minus the per capita incidence of the carbon charge that was shown in Table 7.2. The last three columns of Table 7.3 show the charge, dividend and net benefit as a percentage of household expenditures.

Clearly, the combined effect of the carbon charge and dividend redistribution is strongly progressive. Nationwide, the bottom seven expenditure deciles would receive positive net benefits from the sky trust, while the top three deciles would pay more into the fund than they would get back in dividends. As noted in Chapter 6, even in the United States, where the carbon charge on its own would be regressive, an equal per capita payout of 75 percent of the revenue in a cap-and-dividend policy would yield a progressive net effect. In China, where the carbon intensity of consumption is lower for low-income households than for high-income households, the progressive effect is even stronger.

The majority of China's population (roughly 70 percent) would be net beneficiaries from the sky trust in purely financial terms, not counting any benefits associated with improvements in environmental quality. As a percentage of household expenditure, the net benefits to the lower deciles are greater than the net losses to the higher deciles, reflecting the simple fact that any lump-sum redistribution from rich to poor increases the incomes of the poor by a greater percentage than it decreases the incomes of the rich.

The magnitude of redistribution depends on the size of the carbon charge. At 300 yuan per tC, the households in China's poorest decile would see their incomes rise by the equivalent of 10.3 percent of total expenditure. A higher charge would redistribute more from the top to lower deciles, and a smaller charge would redistribute less, but there would be no change in which deciles would gain and lose, or in the relative sizes of their benefits and losses.

The breakdown between rural and urban households again reveals striking differences. In urban China, the top nine deciles would incur net losses of income and only the bottom decile would benefit, while in rural China the bottom nine deciles would benefit and the top decile would break even. This reflects the fact that rural areas have both lower total expenditures and a less carbon-intensive pattern of expenditure than urban areas.

Effects of a Sky Trust on Poverty

A Chinese sky trust would substantially reduce poverty, especially in rural China. Table 7.4 shows the effect it would have on poverty rates, using a poverty line of 810 yuan for rural China and 1604 yuan for urban China.[27] Before implementing a sky trust, 14.7 percent of our sample had

Table 7.4   Effect on poverty of a Chinese sky trust

	All households	Rural households	Urban households
Headcount poverty rate: Before	14.67	19.11	3.84
Headcount poverty rate: After	11.65	14.88	3.75
Difference	3.03	4.23	0.08
Poverty gap: Before	3.06	3.99	0.78
Poverty gap: After	2.20	2.81	0.72
Difference	0.85	1.18	0.06
Squared poverty gap: Before	1.02	1.34	0.26
Squared poverty gap: After	0.67	0.85	0.23
Difference	0.35	0.48	0.03

expenditures below this poverty line: 19.1 percent in rural areas and 3.8 percent in urban areas. The net effect of a sky trust, with the carbon charge set at 300 yuan *per* tC, is a 21 percent reduction in the headcount poverty rate, from 14.7 percent to 11.6 percent. A total of 36.4 million rural people and 292,000 urban people would be lifted out of poverty as a result.

Table 7.4 also shows the effect of the sky trust on two other poverty measures that are now widely used by economists. The first, known as the 'poverty gap,' measures not only the number of people below the poverty line but also the depth of their poverty, that is, how far the poor are below the poverty line. Implementing a sky trust of the magnitude examined here would reduce the poverty gap nationwide by 28 percent. The second, the 'squared poverty gap,' puts greater weight on the gaps of the poorest. By this measure, the impact of the sky trust is even stronger, reducing poverty by 34 percent, with the biggest impact in rural China.

CONCLUSIONS

In China, the introduction of carbon charges on fossil fuels would have a progressive distributional effect: high-income households would pay a larger percentage of their income than low-income households. This is in contrast to the regressive impact found in most studies of industrialized countries. Our results suggest that findings on the incidence of carbon charges in industrialized countries cannot be readily generalized to developing countries, due to differences in patterns of expenditure on personal transportation, home heating, industrial goods and the use of biofuels.

If the revenues from carbon charges were recycled to the populace on an equal per capita basis through a sky trust, the progressive impact of the policy would be further enhanced. With a charge set at 300 yuan per tC, the poorest decile would receive a net income gain equivalent to 10.3 percent of total expenditure, while the richest decile would see a 2.3 percent decline. Countrywide, roughly 70 percent of China's population would emerge as net winners from the sky trust, with more money in their pockets after the policy than before. Poverty would be reduced by 21 percent by the simple headcount measure, and even more substantially by measures that take into account the depth of poverty as well as its breadth.

China's wide urban-rural income disparities play a key role in these results. While 90 percent of rural people would be net winners, 90 percent of urban households would be net losers. Given the size of China's urban-rural income gap, the negative net impact on most urban households may be regarded as acceptable from an equity standpoint. Politically, however, this may prove to be a liability. One strategy to address this concern would be to modify the policy so as to ease or reverse adverse impacts on the lower deciles in urban areas.[28]

We have made no attempt in this chapter to measure the welfare gains that would accrue to the Chinese people from the environmental benefits of reduced use of fossil fuels, including lower greenhouse gas emissions and lower emissions of other pollutants such as sulfur dioxide. These could be substantial, and they would add to the attractions of a Chinese sky trust.

The policy relevance of these results extends beyond China. In other developing countries, too, carbon consumption patterns may more closely resemble those of China than those of the industrialized countries. In addition, there may be scope for the international community to encourage adoption of carbon-charge systems in China and elsewhere. Under the Clean Development Mechanism established by the Kyoto Protocol, for example, industrialized-country signatories could reimburse developing countries for implementing measures to cut carbon emissions, using these reductions to fulfill part of their Kyoto obligations. This would provide additional resources that could be used to offset income losses (for example, to China's urban lower and middle deciles), invest in renewable energy and provide transitional adjustment assistance to coal-mining regions (Gielen and Changhong 2001). International aid donors also could use green conditionality to encourage developing country governments to introduce sky trust policies (see Chapter 5). Funds from the GEF could be used to underwrite the initial costs of establishing sky trusts.[29]

There are several reasons why Chinese policy-makers may decide to take measures to curb the country's use of fossil fuels: shortfalls in domestic supplies; the country's vulnerability to climate change; the health and environmental benefits of reduced pollution; the weight of international opinion; and the fact that the government is already developing the capacity to administer pollution charges. This chapter suggests that an appropriately designed policy can provide an additional reason to act: a policy to reduce fossil fuel consumption can also help to reduce the wide economic disparities between rich and poor, and between urban and rural China.

NOTES

*   This chapter is a revised version of an article originally published in *Energy Policy* (2007), **35**(3), 1771–84.

1.   In this chapter we use metric tons of carbon (tC) rather than metric tons of carbon dioxide (tCO_2) as a unit of measurement. Both measures have been widely used in the literature, and the conversion between them is straightforward: 1 tC = 3.67 tCO_2.

2. See Zhang (2000, p. 745). Official figures may somewhat understate the rise in China's use of fossil fuels, since some local governments apparently responded to central directives to shut down small low-grade coal mines and heavily polluting power plants simply by ceasing to report their operations to the central government (Bradsher 2003; see also Sinton 2001).

3. Oceanic sinks and terrestrial sinks each absorb roughly 1900 million tC per year; but land-use changes (especially deforestation) release roughly 1700 tC per year; in net terms, oceanic sinks therefore account for close to 90 percent of annual carbon sequestration (Sarmiento and Gruber 2002). Agarwal and Narain (1991) argue that the Earth's reabsorptive capacities should be allocated on an equal per capita basis. Using this formula, the contributions of populous nations like China and India to the world's net carbon emissions is reduced relative to that of the United States and other industrialized economies.

4. See World Bank (1997) and Bradsher (2003). In an effort to limit China's growing dependence on imported oil, in 2004 the government introduced new fuel economy standards for automobiles that are more stringent than those in the United States (Bradsher 2004).

5. See Zhang (2000). A study of regional differences in global warming damages found that damages in China would be equivalent to 6.1 percent of gross national product (GNP), versus a world average of 1.5 percent (Fankhauser and Pearce 1994, p. 76, cited by OECD 1995, p. 34).

6. In the case of Pakistan, for example, Shah and Larsen (1992) estimated that the benefits of reductions in local environmental externalities would more than offset the output losses from a carbon tax. The World Bank (1997, p. 54) estimates that inclusion of the health costs of coal use in Beijing would double its price.

7. For example, US President George W. Bush cited the absence of emission reduction targets for China and other developing countries in rejecting the Kyoto agreement as 'fatally flawed' (Bush 2001).

8. Khan and Riskin (2001, pp. 17 and 20). In a subsequent paper (Khan and Riskin 2008), the authors report that in 2002 the urban-rural average income gap had widened to a 3:1 ratio. The national-level Gini coefficient remained unchanged, however, as widening urban-rural inequality was offset by greater equality within both sectors.

9. Khan and Riskin (2001, pp. 66 and 71). The authors estimate headcount poverty for three different poverty lines in both rural and urban China. We report poverty rates for what they term the 'Unadjusted Intermediate Poverty Threshold.' For further discussion of rural-urban disparities, see Knight et al. (2006).

10. In 1995, the year to which the data reported in this chapter pertain, total household consumption in China (estimated from the survey data presented below) amounted to 3301 billion yuan, equivalent to 57.6 percent of GNP as reported in the national income accounts (Khan and Riskin 2001, p. 25). While carbon emissions per yuan may differ somewhat between the household and non-household sectors, this gives a rough approximation of the household sector's importance in the carbon economy.

11. We call these 'charges' rather than 'taxes,' because their effect is to reduce or eliminate a de facto subsidy: free use of the limited carbon absorptive capacity of the biosphere.

12. An exception is a recent study of Italy's carbon tax (Tiezzi 2005), which finds that it has a progressive incidence by virtue of the fact that it hits transport fuels harder than domestic fuel use and that higher-income households reduce their consumption less in response to higher prices.

13. If it is assumed that carbon charges are not fully passed on to consumers, but instead are partly absorbed by producers via reduced profit margins, the result is less regressive since capital ownership is concentrated in upper-income households (see Dinan and Rogers 2002; Parry 2004). For further discussion of methodologies for assessing the distributional incidence of carbon taxes, see Speck (1999).

14. In the case of China, for example, Wang and Feng (1999, p. 97) report that biomass accounts for 60–90 percent of rural household energy consumption.

15. Addison and Osei (2001) question the conclusion that petroleum taxes are progressive in Ghana, however, arguing that adverse spillover effects via higher transport costs adversely affect the rural poor.

16. The sky trust is an extension of the 'feebate' concept, whereby fees are paid according to the extent of individual resource use, and the proceeds rebated equally to all use-rights holders. This idea has been applied to a variety of environmental problems; see, for example, Puig-Ventosa (2004). For an early application to gasoline taxes, see Shepard (1976).

17. In the United States, this would translate into roughly 2000 collection points (Kopp et al. 1999; US Congressional Budget Office 2001). Smulders and Vollebergh (2001, p. 116) report that the administrative costs of petroleum taxes and excise duties range from 0.12 to 0.25 percent of revenue, lower than most other taxes; see also Fisher et al. (1998). As the US Congressional Budget Office (2001, p. 19) notes, administrative costs would increase if charges were levied not only on fossil fuels, but also on imports of carbon-intensive products (such as aluminum) so as to avoid placing domestic producers at a disadvantage in the absence of similar carbon policies in the exporting countries.

18. In theory, one can design alternative uses of carbon-charge revenues that are superior to lump-sum redistribution on efficiency or distributional grounds, as Zhang and Baranzini (2004, pp. 511–12) discuss. In practice, these alternatives arguably would be more open to political manipulation than a sky trust. Moreover, they would not share the first advantage identified here: affirmation of the principle of equal rights to nature's common wealth.

19. US Congressional Budget Office (2000). The give-away allocation option, sometimes referred to as 'grandfathering,' was the main method adopted in the United States when sulfur dioxide emissions permits were introduced in the 1990s. Insofar as permit rents are taxed, this method does generate some government revenue. Parry (2004) analyses the impact of grandfathered carbon emissions permits in the United States with rents taxed at the rate of 35 percent; even when coupled with lump-sum redistribution of the proceeds, he finds that the distributional impact is regressive due to the highly skewed distribution of profit income.

20. The stronger distributional effects in the Dinan and Rogers study arise mainly from (1) incorporation of an estimated 'deadweight loss' in factor markets due to the impact of higher carbon prices on real returns to capital and labor; and (2) use of a lower value for average income in the lowest quintile.

21. For details on the sampling methodology, see Brenner et al. (2007).

22. See Brenner et al. (2007) for details on the calculation of carbon loading factors.

23. Baranzini et al. (2000). Purchasing power parity-adjusted exchange rates were used to convert to yuan equivalents.

24. Of course, one aim of carbon charges is precisely to shift expenditure toward less carbon-intensive goods and services. If the price elasticity of demand for carbon varies across deciles, this would affect the incidence of carbon charges. Because we do not have the data needed to incorporate this effect, we assume the price elasticity of demand to be constant across deciles. West and Williams (2002), using data from the United States, find that price responsiveness to gasoline taxes is inversely related to income; that is, in response to a higher price, lower-income households reduce consumption more than upper-income households, and hence 'studies that do not consider demand responses will substantially overstate the regressivity of the gas tax' (p. 6). A similar finding is reported for Italy by Tiezzi (2005). If this pattern were to apply to carbon charges in China, their progressivity would be even stronger than reported here.

25. Note that this is slightly different from taking the average charge for the decile and dividing it by the average expenditure for the decile. For this reason, the charge/expenditure column does not exactly equal the ratio between the two preceding columns. We chose to take the average of the ratios, rather than the ratio of the averages, in order

to weigh the effect on each individual evenly when calculating the averages rather than assigning a higher weight to people with higher expenditures. The choice of method does not have a significant effect on the results, as can be seen in Brenner et al. (2007, appendix I).

26. Within the rural and urban areas, the carbon charge is roughly proportional to expenditures. Every decile in the urban areas pays between 3.2 percent and 3.5 percent of their expenditures into the charge, while every decile in rural areas pays between 1.8 percent and 2.1 percent. Behind these results are offsetting trends in the different expenditure categories: the most energy-intensive category, fuels and electricity, accounts for a larger share of expenditures for the poorer households in both areas, but the other two energy-intensive consumption categories, transportation and industrial goods, form a larger part of the expenditures of the richer households.

27. These poverty lines are adapted from the intermediate poverty thresholds used by Khan and Riskin (2001). In their work, Khan and Riskin examine income poverty, whereas we are focused on expenditure poverty. To shift from income to expenditure poverty thresholds, we calculated the average per capita expenditures of all individuals who were within 5 percent of the per capita income poverty threshold defined by Khan and Riskin.

28. In a similar fashion, Holland's tax on energy use exempts certain small consumers (Zhang and Baranzini 2004, p. 511).

29. This would be consistent with the guidelines for use of GEF resources recommended by Johnson et al. (1996).

REFERENCES

Addison, Tony and Robert Osei (2001), 'Taxation and fiscal reform in Ghana,' World Institute for Development economics research discussion paper no. 2001/97, Helsinki.

Agarwal, Anil and Sunita Narain (1991), *Global Warming in an Unequal World*, New Delhi: Centre for Science and the Environment.

Baranzini, Andrea, José Goldemberg and Stefan Speck (2000), 'A future for carbon taxes,' *Ecological Economics*, **32**, 395–412.

Barnes, Peter (2001), *Who Owns the Sky? Our Common Assets and the Future of Capitalism*, Washington, DC: Island Press.

Barnes, Peter and Marc Breslow (2003), 'The sky trust: the battle for atmospheric scarcity rent,' in James K. Boyce and Barry G. Shelley (eds), *Natural Assets: Democratizing Environmental Ownership*, Washington, DC: Island Press, pp. 135–49.

Boyce, James K. and Matthew E. Riddle (2007), 'Cap and dividend: how to curb global warming while protecting the incomes of American families,' Political Economy Research Institute working paper no. 150, Amherst, MA.

Boyce, James K. and Matthew E. Riddle (2008), 'Keeping the government whole: the impact of a cap-and-dividend policy for curbing global warming on government revenue and expenditure,' Political Economy Research Institute working paper no. 188, Amherst, MA.

Boyce, James K. and Matthew E. Riddle (2009), *Cap and Dividend: A State-by-State Analysis*, Amherst, MA and Portland, OR: Political Economy Research Institute and Economics for Equity and Environment.

Bradsher, Keith (2003), 'China prospering but polluting: dirty fuels power economic growth,' *International Herald Tribune*, 22 October, pp. 1, 6.

Bradsher, Keith (2004), 'China tries to reduce thirst for gas,' *International Herald Tribune*, 23 September, p. 11.

Brännlund, Runar and Jonas Nordström (2004), 'Carbon tax simulations using a household demand model,' *European Economic Review*, **48**, 211–33.

Brenner, Mark, Matthew E. Riddle and James K. Boyce (2007), 'A Chinese sky trust? Distributional impacts of carbon charges and revenue recycling in China,' *Energy Policy*, **35**, 1771–84.

Bush, George W. (2001), 'President Bush discusses global climate change,' press conference, 11 June.

Cornwell, Antonia and John Creedy (1996), 'Carbon taxation, prices and inequality in Australia,' *Fiscal Studies*, **17**(3), 21–38.

Cramton, Peter and Suzi Kerr (1999), 'The distributional effects of carbon regulation: why auctioned carbon permits are attractive and feasible,' in Thomas Sterner (ed.), *The Market and the Environment*, Cheltenham, UK and Northampton, MA, USA: Edward Elgar Publishing, pp. 255–71.

Dinan, Terry M. and Diane Lim Rogers (2002), 'Distributional effects of carbon allowance trading: how government decisions determine winners and losers,' *National Tax Journal*, **55**, 199–222.

Fankhauser, S. and D.W. Pearce (1994), 'The social costs of greenhouse gas emissions,' in Organisation for Economic Co-operation and Development (OECD) (ed.), *The Economics of Climate Change: Proceedings of an OECD/IEA Conference*, Paris: OECD.

Fisher, Carolyn, Suzi Kerr and Michael Toman (1998), 'Using emissions trading to regulate US greenhouse gas emissions: design and implementation issues,' *National Tax Journal*, **51**(3), 453–64.

Gielen, Dolf and Chen Changhong (2001), 'The CO_2 emission reduction benefits of Chinese energy policies and environmental policies: a case study for Shanghai, period 1995–2020,' *Ecological Economics*, **39**, 257–70.

Hamilton, Kirk and Grant Cameron (1994), 'Simulating the distributional effects of a Canadian carbon tax,' *Canadian Public Policy*, **20**(4), 385–99.

Jensen, Jesper and David Tarr (2002), 'Trade, foreign exchange, and energy policies in the Islamic Republic of Iran: reform agenda, economic implications, and impact on the poor,' January, World Bank.

Johnson, Todd M., Junfeng Li, Zhongxiao Jiang and Robert P. Taylor (1996), *China: Issues and Options in Greenhouse Gas Emissions Control*, report of a joint study team from the National Environmental Protection Agency of China, the State Planning Commission of China, United Nations Development Programme and the World Bank, Washington, DC: World Bank.

Khan, Azizur R. and Carl Riskin (2001), *Inequality and Poverty in China in the Age of Globalization*, Oxford and New York: Oxford University Press.

Khan, Azizur R. and Carl Riskin (2008), 'Growth and distribution of household income in China between 1995 and 2002,' in B.A. Gustafsson, L. Shi and T. Sicular (eds), *Inequality and Public Policy in China*, Cambridge: Cambridge University Press, chapter 3.

Klinge Jacobsen, H., K. Birr-Pedersen and M. Wier (2003), 'Distributional implications of environmental taxation in Denmark,' *Fiscal Studies*, **24**(4), 477–99.

Knight, John, Li Shi and Lina Song (2006), 'The rural-urban divide and the evolution of political economy in China,' in James K. Boyce, Stephen Cullenberg, Prasanta Pattanaik and Robert Pollin (eds), *Egalitarian Development in the*

Era of Globalization: Essays in Honor of Keith Griffin, Cheltenham, UK and Northampton, MA, USA: Edward Elgar Publishing, chapter 2.

Kopp, Raymond, Richard Morgenstern, William Pizer and Michael Toman (1999), *A Proposal for Credible Early Action in US Climate Policy*, Washington, DC: Resources for the Future.

Metcalf, Gilbert E. (1999), 'A distributional analysis of green tax reforms,' *National Tax Journal*, **52**(4), 655–81.

Organisation for Economic Co-operation and Development (OECD) (1995), *Climate Change, Economic Instruments and Income Distribution*, Paris: OECD.

Parry, Ian W.H. (2004), 'Are emissions permits regressive?' *Journal of Environmental Economics and Management*, **47**, 364–87.

Puig-Ventosa, Ignasi (2004), 'Potential use of feebate systems to foster environmentally sound urban waste management,' *Waste Management*, **24**, 3–7.

Sarmiento, Jorge L. and Nicolas Gruber (2002), 'Sinks for anthropogenic carbon,' *Physics Today*, **55**(6), 30–36.

Shah, Anwar and Bjorn Larsen (1992), 'Carbon taxes, the greenhouse effect, and developing countries,' World Bank policy research working paper no. 957, Washington, DC.

Shepard, Lawrence (1976), 'The short-run incidence of a gasoline tax rebate plan,' *Journal of Economic Issues*, **10**(1), 169–72.

Sinton, Jonathan E. (2001), 'Accuracy and reliability of China's energy statistics,' *China Economic Review*, **12**, 373–83.

Smulders, Sjak and Herman R.J. Vollebergh (2001), 'Green taxes and administrative costs,' in Carlo Carraro and Gilbert E. Metcalf (eds), *Behavioral and Distributional Effects of Environmental Policy*, Chicago, IL: University of Chicago Press, pp. 92–129.

Speck, Stefan (1999), 'Energy and carbon taxes and their distributional implications,' *Energy Policy*, **27**, 659–67.

Symons, Elizabeth, John Proops and Philip Gay (1994), 'Carbon taxes, consumer demand and carbon dioxide emissions: a simulation analysis for the UK,' *Fiscal Studies*, **15**(2), 19–43.

Symons, Elizabeth, Stefan Speck and John Proops (2000), 'The effects of pollution and energy taxes across the European income distribution,' Keele University economics research paper no. 2000/05.

Tiezzi, Silvia (2005), 'The welfare effects and the distributive impact of carbon taxation on Italian households,' *Energy Policy*, **33**, 1597–612.

US Congressional Budget Office (CBO) (2000), *Who Gains and Who Pays Under Carbon-allowance Trading? The Distributional Effects of Alternative Policy Designs*, June, Washington, DC: CBO.

US Congressional Budget Office (2001), *An Evaluation of Cap-and-Trade Programs for Reducing US Carbon Emissions*, June, Washington, DC: CBO.

US Congressional Budget Office (2003), *Shifting the Cost Burden of a Carbon Cap-and-Trade Program*, July, Washington, DC: CBO.

Wang, Xiaohua and Zhenmin Feng (1999), 'Common factors and indicators of rural household energy consumption in China,' *Energy Studies Review*, **9**(2), 96–101.

West, Sarah E. and Robert C. Williams III (2002), 'Estimates from a consumer demand system: implications for the incidence of environmental taxes,' National Bureau of Economic Research working paper 9152, Cambridge, MA.

Wier, Mette, Katja Birr-Pedersen, Henrik Klinge Jacobsen and Jacob Klok (2005),

'Are CO_2 taxes regressive? Evidence from the Danish experience,' *Ecological Economics*, **52**, 239–51.

World Bank (1997), *Clear Water, Blue Skies: China's Environment in the New Century*, Washington, DC: World Bank.

Younger, Stephen (1996), 'Estimating tax incidence in Ghana using household data,' in David E. Sahn (ed.), *Economic Reform and the Poor*, Oxford: Clarendon Press, pp. 231–53.

Younger, Stephen, David Sahn, Steven Haggblade and Paul Dorosh (1999), 'Tax incidence in Madagascar: an analysis using household data,' *World Bank Economic Review*, **13**(2), 303–31.

Zhang, Zhongxiang (1998), *The Economics of Energy Policy in China: Implications for Global Climate Change*, Cheltenham, UK and Lyme, USA: Edward Elgar Publishing.

Zhang, Zhongxiang (2000), 'Decoupling China's carbon emissions increase from economic growth: an economic analysis and policy implications,' *World Development*, **28**(4), 739–52.

Zhang, Zhongxiang and Andrea Baranzini (2004), 'What do we know about carbon taxes? An inquiry into their impacts on competitiveness and distribution of income,' *Energy Policy*, **32**, 507–18.

8. A future for small farms

The small farmer is today an endangered species. In the industrialized countries of the global North, the number of farmers has been dwindling for generations. In the United States, for example, the total number of farms fell from 6.8 million in 1935 to fewer than two million today (Stam and Dixon 2004). Referring to trends in Europe, where the farming population is declining by 3 percent annually, a *New York Times* editorial derides the idea that 'every village that was inhabited in Charlemagne's day must be sustained,' and declares that 'more consolidation, in the form of larger-scale farming and an abandonment of absurdly inefficient production, is inevitable.'[1]

In the developing countries of the global South, governments and international agencies alike appear to be intent on following the same path. Fifty years after the publication of Sir Arthur Lewis's (1954) dual-economy model, in which economic development was identified with the transfer of labor from the 'subsistence' agricultural sector to the 'capitalist' industrial sector, the assumption that small farms are destined for the dustbin of history remains conventional wisdom. 'Those *indios*,' a Guatemalan government official told me, referring to the country's indigenous majority. 'As long as they grow maize just like their grandparents, they'll be poor just like their grandparents.'[2]

Rather than simply letting nature take its ostensible course, governments often seek to speed it along, promoting agricultural 'modernization' by means of subsidies and other policies that favor large-scale farming, purchases of farm machinery and chemical inputs, and more uniformity in the choice of crops and varieties. In a sense, these policies aim to subsume agriculture itself, and not only its erstwhile labor force, into the industrial economy. Even if the demise of the small farm were not a foregone conclusion, these policies could make it a self-fulfilling prophecy.

In the face of these trends, an intrepid band of economists has rallied to the defense of small farms on grounds of both equity and efficiency. Prominent among them is Keith Griffin, who warned in his classic study, *The Political Economy of Agrarian Change* (1979, p. xxii), against policies that could 'lead to the creation of an inefficient and capital intensive agriculture which is incapable of producing an adequate livelihood for the mass of the rural population.' In a recent article co-authored with Azizur Rahman Khan and Amy Ickowitz (2002, p. 320), Griffin insists that 'family farms use resources efficiently and can be just as dynamic as large farms.'

Among economists, the arguments in favor of small farms have gained ground in the last few decades. The efficiency advantages of small farms – rooted in their labor intensity – have won increasing recognition, even in bastions of the development establishment such as the World Bank.[3] Yet policies on the ground have been slow to change. As Griffin (1979, p. 84) observed, the policy mix that favors larger farms is primarily attributable not to ignorance, but rather the political influence of large landowners: 'Governments may claim to rule in the "national interest",' he wrote, 'but in reality they act in behalf of their supporters.' A shift toward pro-small farm policies is unlikely to be brought about by small farmers acting alone.

This chapter offers a further argument on behalf of small farms, based on their role in providing a crucial public good: the conservation of agricultural biodiversity.[4] From the highland maize plots of southern Mexico and Guatemala to the rice paddies of eastern India and Bangladesh, small farmers across the world sustain the crop genetic diversity that underpins humankind's long-term food security. Many of those who provide this public good are desperately poor, and their continued ability and willingness to cultivate diversity can no longer be taken for granted. Policies to reward small farmers for their contributions to global food security would help to ensure both their future and our own.

Of course, this does not mean that all small farms – or, in the *reducto absurdum* phrase of *The Times*, 'every village inhabited in Charlemagne's day,' should endure forever. Nor does it mean that we ought to create living museums where the agricultural landscape is frozen in time. On the contrary, a hallmark of 'traditional' agriculture is precisely its dynamism: in the farmers' fields, the process that Charles Darwin termed 'artificial selection' – natural selection guided by human hands – yields a constant stream of new varieties, adapted to changing needs and changing environmental circumstances.[5] But to say that not all small farms, or all crop varieties, can or should survive is not to say that a world of large, monocultural farms is desirable or feasible as the endpoint of agricultural history. A productive and resilient world agriculture requires a diverse mix of crop varieties, agricultural techniques and farming systems. In this mix, there is a future for small farms.

HUMANS AS A KEYSTONE SPECIES

As early as the 1500s, Spanish settlers began to arrive in the valley of the upper Rio Grande, in what is now the southwestern United States. To irrigate the semi-arid lands they found, the settlers constructed *acequias*, earthen channels that divert river water and carry it to valley slopes downstream. These gravity-fed irrigation systems transformed the landscape into a diverse agroecosystem that includes wetlands, fields and orchards with unique varieties of beans and fruit trees, riparian corridors for wildlife movement and fertile soils built by generations of careful land stewardship.

Anthropologist Devon Peña (2003, p.169) describes humans as the 'keystone species' of this *acequia* landscape mosaic – 'a species so central to the health of the ecosystem that without it many other species could not survive.' The idea that humans can act as a keystone species – playing a role in nature akin to that of beavers in the Canadian forests, or corals in ocean reefs – marks a profound departure from the image, widespread among environmentalists, of human beings as alien intruders whose 'ecological footprint' invariably tramples upon the fragile shoots of the natural world. Instead, it evokes a more balanced assessment of the relationship between humans and nature, one in which humans can have positive impacts, as well as negative ones, on the richness and diversity of life.

Another striking illustration of the potential for positive human impacts has come to light in recent years in South America. About 10 percent of the Amazonian region – with an area roughly the size of France – is covered by deep, dark soil known locally as *terra preta do indio* (dark earth of the Indians) that is prized for its long-lasting fertility. *Terra preta* is a remarkable exception to the general rule that tropical rainforest soils are poor in nutrients, and hence subject to rapid degradation once the forest cover is removed. Soil scientists have concluded that *terra preta* was created by the indigenous people who practiced 'slash-and-char' agroforestry in the region for two millennia.[6] An astonishing feature of *terra preta* is its capacity to regenerate itself: 'In a process reminiscent of dropping microorganism-rich starter into plain dough to create sourdough bread,' scientists hypothesize that 'Amazonian peoples inoculated bad soil with a transforming bacterial charge' (Mann 2002b, p.52).

Indeed, it is not an exaggeration to say that most people today depend for their very survival on the fruits of past human interactions with nature. If we pause to give thanks before we eat a meal, our gratitude should extend to our predecessors who first domesticated plants and animals and over the millennia created the many thousands of varieties of these species that underpin the world's agriculture. Crops such as wheat, rice, maize, potatoes and cotton did not appear on Earth by some happy circumstance. These and the other species on which we rely for our food and fiber arose in a process of 'co-evolution' with human cultures. Beginning some 10,000 years ago, the inhabitants of Asia Minor domesticated wheat and barley, grains whose seeds have the key property of not 'shattering' and falling to the ground as they ripen. Their counterparts in Asia gave us rice, a versatile plant whose roots can survive in continuously flooded fields. In the Andes, early Americans gave us the potato. In Mesoamerica, perhaps most remarkably of all, the forebearers of today's Mayan *campesinos* evolved maize from its wild relative, teosinte.[7] Were humans to vanish from the planet, these species would vanish in short order too.

To term these developments beneficial is, of course, to make a normative judgment. From a 'deep ecology' perspective in which humans are just another species, whose survival is of no greater consequence than that of any other, the judgment that the *acequia* ecosystem, or *terra preta*, or food crops can be termed positive achievements might be questioned. If, however, our value system embraces a concern for the biosphere's capacity to sustain human well-being, then I think these deserve to be called improvements in the state of nature. To be sure, there are plenty of counter-examples where human activities have had negative environmental impacts. But positive impacts are part of our story too.

SMALL FARMERS: CULTIVATORS OF DIVERSITY

Today, perhaps the single most important examples of humans acting as a keystone species are the agroecosystems that maintain the world's crop genetic diversity. Most of the keystone people are small farmers. In part, this is because agricultural biodiversity is concentrated in regions of the world where small farms still predominate. In part, too, it is because small farmers have comparative advantages in the cultivation of diversity.

Centers of Agricultural Biodiversity

The centers of origin of the world's crops are concentrated in a few places, known as 'Vavilov centers' after the great Russian botanist of the early twentieth century, Nikolai Vavilov. Most of the Vavilov centers are in the developing countries of the global South (Figure 8.1). Vavilov hypothesized that the ancient centers of crop origin tend to be the modern centers of crop diversity, a suggestion that, by and large, has stood the test of time. The logic behind this correlation is straightforward: crops evolve as farmers select seed for replanting from those individual plants that perform best in

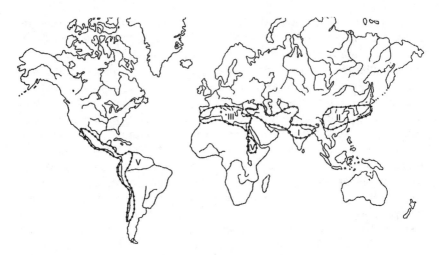

Key: I Southwestern Asia; II Eastern Asia; III Mediterranean area; IV Abyssinia and Egypt; V Mountainous areas of Mexico, Central America and South America.

Source: Vavilov (1926 [1992], p. 127).

Figure 8.1   Centers of origin of crops

the face of local variations in soils, rainfall, altitude, pest populations and so on. Diversity tends to be greatest where this process has had the longest time to unfold. In the Bengal delta, for example, where 'a few inches difference in elevation in relation to expected flooding depth and duration can cause farmers to plant different rice varieties,' some 10,000 different varieties of rice were being grown in the 1970s (Brammer 1980, p. 25).

Darwin described this process in the opening chapter of *The Origin of Species*: 'The key is man's power of accumulative selection: nature gives successive variations; man adds them up in certain directions useful to him.' One of Darwin's examples was the strawberry, a fruit that was growing in popularity at the time: 'Gardeners picked out individual plants with slightly larger, earlier, or better fruit, and raised seedlings from them, and again picked out the best seedlings and bred from them.' In this way, Darwin explained, 'those many admirable varieties of the strawberry were raised which have appeared during the last half-century' (Darwin 1859 [1952], pp. 18, 23).

As Vavilov documented, crop genetic diversity is distributed very unevenly across the globe. The available data on this point are remarkably sparse, but a rough indicator is the sources of seed samples that are stored in the world's largest 'gene banks', *ex situ* (off-site) collections maintained for possible future use by scientists and plant breeders. In the case of maize, for example, Mexico accounted for 4220 of the maize accessions held at the International Maize and Wheat Improvement Center (known by its Spanish acronym, CIMMYT) in the mid-1990s, and Guatemala for another 590; by contrast, the United States, with more than three times the maize acreage of Mexico and Guatemala combined, accounted for only 43 (Boyce 1996). Mexican farmers today are believed to grow roughly 5000 different varieties of maize, whereas in the United States – where corn is sown on roughly 70 million acres – more than 70 percent of the acreage is planted with varieties 'based on no more than half a dozen inbred lines' (Goodman 1995, p. 200).[8]

Comparative Advantages of Small Farmers in Cultivating Diversity

Around the world, it is generally small farms – especially those in the Vavilov centers – that practice high-diversity agriculture. Not only do individual small farmers often choose to cultivate several varieties of the same crop, but also, and probably more importantly, different farmers in a given locality often cultivate different varieties. Large farms, in contrast, are more likely to sow a single variety over a wide area. This inverse relationship between farm size and varietal diversity has several explanations.

First, high-diversity farming is generally more labor-intensive than low-diversity farming. It takes more time and effort to cultivate varieties with different sowing dates, harvest times and other requirements than to practice varietal monoculture. Considerable labor also is needed to maintain the physical infrastructure – such as watercourses and terraces – that often supports high-diversity agriculture. As we know from the many studies of the relationship between farm size and labor use, smaller farms have a comparative advantage in labor-intensive operations. This is because they rely more on family labor, the 'real cost' of which is lower than the wage of hired labor, and because insofar as they do use hired laborers, small farmers have fewer supervision problems (not only is supervision easier on small farms, but also the need for supervision may be less by virtue of the narrower social distance between employer and employee).[9]

Second, high-diversity agriculture depends on the farmers' knowledge of different crop varieties and their relationships to microhabitat variations. Small farmers are the repositories of this knowledge. Without them, it would be harder not only to sustain agricultural biodiversity, but also know the attributes of the varieties that are being sustained. Indigenous cultures often are particularly rich in this knowledge. For example, the Mixe language, spoken by maize farmers in southern Oaxaca, Mexico, has words for 'a greater and richer number of stages of plant development (germination, flowering, leaf and whorl development, appearance of black color at base of kernels, etc.) than those existing in conventional scientific literature.'[10]

Third, small farmers often predominate in 'marginal' agricultural environments where the spread of modern varieties has been held in check by unfavorable growing conditions. Hilly terrain, as in the highlands of southern Mexico and Guatemala, is less suitable for monoculture and mechanization; similarly, in deeply flooded parts of the Bengal delta, the short-statured 'high-yielding' (that is, highly fertilizer-responsive) varieties cannot be grown. Such lands are relatively unattractive targets for appropriation and concentration by landowning elites. At the same time, they often have exceptionally high degrees of microenvironmental variation, which favors varietal diversification. In a single village in Oaxaca, for example, researchers Raúl and Luis García-Barrios (1990) found that the *campesinos* distinguished among 17 different environments in which they grew 26 distinct varieties of maize. Similarly, Maori weavers in New Zealand recognize more than 80 distinct varieties of flax (Shand 1997, p. 11, citing Heywood 1995).

As already noted, traditional agriculture is by no means static. The artificial selection process that created crop genetic diversity continues unabated in farmers' fields, leading botanists to refer to these fields as 'evolutionary gardens.'[11] In this process, the line between 'traditional' and 'modern' agriculture often becomes blurred, as small farmers adopt and adapt new varieties released by professional public-sector and private-sector plant breeders.[12] As Stephen Brush (1995), among others, has observed, traditional varieties can co-exist with modern varieties. Moreover, even after the introduction of new varieties, the processes of cross-pollination, mutation and artificial selection continue to give rise to successive generations adapted to local conditions. In Bangladesh, for example, by selecting seed from the tallest plants in fields of short-statured 'green-revolution' rice varieties, farmers developed in the space of a few years new varieties that are suitable for more deeply flooded fields.[13] Given the dynamic character of traditional agriculture, the 'traditional-modern' dichotomy is better described as a contrast between high-diversity and low-diversity agricultural ecosystems.

DIVERSITY AND EFFICIENCY

There is a fundamental tension between the 'efficiency' promoted by markets and a broader notion of efficiency, founded on long-term human well-being, that (1) encompasses externalities, both positive and negative, and (2) puts the welfare of future generations on a par with present-day welfare, rather than discounting it toward zero. The logic of the market puts little value on crop genetic diversity. Instead, it dictates that in any given time and place all farmers should grow the same 'optimal' variety, tempered only by local differences in soils, climate and so on. Apart from some variations in response to local differences, the market puts no value on diversity per se: less profitable varieties are driven out by more profitable varieties. Yet in the long run, diversity is crucial if agriculture is to be resilient. The farmers who maintain diversity thus provide a positive externality, a social benefit that the market fails to reward.

The Varietal Relay Race

The basic problem with low-diversity agriculture is that time and nature do not stand still. Among the insects and plant pathogens that thrive in the green blanket of corn that covers the midsection of the United States every summer, the Darwinian process of survival of the fittest proceeds, favoring the evolution of new strains of pests that are particularly well adapted to the handful of corn varieties being grown on millions of acres of farmland. State and federal agricultural officials monitor the fields for outbreaks of new insect and plant disease threats. Plant breeders respond by screening their breeding lines for varieties with resistance to these new strains, and incorporating this resistance into the next generation of cultivars (cultivated varieties). The average commercial lifespan of a newly released corn variety in the United States is only seven years, after which it is rendered obsolete by the emergence of new strains of insects or plant diseases (Duvick 1984, p. 164). Surveys of a number of major crops undertaken for the UK Department of the Environment in the mid-1990s found that 'the viability of any given product is only about five years, with pests and disease being the primary factors for the obsolescence' (Swanson and Luxmoore 1997, p. 98).

The same process occurs wherever agricultural 'modernization' results in a high degree of varietal uniformity. In the case of Asian rice agriculture, for example, 'under the intensive cultivation practices, insect pests of short life span and heterogeneous population structure, such as the brown planthopper, can quickly adapt their genetic population structure in response to the resistance gene in the most widely grown cultivar' (Chang 1995, p. 154). Rice breeders at the International Rice Research Institute (IRRI) in the Philippines and at national agricultural research institutions again must respond by releasing new varieties with resistance to the new threats.

Monocultural optimization not only creates an environment that favors evolution of virulent new pests and diseases. It also creates one in which, if and when such organisms emerge, they can trigger widespread crop failures. This genetic vulnerability – arising from the eggs-in-one-basket syndrome – is the soft underbelly of low-diversity agriculture. To cope with this vulnerability, plant breeders rely on 'diversity through time,' constantly breeding and releasing new crop varieties (Duvick 1984; Duvick et al. 2004). In a sense, then, 'low-diversity' agriculture is a misnomer: the viability of modern agriculture rests on the substitution of time-series variation for cross-sectional variation.

The stakes in this varietal relay race are high, as was demonstrated in the United States in 1970 when the southern corn leaf blight destroyed one billion bushels of maize, including as much as half the harvest in some southern states. The epidemic was caused by a new strain of a fungus, *Bipolaris maydis*, which was virulent on plants with a genetic makeup shared by 85 percent of the maize grown in the United States at the time. Plant breeders were able to respond in the following year by incorporating genetic resistance they found in some maize varieties grown in Africa. Scientists were 'shaken by how close the system had come to disaster,' Mann (2004, p. 7) reports. 'They had been lucky that the problem was quickly contained, and luckier still that the African maize had not been supplanted by vulnerable modern hybrids.'

As the corn leaf blight example illustrates, the raw material for the varietal relay race ultimately comes from the crop genetic diversity bequeathed to us by previous generations. Today, small farmers around the world sustain this diversity. In other words, the long-run sustainability of low-diversity agriculture rests on a continuing flow of biological inputs from the high-diversity agriculture. The irony is that by virtue of its superior short-run 'efficiency,' modern agriculture is undermining the economic viability of traditional agriculture: the small farmers who cultivate diversity face increasing competition from the 'green revolution' at home and from cheap agricultural imports from the industrialized countries. In the quest for high productivity, botanist Garrison Wilkes explains, we have 'built our roof with stones from the foundation.'[14]

The Need for *In Situ* Diversity

The seed collections held at public-sector agricultural research institutions around the world are storehouses of crop genetic diversity. When dried and kept under controlled temperature and humidity conditions, the seeds can remain viable for a number of years (often around three decades); if then planted, with care to prevent cross-pollination, the seed can be replicated and stored again. These *ex situ* 'gene banks' – including the wheat and maize collections at CIMMYT in Mexico; the rice collection at IRRI in the Philippines; the potato collection at the International Potato Center in Peru; and the US Department of Agriculture's National Seed Storage Laboratory (NSSL) in Fort Collins, Colorado – are public goods of immense value to humankind. They do not represent an adequate substitute for *in situ* (in-the-field) diversity, however, for several reasons.

First, the gene banks are not completely secure. Accidents, wars and chronic underfunding all make the survival of the stored seeds precarious. The world's largest *ex situ* collection of crop varieties is – or was – at the Vavilov Institute in what for a time was called Leningrad and now once again is called St Petersburg. In their book, *Shattering* (1990), Cary Fowler and Pat Mooney recount the drama that unfolded at the Vavilov Institute during the siege of Leningrad in World War II. With food supplies cut off by the German army, people ate dogs, cats and even grass in an effort to survive. In the end, more than half a million of the city's residents starved to death. The dead included staff members of the Institute, who took extraordinary measures to safeguard seeds that they could have eaten to prolong their own lives. 'When all the world is in the flames of war,' a survivor recalls the staff telling each other, 'we will keep this collection for the future of all people' (Fowler and Mooney 1990, pp. 221–2).

Today, plant breeders believe that most of the seeds held at the Vavilov Institute are no longer viable – in other words, they are dead. The reason is the inadequate maintenance and replication of the collection in the years before and after the breakup of the Soviet Union. A similar fate may have befallen what was once the world's second largest maize collection (after that of the Vavilov Institute) in Belgrade, the capital of the former Yugoslavia (Plucknett et al. 1987, p. 120). Even in relatively prosperous and stable nations, like the United States, accidents and funding shortages make the *ex situ* collections less than perfectly secure.[15]

A second reason why *ex situ* collections cannot adequately replace *in situ* diversity is that, at best, gene banks conserve only the existing stock of crop genetic diversity. They cannot mimic the ongoing flow of new varieties that happens in the farmer's field under the pressures of natural and artificial selection. 'A main object of *in situ* conservation,' Brookfield (2001, p. 248) concludes, 'should be to enhance the processes that create genetic diversity, not to protect any actual body of genetic material.' It would require great hubris to imagine that we can safely terminate the co-evolutionary process that small farmers have carried forward for thousands of years, and henceforth delegate all crop breeding to professional scientists mining the existing stock of diversity held in seed collections.

Finally, there is a world of difference between having a seed 'in the bank' and knowing what you have. Many genetic attributes can be observed only by growing plants in the microhabitats from which they come. The fact that a certain maize variety can withstand intermittent drought at four-week intervals, for example, or that is resistant to a particular strain of fungus, is not apparent unless it is grown in circumstances that reveal these qualities. Relying on artificial growth chambers to obtain this information would be very expensive. In effect, knowledge of the attributes of diverse varieties – knowledge that resides in the farmers who grow them – is a vital component of diversity itself. As Garrison Wilkes puts it, 'sun, soil, seeds, and smarts' are the 'four S's of farming.'[16]

None of the foregoing is meant to disparage the importance of *ex situ* collections or minimize the need for their adequate financial support. *Ex situ* collections provide a conduit for plant breeders to access diversity, and they provide insurance against losses of diversity in the field. For example, Cambodian rice varieties that were lost during the war and the disruption of the Khmer Rouge period subsequently were reintroduced using seeds that had been stored at IRRI.[17] But the insecurity of *ex situ* collections, the importance of continued evolution in the field and the need for information about varietal attributes all mean that the world needs *in situ* diversity too. In short, *in situ* and *ex situ* diversity are complements, not substitutes.

SMALL FARMERS AS AN ENDANGERED SPECIES

From the highlands of Mesoamerica to the river deltas of south Asia, the ability of small farmers to sustain agricultural biodiversity is threatened by their lack of livelihood security. For example, in Mexico – where there is a striking geographical correlation between maize diversity and the prevalence of infant malnutrition (Figure 8.2) – outmigration from rural areas is highest 'where corn production is carried out in small plots, with local varieties, and where poverty is pervasive' (Nadal 2000, p. 8).[18] Rural outmigration has been limited by Mexico's economic crisis and the lack of urban employment opportunities, but this could change quickly if the economy improves (Ackerman et al. 2003). Poverty cannot provide a durable basis for conserving *in situ* diversity.

Outmigration of farmers is propelled by 'pull' factors and 'push' factors. On the pull side are the lures of urban employment, the 'bright lights' of the city and better access to education and health services. Yet the fate of displaced small farmers in urban areas is often grim: the work that awaits them is often low-paid, insecure and hazardous; their housing is precarious and inadequate; and they no longer have access to land for subsistence production. To understand what makes these urban options seem attractive in comparison to farming, we must also look at the push side of the

Landraces in corn production by state, 1990

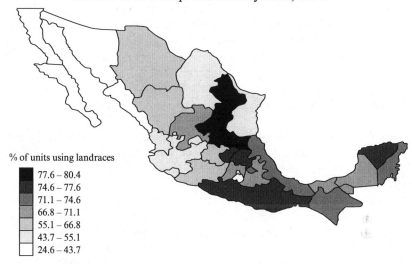

% of units using landraces

77.6 – 80.4
74.6 – 77.6
71.1 – 74.6
66.8 – 71.1
55.1 – 66.8
43.7 – 55.1
24.6 – 43.7

Infant malnutrition, 1996

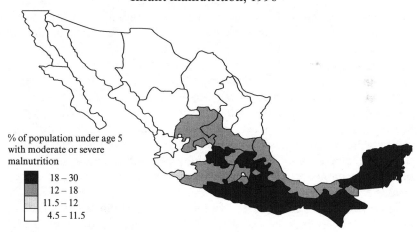

% of population under age 5
with moderate or severe
malnutrition

18 – 30
12 – 18
11.5 – 12
4.5 – 11.5

Source: Nadal (2000, pp. 50, 90).

Figure 8.2   Maize diversity and infant malnutrition in Mexico

migration equation. Two factors that help to explain why small farmers find it increasingly difficult to earn a living on the land are agricultural 'modernization' and international agricultural trade. On a level playing field, neither of these necessarily would be inimical to the small farmer. All too often, however, both are played out on a terrain that is tilted against small farmers.

Agricultural 'Modernization'

Agricultural 'modernization' is often spearheaded by the introduction and diffusion of highly fertilizer-responsive crop varieties, a process epitomized by the 'green revolution' in rice and wheat agriculture that was launched in Asia and Latin America in the 1960s. In principle, this technology was divisible and labor-intensive, and thus well suited to small farms. In practice, as Keith Griffin documented in *The Political Economy of Agrarian Change* (1979), large landowners often reaped the lion's share of the benefits. Small farmers lost out not only in relative terms, but also absolutely insofar as large farmers were able to expand operations at their expense.

This polarization occurred for several reasons. First, the new varieties were best suited to regions well endowed with water-control infrastructure, such as the states of Punjab and Haryana in India, leaving producers in poorer regions to face adverse effects from falling output prices and/or rising input prices. Second, within regions, large farmers had preferential access to irrigation hardware and subsidized credit, positioning them to reap windfall gains as early adopters of the new technology. Third, large farmers used their political power, bolstered by these income gains, to extract further state support, including subsidies for farm machinery that helped to offset the labor-cost advantages of small farmers. Fourth, in settings where land often changes hands through transactions that involve some degree of 'extra-economic' coercion, the green revolution enhanced both the incentive for large landowners to wrest control of lands from smaller farmers, and their power to do so.[19]

Insofar as agricultural modernization triggers displacement of small farmers, it undermines the social basis for agricultural biodiversity. To be sure, new technologies can lead to genetic erosion on small farms, independently of changes in the agrarian structure, if small farmers themselves decide to replace numerous local varieties with fewer new ones.[20] As noted above, however, it is possible for traditional crop varieties and farming practices to co-exist with new ones. Indeed, one can imagine situations where the introduction of new varieties enhances diversity rather than diminishing it.[21] The impact of modernization on agricultural biodiversity hinges, in no small measure, on how it affects the livelihood security of small farmers. As the small farmer goes, so goes diversity.

International Agricultural Trade

A second push factor arises from the growth of international agricultural trade. Small farmers in the developing countries of the global South face intensifying competition from cheap grain imported from the industrialized countries of the global North. A striking example is Mexico's imports of maize from the United States: since the NAFTA went into effect in 1994, imports have risen from one million metric tons per year to more than six million, a volume equivalent to roughly one-quarter of Mexico's annual consumption (Audley et al. 2004, p. 22). These imports, coupled with the Mexican government's withdrawal of price supports for maize farmers, caused real producer prices to plummet by 70 percent (Oxfam 2003, p. 2).

The competitive edge that permits US corn to capture Mexican markets has several sources. Genuine comparative advantage is part of the story: the regular rainfall, fertile soils and harsh winters that suppress pest populations help to make the midwestern US corn belt a good place to grow maize. The broad array of agricultural support policies and subsidies in the United States also makes a contribution.[22] The failure of market prices to internalize environmental costs ('negative externalities') confers a further advantage to US agriculture; the supply price of US maize does not include, for example, the social costs of widespread contamination of groundwater and surface waters by the herbicide atrazine.[23] Last, but not least, the failure of market prices to internalize the environmental benefits of *in situ* conservation of crop genetic diversity (a 'positive externality') hobbles the competitive position of small-scale Mexican farmers.

International trade thus allows low-diversity agriculture in the North to displace high-diversity agriculture in the South. Trade reform efforts – for example, efforts to curtail US and European Union policies that foster overproduction and the dumping of agricultural products on world markets – would help to level the playing field for small farmers. But as long as externalities are left out of the picture, systematic biases against small farmers will persist. For small farmers in the global South, and above all in the centers of diversity, policies to reward the environmental service of *in situ* conservation are of key importance. In effect, these small farmers subsidize modern agriculture and food consumers worldwide. The way to end this subsidy is not to eliminate the environmental service by driving small farmers off the land, but instead to reward their contributions to world food security.

WHAT IS TO BE DONE?

A wide range of policies can be envisioned that would reward small farmers for sustaining agricultural biodiversity. Such policies would both strengthen rural livelihood security and provide incentives for continued *in situ* conservation. In other words, rather than posing a tradeoff between poverty reduction and environmental protection, these are policies that would advance both goals simultaneously.[24]

1. *Removal of anti-small farmer policy distortions.* As noted above, the competitive advantage of large farmers and low-diversity agriculture rests, in part, on government policies that favor capital-intensive agricultural technologies and promote the dumping of surplus agricultural products on world markets. While the removal of these distortions would not eliminate other biases that arise from neglect of externalities, this would be a step in the right direction.
2. *Social recognition.* Another important step would be to promote 'non-economic' rewards for the conservation of agricultural biodiversity. At the annual *feria del elote* (corn fair) in Jala, Mexico, for example, farmers get prizes for producing the finest examples of the valley's traditional landrace maize. Such recognition not only makes farmers feel good, it also helps to create public awareness of the need for policies to provide economic rewards.
3. *Market development.* 'A rose is a rose is a rose,' wrote the poet Gertrude Stein. However that may be (and rose lovers no doubt would have something to say about this), one ear of corn is not the same as any other. Traditional varieties of grains, vegetables and fruits not only have different genetic attributes than modern varieties, they also look different, and most importantly, taste different. In part, for this reason – and in part, by virtue of commitments to environmental values – there is scope for development of domestic and international markets in which traditional varieties command a price premium. Labeling systems, like the denominations of origin established for French wines in 1935, can assist in creating such markets (Mann 2004). Again, this could not only provide direct rewards to growers, but also help to raise public consciousness of the importance of diversity and the need for public policies to sustain it.[25]
4. *Provision of local public goods.* Outmigration of small farmers is propelled in part by lack of local public goods, such as schools and health clinics. To encourage small farmers to remain on the land, and to provide tangible evidence of the value society places on the environmental services they provide, governments and international agencies

could invest in local public goods. Even in the absence of concerns over the erosion of agricultural biodiversity, there are compelling equity and efficiency arguments for such investments. The need to conserve diversity merely adds to the case.

5. *Payments for environmental services.* A further possibility that warrants serious exploration is payments to farmers who provide the environmental service of *in situ* conservation. For such payments to become a part of the policy mix, two main questions would need to be resolved: how to structure the payments and how to finance them. Payments could take the form of a 'bonus' per unit output (as suggested by Nadal 2000, p. 104), or a payment per unit area under the crop, which would have the advantage of removing biases against varieties with low yields per unit area. In determining which individuals or communities should receive payments, there may be tradeoffs between precision and inclusivity, and a good case can be made for the latter. 'When money falls from heaven into a poor community,' Peter Rosset comments, 'it often ends up accentuating the power and wealth differences in the community,' and can 'even lead to violence.'[26] Structuring payments so as to strengthen rural communities will be a key challenge.[27] With regard to sources of finance, the fact that the benefits of agricultural biodiversity are truly global means that local and national governments should not have to bear the entire cost of sustaining it. There is a need to mobilize international resources, perhaps under the aegis of the GEF.[28]

6. *Policies to encourage part-time farming.* Finally, we should recognize that farming need not be an all-or-nothing occupational choice. In Japan, for example, only 15 percent of the country's three million farm households (a number that was down from six million in 1960) earn their livelihoods entirely from farming; three-quarters derive most of their income from non-farm sources (Figure 8.3). Just as the adoption of modern crop varieties does not necessarily eliminate traditional varieties, so the expansion of non-farm employment does not necessarily eliminate farming. Policies that help to generate part-time, off-farm employment opportunities in rural areas can help to sustain small farms. So can policies that promote agriculture-friendly tourism, thereby internalizing another positive externality often generated by small-farm landscapes: scenic beauty.[29] In supporting small farms, such policies could help to sustain agricultural biodiversity, especially if accompanied by other policies that recognize and reward the social value of *in situ* conservation.

These policies are not mutually exclusive, nor is any one policy alone likely to be sufficient. Taken together, however, they could do a great deal to support small farms and stewardship of agricultural biodiversity.

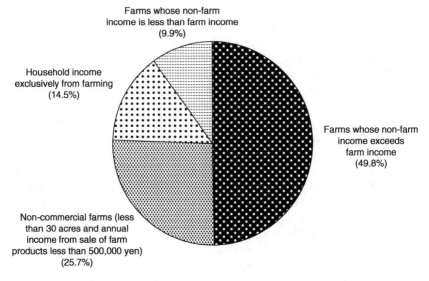

Farms whose non-farm
income is less than farm income
(9.9%)

Household income
exclusively from farming
(14.5%)

Farms whose non-farm
income exceeds
farm income
(49.8%)

Non-commercial farms (less
than 30 acres and annual
income from sale of farm
products less than 500,000 yen)
(25.7%)

Source: Government of Japan (2003, p. 57).

Figure 8.3   Distribution of farm households in Japan

CONCLUSION

There is a future for small farms. Or, to be more precise, there can be and should be a future for them. Owing to the dependence of modern low-diversity agriculture on traditional high-diversity agriculture, the long-term food security of humankind will depend on small farms and their continued provision of the environmental service of *in situ* conservation of crop genetic diversity. Policies to support small farms can be advocated, therefore, not merely as a matter of sympathy, or nostalgia, or equity. Such policies are also a matter of human survival.

The diversity that underpins the sustainability of world agriculture did not fall from the sky. It was bequeathed to us by the 400 generations of farmers who have carried on the process of artificial selection since plants were first domesticated. Until recently, we took this diversity for granted. The ancient reservoirs of crop genetic diversity, plant geneticist Jack Harlan (1975, p. 619) wrote three decades ago, 'seemed to most people as inexhaustible as oil in Arabia.' Yet, Harlan warned, 'the speed with which enormous crop diversity can be essentially wiped out is astonishing.'

The central message of this chapter is that efforts to conserve *in situ* diversity must go hand in hand with efforts to support the small farmers around the world who sustain this diversity. Economists and environmentalists alike, by and large, have neglected this issue. In thrall to a myopic notion of efficiency, many economists fail to appreciate that diversity is the *sine qua non* of resilience and sustainability. In thrall to a romantic notion of 'wilderness,' many environmentalists fail to appreciate that agricultural biodiversity is just as valuable – indeed, arguably more valuable from the standpoint of human well-being – as the diversity found in tropical rainforests or the spotted owls found in the ancient forests of the northwestern United States.

Today, a formidable nexus of market forces and political forces threatens both small farmers and the agricultural biodiversity they sustain. Several countervailing public policies have been suggested here: removal of policy biases against small farmers; social recognition of the contribution of *in situ* conservation to human well-being; development of markets for traditional varieties; provision of local public goods in areas where farmers cultivate diversity; payments for the environmental service of on-farm conservation; and policies to support part-time farming as a component of household livelihood strategies.

Only an awakened and mobilized public opinion can bring such policies into being. Small farmers cannot do it alone. They need allies. A process of 'artificial selection' is needed in the policy arena to yield outcomes that will not come about from 'natural selection' by market forces and the political influence of the powerful.

No less than farming itself, ensuring a sustainable future requires human intelligence and human agency. In the present era of globalization, all of us share responsibility for the cultivation of agricultural biodiversity.

NOTES

*   This is a revised version of a chapter originally published in James K. Boyce, Stephen Cullenberg, Prasanta K. Pattanaik and Robert Pollin (eds), *Human Development in the Era of Globalization: Essays in Honor of Keith B. Griffin* (2006), Cheltenham, UK and Northampton, MA, USA: Edward Elgar Publishing, pp. 83–104.
1.   'A French roadblock to free trade,' *New York Times,* 3 August 2003.
2.   Personal interview, Guatemala City, December 1997.
3.   For the incorporation of this recognition into recent thinking at the World Bank, see Deininger (2003).
4.   The term 'agricultural biodiversity' is often used to refer not only to crop genetic diversity, but also other related forms of biodiversity, including pathogens, insects and soil microorganisms (see, for example, Wood and Lenné 1999). Here my focus is crop genetic diversity and I shall use the terms interchangeably. Much of the discussion could be generalized, however, to other forms of agricultural biodiversity.
5.   Wilkes (1995, p. 207) suggests that we call this process 'anthro-selection,' in recognition of the human-centered nature of the process.

6. See Mann (2002a). See also Brookfield (2001, pp. 96–7) for discussion of this and other examples of 'manufactured soils.'
7. For discussions of the origins of these and other crop plants, see MacNeish (1992), Harlan (1995), Smartt and Simmonds (1995) and Smith (1995).
8. For more on the contrasts between Mexican and US maize agriculture, see Boyce (1996).
9. For discussion of differences in the real cost of family labor versus hired labor, see Sen (1975). For discussion of farm size and labor supervision, see Boyce (1987, pp. 39–40, 213).
10. Nadal (2000, p. 122), citing Ortega Paczka (1997). Women often play a particularly important role in agricultural biodiversity conservation. For example, surveys in indigenous communities in the Guatemalan highlands have found that women often select the seed for the next production cycle, doing so on the basis of culinary requirements and Mayan cosmology as well as agronomic characteristics (FAO and IPGRI 2002, pp. 22, 39–40).
11. The term 'evolutionary gardens' is used by Wilkes (1992, pp. 24–6) to describe the hilly, rain-fed *milpa* plots cultivated by the *campesinos* of Mesoamerica.
12. Most plant breeding is still performed in the public sector, notwithstanding the growing importance of private-sector breeders and the publicity that has accompanied this trend.
13. See Brammer (1980) and Biggs (1980). See also Bellon et al. (1997).
14. Quoted by Fowler and Mooney (1990, p. xii).
15. In the late 1960s, for example, CIMMYT sent 'back-up copies' of about 5000 varieties of Latin American maize to the NSSL in Fort Collins. When CIMMYT asked for some of these back, having lost some of its own samples in a period of budgetary shortfalls, it turned out that most of the seeds sent to the NSSL had been inadvertently discarded (Raeburn 1995, pp. 62–3). See also Brookfield (2001, p. 247), who concludes that 'a high proportion of the world's seed storage has substandard conditions, and there is concern about the viability of many collections.'
16. Personal communication, May 2004.
17. Personal interview with Joel Charny, who retrieved the seed samples from the IRRI while working for Oxfam-America in the 1980s.
18. For examples of genetic erosion associated with this outmigration, see Nadal (2000, pp. 90–1).
19. For further discussion, see Griffin (1979; 1999, chapter 6) and Boyce (1993, chapters 3–5).
20. For examples in the case of potato cultivation in the Andes, see Ochoa (1975).
21. For discussion, see Qualset et al. (1997), Wood and Lenné (1997), Edwards et al. (1999) and Jana (1999).
22. For discussion, see Wise (2004).
23. See Boyce (1996) and Ackerman (2002).
24. The policies sketched here are examples of the 'internalization' route to building natural assets in the hands of the poor (Boyce 2003). For further discussion of these policies, see also Thrupp (1998) and Brush (2000).
25. For examples from Switzerland, see Bardsley and Thomas (2004). For discussion, see also Smale et al. (2004, pp. 130–1).
26. Quoted by Mann (2004, p. 23).
27. In Guatemala's western highlands, for example, small farmers who cultivate traditional maize varieties also invest in labor-intensive land improvements such as terracing and the cultivation of live barriers to control soil erosion, despite lack of formal land titles. Elizabeth Katz (2000, p. 124) attributes their willingness to undertake these investments to 'informal social recognition of property rights – a manifestation of social capital – at the community level, which effectively replaces formal legal title.' If payments for environmental services were to erode this social capital, the net effect paradoxically could be to undermine such investments. See also Rosa et al. (2007).

28. The GEF has begun to contemplate work in this area; see GEF (2000).
29. In some cases, agricultural biodiversity itself has tourism value. For example, in Cusco, Peru, tour groups can visit a potato museum, demonstration plots and restaurants featuring traditional produce (Cromwell et al. 1999, p. 35).

REFERENCES

Ackerman, Frank (2002), *Is the United States a Pollution Haven?*, Silver City, NM: Interhemispheric Resource Center.

Ackerman, Frank, Timothy A. Wise, Kevin P. Gallagher, Luke Ney and Regina Flores (2003), 'Free trade, corn, and the environment: environmental impacts of US–Mexico corn trade under NAFTA,', Tufts University Global Development and Environment Institute working paper no. 03-06, Medford, MA.

Audley, John J., Demetrios G. Papademetriou, Sandra Polaski and Scott Vaughan (2004), *NAFTA's Promise and Reality: Lessons from Mexico for the Hemisphere*, Washington, DC: Carnegie Endowment for International Peace.

Bardsley, D. and I. Thomas (2004), 'In situ agrobiodiversity conservation in the Swiss Inner Alpine Zone,' *GeoJournal*, **60**(2), 99–109.

Bellon, M.R., J.-L. Pham and M.T. Jackson (1997), 'Genetic conservation: a role for rice farmers,' in N. Maxted, B. Ford-Lloyd and J.G. Hawkes (eds), *Plant Genetic Conservation: The In Situ Approach*, London: Chapman & Hall, pp. 263–89.

Biggs, Stephen D. (1980), 'Informal R&D,' *Ceres*, publication of the Food and Agriculture Organization, Rome, **13**(4), 23–6.

Boyce, James K. (1987), *Agrarian Impasse in Bengal: Institutional Constraints to Technological Change*, Oxford: Oxford University Press.

Boyce, James K. (1993), *The Philippines: The Political Economy of Growth and Impoverishment in the Marcos Era*, London: Macmillan.

Boyce, James K. (1996), 'Ecological distribution, agricultural trade liberalization, and *in situ* genetic diversity,' *Journal of Income Distribution*, **6**(2), 263–84.

Boyce, James K. (2003), 'From natural resources to natural assets,' in James K. Boyce and Barry G. Shelley (eds), *Natural Assets: Democratizing Environmental Ownership*, Washington, DC: Island Press, chapter 1.

Brammer, Hugh (1980), 'Some innovations don't wait for experts,' *Ceres* publication of the Food and Agriculture Organization, Rome, **13**(2), 24–8.

Brookfield, Harold (2001), *Exploring Agrodiversity*, New York: Columbia University Press.

Brush, Stephen B. (1995), 'In situ conservation of landraces in centers of crop diversity,' *Crop Science*, **35**, 346–54.

Brush, Stephen B. (ed.) (2000), *Genes in the Field: On-farm Conservation of Crop Diversity*, Rome: International Plant Genetic Resources Institute.

Chang, T.T. (1995), 'Rice,' in J. Smartt and N.W. Simmonds (eds), *Evolution of Crop Plants*, 2nd edn, Harlow: Longman Scientific & Technical, pp. 147–55.

Cromwell, Elizabeth, David Cooper and Patrick Mulvany (1999), *Agriculture, Biodiversity and Livelihoods: Issues and Entry Points for Development Agencies*, London: Overseas Development Institute.

Darwin, Charles (1859 [1952]), *The Origin of Species by Means of Natural Selection*, Chicago, IL: Encyclopaedia Britannica.

Deininger, Klaus (2003), *Land Policies for Growth and Poverty Reduction*, Oxford: Oxford University Press.

Duvick, Daniel N. (1984), 'Genetic diversity in major farm crops on the farm and in reserve,' *Economic Botany*, **38**(2), 161–78.

Duvick, Daniel N., J.S.C. Smith and M. Cooper (2004), 'Changes in performance, parentage, and genetic diversity of successful corn hybrids, from 1930 to 2000,' in C.W. Smith, J. Betrán and E.C.A. Runge (eds), *Corn: Origin, History, Technology, and Production*, New York: John Wiley & Sons, pp. 65–97.

Edwards, P.J., J. Kollmann and D. Wood (1999), 'Determinants of agrobiodiversity in the agricultural landscape,' in David Wood and Jillian M. Lenné (eds), *Agrobiodiversity: Characterization, Utilization and Management*, Wallingford: CABI Publishing, pp. 183–210.

Food and Agriculture Organization of the United Nations (FAO) and International Plant Genetic Resources Institute (IPGRI) (2002), *The Role of Women in the Conservation of the Genetic Resources of Maize*, Rome: FAO and IPGRI.

Fowler, Cary and Pat Mooney (1990), *Shattering: Food, Politics, and the Loss of Genetic Diversity*, Tucson, AZ: University of Arizona Press.

García-Barrios, Raúl and Luis García-Barrios (1990), 'Environmental and technological degradation in peasant agriculture: a consequence of development in Mexico,' *World Development*, **18**(11), 1569–85.

Global Environment Facility (GEF) (2000), *Elements of a GEF Operational Program on Conservation and Sustainable Use of Biological Diversity Important to Agriculture*, April.

Goodman, Major M. (1995), 'Maize,' in J. Smartt and N.W. Simmonds (eds), *Evolution of Crop Plants*, 2nd edn, Harlow: Longman Scientific & Technical, pp. 193–202.

Government of Japan (2003), *Statistical Handbook of Japan, 2003*, Tokyo: Ministry of Public Management, Home Affairs, Post and Telecommunications, Statistics Bureau.

Griffin, Keith (1979), *The Political Economy of Agrarian Change*, 2nd edn, London: Macmillan.

Griffin, Keith (1999), *Alternative Strategies for Economic Development*, 2nd edn, London: Macmillan.

Griffin, Keith, Azizur Rahman Khan and Amy Ickowitz (2002), 'Poverty and the distribution of land,' *Journal of Agrarian Change*, **2**(3), 279–330.

Harlan, Jack R. (1975), 'Our vanishing genetic resources,' *Science*, **188**(4188), 617–21.

Harlan, Jack R. (1995), *The Living Fields: Our Agricultural Heritage*, Cambridge: Cambridge University Press.

Heywood, V.H. (1995), *Global Biodiversity Assessment*, Cambridge: Cambridge University Press.

Jana, S. (1999), 'Some recent issues on the conservation of crop genetic resources in developing countries,' *Genome*, **42**, 562–9.

Katz, Elizabeth (2000), 'Social capital and natural capital: a comparative analysis of land tenure and natural resource management in Guatemala,' *Land Economics*, **76**(1), 114–32.

Lewis, W. Arthur (1954), 'Economic development with unlimited supplies of labor,' *The Manchester School of Economic and Social Studies*, **22**, 139–91.

MacNeish, Richard S. (1992), *The Origins of Agriculture and Settled Life*, Norman, OK: University of Oklahoma Press.

Mann, Charles (2002a), 'The real dirt on rainforest fertility,' *Science*, **297**, 920–23.

Mann, Charles (2002b), '1491,' *Atlantic Monthly*, March, 41–53.

Mann, Charles (2004), *Diversity on the Farm*, New York and Amherst, MA: Ford Foundation and Political Economy Research Institute.

Nadal, Alejandro (2000), *The Environmental and Social Impacts of Economic Liberalization on Corn Production in Mexico*, Oxford and Gland: Oxfam and WWF International.

Ochoa, Carlos (1975), 'Potato collecting expeditions in Chile, Bolivia and Peru, and the genetic erosion of indigenous cultivars,' in O.H. Frankel and J.G. Hawkes (eds), *Crop Genetic Resources for Today and Tomorrow*, Cambridge: Cambridge University Press, pp. 167–74.

Ortega Paczka, Rafael A. (1997), *Maíz en el Tratado de Libre Comercio: Implicaciones para el medio ambiente. Recursos genéticos*, consultant's report to the Commission for Environmental Cooperation, Montreal, QC.

Oxfam (2003), 'Dumping without borders: how US agricultural policies are destroying the livelihoods of Mexican corn farmers,' Oxfam briefing paper no. 50, August, Oxford.

Peña, Devon (2003), 'The watershed commonwealth of the Upper Rio Grande,' in James K. Boyce and Barry G. Shelley (eds), *Natural Assets: Democratizing Environmental Ownership*, Washington, DC: Island Press, chapter 9.

Plucknett, D.L., Nigel J.H. Smith, J.T. Williams and N. Murthi Anishetty (1987), *Gene Banks and the World's Food*, Princeton, NJ: Princeton University Press.

Qualset, C.O., A.B. Damania, A.C.A. Zanatta and S.B. Brush (1997), 'Locally based crop plant conservation,' in N. Maxted, B. Ford-Lloyd and J.G. Hawkes (eds), *Plant Genetic Conservation: The In Situ Approach*, London: Chapman & Hall, pp. 160–75.

Raeburn, Paul (1995), *The Last Harvest*, New York: Simon & Schuster.

Rosa, Herman, Susan Kandel, Leopoldo Dimas and Deborah Barry (2007), 'Compensation for environmental services and rural communities: lessons from the Americas,' in James K. Boyce, Sunita Narain and Elizabeth A. Stanton (eds), *Reclaiming Nature: Environmental Justice and Ecological Restoration*, London and New York: Anthem Press, chapter 9.

Sen, Amartya (1975), *Employment, Technology, and Development*, Oxford: Oxford University Press.

Shand, Hope (1997), *Human Nature: Agricultural Biodiversity and Farm-based Food Security*, Ottawa, ON: Rural Advancement Foundation International.

Smale, Melinda, Mauricio R. Bellon, Devra Jarvis and Bhuwon Sthapit (2004), 'Economic concepts for designing policies to conserve crop genetic resources on farms,' *Genetic Resources and Crop Evolution*, **51**, 121–35.

Smartt, J. and Simmonds, N.W. (eds) (1995), *Evolution of Crop Plants*, 2nd edn, Harlow: Longman Scientific & Technical.

Smith, Bruce D. (1995), *The Emergence of Agriculture*, New York: Scientific American Library.

Stam, Jerome M. and Bruce L. Dixon (2004), 'Farmer bankruptcies and farm exits in the United States, 1899–2002,' US Department of Agriculture Economic Research Service agriculture information bulletin no. 788, Washington, DC.

Swanson, T.M. and R.A. Luxmoore (1997), *Industrial Reliance on Biodiversity*, Biodiversity Series No. 7, Cambridge: World Conservation Monitoring Centre.

Thrupp, Lori Ann (1998), *Cultivating Diversity: Agrobiodiversity and Food Security*, Washington, DC: World Resources Institute.

Vavilov, Nikolai I. (1926 [1992]), *Origin and Geography of Cultivated Plants*, Cambridge: Cambridge University Press.

Wilkes, Garrison (1992), *Strategies for Sustaining Crop Germplasm Preservation, Enhancement, and Use*, Washington, DC: Consultative Group on International Agricultural Research.

Wilkes, Garrison (1995), 'The ethnobotany of artificial selection in seed plant domestication,' in Richard E. Schultes and Siri von Reis (eds), *Ethnobotany: Evolution of a Discipline*, Portland, OR: Dioscorides Press, pp. 203–8.

Wise, Timothy A. (2004), 'The paradox of agricultural subsidies: measurement issues, agricultural dumping, and policy reform,', Tufts University Global Development and Environment Institute working paper no. 04-02, Medford, MA.

Wood, David and Jillian M. Lenné (1997), 'The conservation of agrobiodiversity on-farm: questioning the emerging paradigm,' *Biodiversity and Conservation*, **6**, 109–29.

Wood, David and Jillian M. Lenné (1999), *Agrobiodiversity: Characterization, Utilization and Management*, Wallingford: CABI Publishing.

9. Globalization and our environmental future

In the early 1990s, the environmental movement in the United States underwent an acrimonious split over whether to support the North American Free Trade Agreement. Some environmental groups backed the treaty, maintaining that 'the best way to ensure that Mexico's environment is cleaned up is to help Mexico become a prosperous country, and that means NAFTA.'[1] Others opposed it, arguing that 'the competition to attract investment will result in a lowest common denominator for environmental statutes' and that 'the country with the least restrictive statutes will become the floor, and others will harmonize downward to that floor.'[2]

Despite their differences, both sides shared a common assumption: Mexico's environmental practices were inferior to those of the United States and Canada. The only point of contention was whether free trade would pull the United States and Canada down to Mexico's level, or lift Mexico to the plane of its northern neighbors. Partly as a result, both sides were oblivious to what may turn out to be NAFTA's most serious environmental impact, discussed in the preceding chapter: the erosion of Mexico's rich biological diversity in maize ('corn' in US parlance), as Mexican *campesino* farmers abandon traditional agriculture in the face of competition from cheap corn imported from the United States.

In this chapter, I question the assumption that the global North is relatively 'green' and the global South relatively 'brown.' I also argue that neither theoretical reasoning nor empirical evidence supports axiomatic claims that globalization must inexorably lead to a convergence across countries toward better environmental practices or toward worse ones.

UNEVEN GLOBALIZATION

Globalization, here defined as the integration of economic activities around the world, has long been an uneven process, not only across regions but also across the social spheres that structure economic activity. In general, globalization has proceeded furthest in the sphere of the market – more precisely, in capital and product markets, since labor mobility remains far more constrained by national borders. In the sphere of governance, globalization generally has not proceeded as far.[3] Geographical disparities in the extent of globalization have been well documented (see, for example, Sutcliffe 2004). My focus here is institutional disparities between globalization of the market and globalization of governance, particularly as these affect environmental quality.

Both markets and governance are integral parts of economies. Markets are nested within social institutions that both enable them to function and temper their effects. The rise of capitalism was characterized by what Karl Polanyi (1944 [1957], p. 132) called a 'double movement': the expansion of the market, coupled with the expansion of 'social protection aiming at the conservation of man and nature as well as productive organization.' The latter includes what today we call 'environmental protection' – measures that aim to redress environmental market failures associated with public goods and externalities.

Globalization likewise entails the integration not only of markets, but also of governance, institutions 'capable of resolving conflicts, facilitating cooperation, or, more generally, alleviating collective-action problems in a world of interdependent actors' (Young 1994, p. 15). The globalization of governance includes formal international agreements, such as the 1987 Montreal Protocol, which curtailed the use of chemicals that deplete the Earth's protective ozone layer; supranational institutions such as the European Union, which recently adopted regulations that shift onto manufacturers the burden of proof for safety of industrial chemicals released into the environment;[4] and informal governance by 'global civil society' (Lipschutz and Mayer 1996; Sonnenfeld and Mol 2002) and by decentralized 'networks' encompassing both state and non-state actors (Haas 2004).

When trade occurs at prices that do not capture external costs and external benefits, market integration is accompanied by the globalization of market failure. Yet the absence of corrective policies also represents a governance failure. Institutions of governance can fail to redress market failures for reasons of both inability (for example, bureaucratic incompetence) and unwillingness (for example, the political influence of those who would bear the costs of internalization).[5] The unevenness in the globalization of markets and governance exacerbates the ability side of the problem. As discussed below, it may also create new impediments on the willingness side.

ENVIRONMENTAL CONVERGENCE: FOUR SCENARIOS

In debates on North-South trade, it is often assumed that production processes in the global South tend to be more environmentally degrading than those in the global North, by virtue of weaker demand for environmental quality (ascribed to low incomes), the weaker ability of governments to promulgate and enforce environmental regulations, or both. Hence, trade occurs on a tilted playing field, where Southern producers have a competitive advantage over their Northern counterparts, thanks to their greater scope for externalization of costs.

Economic theory is often invoked to maintain that a level playing field – one with no international differences in environmental standards – is not necessarily optimal: the marginal costs and benefits of environmental quality are likely to vary across locations.[6]

Two points should be noted in this connection. First, this does not imply that existing variations in standards across countries are optimal, nor that moves toward greater harmonization would not be welfare-improving in conventional terms. Second, international differences in the 'optimal' level of environmental quality are partly – perhaps mainly – attributable to differences in ability to pay, in the sense that it is 'efficient' for poorer people to breathe dirtier air. This distribution-blind notion of optimality is unexceptional in neoclassical economics, but its wider normative appeal as a basis for policy is questionable. Elsewhere I have suggested that a rights-based allocation of access to a clean and safe environment – a principle enshrined in dozens of national constitutions around the world – is an attractive alternative to the wealth-based allocation principle founded on willingness to pay (Boyce 2000).

Here, however, our concern is not normative prescription but rather positive description. As in the NAFTA debate, the question is whether economic integration will lead to 'harmonization upward,' in which the South becomes more like the North, or a 'race to the bottom,' in which the opposite occurs. These opposing outcomes are labeled 'ecological modernization' and 'environmental protectionism,' respectively, in Figure 9.1, based on prominent schools of thought that have emphasized these possibilities.

In principle, we can distinguish two further paths of convergence, in which the North-South environmental gradient is reversed: that is, Southern production is cleaner and more sustainable than that of competing sectors in the North. That this is not a purely hypothetical possibility is illustrated below. In Figure 9.1, these paths are labeled 'greening the North' (when the North moves up the gradient, becoming more like the

Direction of change / Environmental quality gradient	'Harmonization upward'	'Race to the bottom'
North > South	Ecological modernization	Environmental protectionism
South > North	Greening the North	Environmental imperialism

Figure 9.1   Environmental convergence: four scenarios

South) and 'environmental imperialism' (when the South moves down the gradient to become more like the North).

Of course, these stylized scenarios simplify complex processes. One scenario need not fit all environmental problems; it is quite possible, for example, that in some respects the environmental gradient runs from North to South while in others it runs in the opposite direction. Harmonization may occur not at either end of the spectrum, but rather somewhere in the middle. And in some cases, globalization may promote divergence rather than convergence. To begin mapping out the possibilities, I first consider the four convergence scenarios.

Ecological Modernization

The term 'ecological modernization' was coined in the 1980s by European sociologists to describe recent changes in production and consumption in industrialized countries. In many cases, these changes have reduced the use of natural resources and emissions of pollutants per unit output, and in some cases these reductions have been substantial enough to generate net environmental improvements alongside economic growth (see, for example, Spaargaren and Mol 1992; Weale 1992).

Ecological modernization theorists interpret these transformations as a response not only to market signals but also, more importantly, to the growth of environmental concerns among the public and policy-makers.[7] Although originally put forward as an analysis of trends in industrialized countries, the theory has been extended globally by some of its proponents. In so doing, most have accepted the conventional premise that the environmental-quality gradient runs from North to South. Thus Mol (2001, p. 157) writes of 'the need to harmonize environmental capacities and regimes up to at least the level that has been achieved in the [Europe-North America-Japan] triad countries.'

Mechanisms identified as vehicles for such harmonization upwards include income growth, foreign direct investment, international agreements and 'governance from below.'

- A positive effect from *income growth* is premised on the view that globalization leads to rising per capita income, and that the latter in turn leads to greater effective demand for environmental quality (often referred to as a better ability to 'afford' a cleaner environment). During the NAFTA debate, for example, Mexican President Carlos Salinas proclaimed, 'Only through widespread prosperity can we have the resources to channel toward the protection of land, air and water' (quoted by Hogenboom 1998, p. 180). Both links – from globalization to rising incomes, and from rising incomes to a better environment – are open to question. With respect to the latter link, it is important to recognize that many aspects of environmental quality are public goods. To be politically effective, demand for environmental quality therefore must be articulated through institutions that overcome both the free-rider problem and political opposition from the beneficiaries of cost externalization. I return to this issue below.

- *Foreign direct investment* is sometimes portrayed as a vehicle for environmental improvement on the grounds that foreign firms have superior technological know-how, derived from production in countries with stricter regulations, and that they find it efficient to use standardized processes to produce standardized products. In addition, foreign firms may be more sensitive to reputational concerns than local firms, and more subject to media scrutiny and pressure from public opinion. In keeping with this prediction, some empirical studies have found evidence of 'pollution halos' – above-average environmental performance – associated with foreign investment.

In a review of this literature, Zarsky (1999, p. 14) concludes that the evidence is mixed, and that 'the most significant determinant of firm performance is community pressure' rather than the origin of investment per se.[8]

- *International agreements* can also promote upward harmonization in environmental practices. Examples of such agreements include the treaties on oceanic pollution, transport of hazardous waste, and ozone-depleting chemicals (Table 9.1). Neumayer (2002) finds that the degree of democracy – as measured by indices of political rights and 'voice and accountability' – is a strong predictor of whether countries will enter into environmental agreements, again pointing to the importance of political variables in determining outcomes.

- *Governance from below* refers to de facto rules that are imposed not by governments, but by civil society and public opinion. A series of studies at the World Bank, for example, has found that 'informal regulation' by local communities can limit industrial pollution even in the absence of formal regulation (see Pargal and Wheeler 1996; Pargal et al. 1997). These studies generally find the average income and education of communities to be strongly correlated with successful informal regulation. Transnational environmental alliances can also increase the bargaining power of local communities (see, for example, Keenan et al. 2007). In addition to directly influencing

Table 9.1   List of major international environmental agreements

Agreement	Date	Issue addressed
International Convention for the Regulation of Whaling	1946	Whale depletion
Nuclear Test Ban Treaty	1962	Atmospheric nuclear weapons testing
Biological and Toxic Weapons Treaty	1972	Chemical and biological weapons
London Convention	1972	Ocean pollution
Montreal Protocol	1987	Ozone-layer depletion
Basel Convention	1989	Transport of hazardous wastes
Convention on Biological Diversity	1992	Biodiversity loss
Kyoto Protocol	1997	Carbon emissions and global climate change
Mine Ban Treaty	1997	Landmines
Stockholm Convention on Persistent Organic Pollutants	2001	Hazardous chemicals

decisions of private firms and government officials, informal actors have developed third-party certification and eco-labeling initiatives that respond to and influence consumer demands (Conroy 2007).

Environmental Protectionism

Instead of harmonization upward, many environmentalists maintain that globalization promotes a race to the bottom, in which competition for private investment undermines environmental regulation. In its weaker variant, this argument holds that global competition impedes new regulation so that Southern countries remain 'stuck at the bottom' (Porter 1999) and Northern countries are 'stuck in the mud' (Zarsky 2002). In its stronger variant, globalization spurs the competitive lowering of standards in the North, ultimately leading to convergence on the lowest common denominator. Hence the claim in the NAFTA debate that the trade agreement would 'sabotage' US environmental laws.[9]

The usual policy recommendation flowing from this analysis is that Northern countries should use compensating tariffs or other trade restrictions to prevent 'ecological dumping' – the sale of products at prices below their marginal social cost of production by virtue of externalization of environmental costs.[10] Hence, this school of thought is here termed 'environmental protectionism.'

The logic rests on the uneven globalization of markets and governance:

> International trade increases competition, and competition reduces costs. But competition can reduce costs in two ways: by increasing efficiency or by lowering standards. A firm can save money by lowering its standards for pollution control, worker safety, wages, health care and so on – all choices that externalize some of its costs . . . Nations maintain large legal, administrative and auditing structures that bar reductions in the social and environmental standards of domestic industries. There are no analogous international bodies of law and administration; there are only national laws, which differ widely. Consequently, free international trade encourages industries to shift their production activities to the countries that have the lowest standards of cost internalization – hardly a move toward global efficiency. (Daly 1993, p. 52)

Empirical studies generally have concluded that environmental regulation does not, in fact, have much effect on firms' competitiveness (for a review, see Jaffe et al. 1995). At the same time, however, studies of 'revealed comparative advantage' in pollution-intensive industries (such as pulp and paper, mining, chemicals and petroleum products) have found that countries in the global South and eastern Europe account for a rising share of world exports.[11] This relocation of 'dirty industries' – a policy infamously recommended by the World Bank's chief economist in the early 1990s (*The*

Economist 1992) – occurs mainly via net additions to the capital stock, given the sunk costs in existing Northern facilities.

Even if there were robust evidence that dirty industries are migrating from North to South, this would not automatically put downward pressure on environmental standards in the North, as envisaged in the strong variant of the race-to-the-bottom logic. It is conceivable that, instead, Northern countries would allow, or even encourage, the displacement of environmental costs to the South, with international trade allowing them to import raw materials, intermediate inputs and final products at prices held down by cost externalization.[12] In other words, the North could maintain higher environmental standards domestically, while reaping 'ecological subsidies' from the South. I return to this possibility below.

Greening the North

I now turn to scenarios where the environmental-quality gradient runs from South to North – that is, where Southern production is cleaner and more sustainable than competing production in the North. At first blush this may seem implausible, given the deeply ingrained assumption that environmental quality is a luxury that only the affluent can afford, or at least a normal good for which demand rises with income. Indeed it is often assumed that the 'bottom billion' – the world's poorest people – 'cause a disproportionate share of environmental degradation' (Myers 1993, p. 23).

This demand-driven model of environmental quality neglects the supply side. We know that the global North's share of world income – and hence of world production and consumption – far exceeds that of the global South. In 2000, the countries with the richest quintile (20 percent) of the world's population, in terms of per capita incomes, accounted for 67 times as much income as the countries with the poorest quintile. The ratio narrows when computed on the basis of purchasing-power parity (PPP), but even then the average income in the richest quintile exceeded that in the poorest quintile by a ratio of 16:1 (Sutcliffe 2003).

Environmental degradation per unit income may vary across countries or income classes. If degradation were sufficiently concave in income – with damage per dollar falling as income rises – the poorest quintile in theory could generate more environmental degradation than the richest quintile. But merely to equal the degradation generated by the top quintile, the environmental degradation per unit PPP-adjusted income in the bottom quintile would have to be 16 times greater than in the top quintile. Such a disparity seems improbable, to say the least. Indeed, in some respects environmental degradation per unit income may even be greater for the rich. Contrast, for example, the pollution generated by automobiles compared to bicycles, or the amount of non-renewable resources used to produce a bushel of grain in the United States compared to India, or the pollution generated in the production and disposal of synthetic as opposed to natural fibers.

If there are gradients along which certain aspects of environmental quality are better in the South than in the North, then an optimistic view of globalization is that it will promote the 'greening of the North' (Sachs et al. 1998). This is akin to the ecological modernization school of thought in that it emphasizes possibilities for harmonization upward, with the notable difference that it reverses the relative positions of North and South.

Broadly speaking, there are two routes by which greening the North could come about. The first is via reductions in Northern consumption levels, a change that could be brought about by either falling incomes or a shift in preferences away from goods in favor of leisure, as advocated by the 'voluntary simplicity' movement in the United States. There is little historical precedent, however, for expecting either to happen on a meaningful scale in the foreseeable future.

The second is via transformations of production and consumption that reduce environmental degradation per unit income. This is the sort of change envisioned by the ecological modernization school. In this scenario, the North 'catches up' with the South in terms of environmental practices.

Several recent trends in agriculture in the industrialized countries illustrate this possibility. In the United States, for example, organically grown products are the fastest-growing segment of the food market, with sales rising at more than 20 percent annually in the final decade of the twentieth century (Dimitri and Greene 2002). Urban agriculture and community-supported agriculture have also grown substantially, and even when these are not 'organic' (in the sense of zero use of agrochemicals), they minimize negative externalities in transportation and generate positive externalities in the form of community amenities (Pinderhughes 2003). On a related front, the 'slow food' movement that originated in Italy in the late 1980s is promoting the conservation and revival of traditional agricultural practices (Petrini 2003). Such greening of the North is by no means a uniform process, however: it has come about partly as a reaction against other features of globalization, such as the use of genetically modified organisms in agriculture and the spread of multinational fast-food restaurant chains.

Environmental Imperialism

In the final convergence scenario, globalization undermines relatively clean and sustainable production in the global South. I term this scenario 'environmental imperialism' to evoke the parallel with economic and political subordination of South to North. To illustrate this possibility, consider two examples: the displacement of jute by polypropylene, and the displacement of Mexican maize by US maize.

1.   Jute versus polypropylene
Since World War II, international markets for renewable natural raw materials such as cotton, jute, sisal and rubber have faced increasingly tough competition from synthetic substitutes.[13] The former are produced mainly in the global South, the latter mainly in the global North. While the production of natural raw materials can have substantial negative environmental impacts (as in the case of pesticide-intensive cotton cultivation), in general synthetics entail greater environmental costs. The competition between jute and polypropylene is a case in point.

Jute, traditionally used to produce hessian (burlap) cloth and carpet backing, is the second most important natural fiber in world trade after cotton. In the late 1960s, stimulated by US military orders for sandbags for the Vietnam war, polypropylene began to compete with jute. Between 1970 and 1992, jute imports to North America and western Europe plummeted from one million to 52,000 tons, and jute's real price fell by 70 percent (Boyce 1995). This collapse hit particularly hard at the incomes of small farmers and agricultural laborers in Bangladesh, the world's premier jute-exporting country.

The environmental impacts of jute production are quite modest. Bangladeshi farmers use only small amounts of chemical fertilizers and little pesticide on the crop. The country's flooded jute fields support diverse fish populations, an important positive externality for rural people. Like all plants, jute sequesters atmospheric carbon, a further positive externality. And at the end of the product life cycle, jute biodegrades easily in the soil.

Polypropylene, jute's main competitor, is manufactured by multinational petrochemical firms. The United States is the world's leading producer. Polypropylene production generates emissions of numerous air pollutants, including particulate matter, sulfur oxides, nitrogen oxides, carbon monoxide, volatile organic compounds and other toxins, in addition to carbon dioxide. Since it is not biodegradable, polypropylene generates further environmental costs in the form of landfill disposal, incineration or litter at the end of the product life cycle.

The price advantage that helped polypropylene to displace jute in world markets arises in no small measure from the failure of market prices to internalize environmental costs.[14] The result of global competition between the two has been the displacement of a relatively 'green' Southern product by a relatively 'brown' Northern product. Even within Bangladesh, plastic shopping bags are now replacing traditional jute bags.

2. Maize: Mexico versus the United States

Maize is the leading crop in both Mexico and the United States. Competition between producers in the two countries has intensified in recent years, as the Mexican government has cut support to small farmers and lowered maize tariffs.

Mexico is the historic center of origin of maize, and the modern center of the genetic diversity in the crop. In the hilly lands of southern and central Mexico, *campesino* farmers grow thousands of different varieties of maize in small plots that botanists call 'evolutionary gardens' (see Chapter 8). On these farms, the maize plant continues to evolve with the assistance of the human hand – the process Darwin called 'artificial selection' – in response to climate change and newly emerging strains of pests and plant diseases. The *campesinos* thus provide a valuable positive externality to humankind – the *in situ* conservation and evolution of genetic diversity in one of our main food crops.

In the United States, fewer than a dozen varieties account for half of total acreage under maize. Only a few hundred varieties, many of them closely related, are commercially available. The crop therefore suffers from genetic vulnerability to catastrophic crop failures, as discussed in the preceding chapter. In the effort to remain a step ahead of evolving pests and pathogens, US plant breeders run a varietal relay race, constantly developing new varieties that incorporate resistance to new threats. The raw material for this race is the genetic diversity found in the evolutionary gardens of traditional agriculture.

US corn farmers are more 'efficient' than Mexican producers, if efficiency is measured only in terms of market prices. Prior to NAFTA, US maize sold at roughly $110 per ton at the border, whereas Mexican growers received $240 per ton.[15] After NAFTA went into effect, Mexico's annual imports of US corn rose from less than one million ton to more than six million tons. At the same time, the price of maize in Mexico fell by more than 70 percent.[16] If these trends persist, they are likely to accelerate genetic erosion – the loss of intraspecific diversity – in the crop.

Some comfort can be taken from the fact that samples of many Mexican maize varieties are stored in 'seed banks' at agricultural research institutes in Mexico and elsewhere. But, as noted in Chapter 8, seed banks are insecure, being subject to the perennial hazards of underfunding, accidents and war. Moreover, having seeds 'in the bank' is not the same as knowing about varietal properties, such as pest resistance and climate sensitivity – information that is most readily obtained in the field. And even at best, seed banks can conserve only the existing stock of genetic diversity; they cannot replicate the ongoing process of evolution that takes place in the farmers' fields.

As in the case of jute and polypropylene, the competition between Mexican and US maize pits relatively clean and sustainable production in the global South against relatively dirty and unsustainable production in the global North. If we view globalization through a long-term lens, looking back to the era of colonialism and the industrial revolution, this may have been the more common type of race to the environmental bottom.

ENVIRONMENTAL POLARIZATION

Rather than convergence, globalization instead could promote polarization: widening disparities in environmental quality across countries. The most likely polarization scenario would combine environmental improvements in the global North together with increasing environmental degradation in the global South. In other words, regardless of whether a 'green' North and 'brown' South is a good description of the world's current situation, it could be a good prediction of where we are headed.

The impacts of pollution and natural resource depletion are often concentrated in specific localities. This fact opens possibilities for 'environmental cost shifting,' so as to separate those who benefit from an economic activity from those who bear its external costs (Opschoor 1992, p. 36). Globalization increases possibilities for environmental cost shifting, by widening the spatial distance across which economic interactions take place. It can also widen what can be termed the 'social distance' between the beneficiaries of cost externalization and those who bear these costs, making the latter less able to influence the actions of the former. The likelihood of polarization hinges on whether globalization also promotes countervailing forces, such as the development of global civil-society networks, that offset these effects by reducing social distance.

To frame the discussion of environmental polarization, I begin with a brief review of the political economy of environmental degradation. In contrast to the neoclassical treatment of environmental problems as simply a result of missing markets and impersonal governance failures, political economy suggests that the identities of those who gain and lose by virtue of cost externalization help to determine the extent of environmental degradation and of corrective action undertaken by institutions of governance. I then review evidence on the impact of power disparities within countries on the magnitude of environmental degradation, before turning to the impacts of globalization on prospects for environmental cost shifting.

Political Economy of Environmental Degradation

Environmentally degrading economic activities generally involve winners who benefit from these activities as well as losers who bear their costs. Without winners, the activities would not occur. Without losers, their environmental impacts would not matter from the standpoint of human well-being.

In analysing the dynamics of environmental degradation, we can therefore ask why it is that the winners are able to impose environmental costs on the losers. When market failures take the form of environmental externalities, why do the institutions of governance fail to remedy them? As discussed in Chapter 2, there are three possible reasons:

- First, the losers may belong to future generations who are not here to defend themselves. In such cases, the only remedy for governance failure is a social commitment to an ethic of intergenerational responsibility.
- Second, the losers may lack adequate information as to the extent or sources of environmental burdens. It is often difficult, for example, to link health problems to pollution, and to track pollution to its source. In such cases, environmental education and right-to-know legislation are crucial elements of a solution.
- Third, the losers may lack sufficient power to alter the behavior of the winners. In such cases, a change in the balance of power between winners and losers is a necessary condition for greater environmental protection.

Here I focus on the third explanation – power disparities – since this is most directly affected by globalization.

In the past two decades, a growing body of literature has documented the uneven distribution of environmental burdens within countries, and their correlation with disparities in political power. In the United States, studies of environmental justice have shown that communities with lower incomes and higher percentages of racial and ethnic minorities tend to face disproportionate environmental hazards.[17] For example, even when controlling for income, Ash and Fetter (2004) find that African-Americans tend to reside not only in metropolitan areas with above-average levels of point-source air pollution, but also in localities that have higher-than-average pollution levels for the metropolitan area.

In their analysis of informal regulation in Indonesia, Pargal and Wheeler (1996) similarly find that communities with lower average incomes and educational attainments tend to have higher levels of industrial water pollution, even after controlling for other variables such as the volume of output and the age of nearby factories. They attribute this to differences in the 'implicit price' of pollution, which they define as 'the expected penalty or compensation exacted by the affected community.' Following this logic, Hettige et al. (2000, p. 452) write that 'cost-minimizing firms with flexible abatement choices will control pollution to the point where their marginal abatement costs equal the "price" exacted for pollution by the affected parties.' The affected parties may include local communities, government officials, non-governmental organizations (NGOs), stockholders and consumers – all of whom are 'in a position to impose some cost on a firm or plant if its emissions exceed the norms adopted by that group.' The resulting implicit price of pollution varies across localities.

Pollutees (those who bear costs from environmental degradation) can influence the decisions of polluters in two broad ways. The first is when their well-being enters directly into the polluters' utility function. This can be termed 'internalization through sympathy.' Following Sen (1975, p. 23), we can represent the degree of sympathy by means of a parameter, h, that indicates the weight placed on the well-being of others relative to one's own well-being. When $h_i = 0$, the polluter is indifferent to the well-being of the ith individual. When $h_i = 1$, the polluter values impacts on the ith individual the same as impacts on himself or herself. If $h_i = 1$ for all i individuals impacted by pollution, there is full internalization.

The second way that pollutees can influence the decisions of polluters is through the political process. This can be termed 'internalization through governance,' with governance understood to encompass both formal and informal rules that constrain behavior. Like sympathy, the ability of pollutees to use governance to alter the behavior of polluters is a matter of degree. Let the parameter π_i represent the power of the ith individual to affect social decisions regarding pollution. Where $\pi_i = 0$ for all pollutees, the price of pollution (set implicitly by informal regulation or formal standards, or explicitly by pollution taxes or tradable permits) is likewise zero.

More generally, we can describe environmental governance outcomes as following a power-weighted social-decision rule, in which decisions aim to maximize net benefits weighted by the power of those to whom they accrue. Mathematically, this can be expressed as follows:

$$\max_i \Sigma \pi_i b_i$$

where b_i = the net benefit that individual i derives from an environmentally degrading activity (or net cost if $b_i < 0$). Where the power of those who benefit – as producers via higher incomes, or as consumers via lower prices – exceeds the power of those who bear net costs, the social-decision rule leads to weaker environmental governance than when the reverse is true.

The power-weighted social-decision rule describes what happens, in contrast to the cost-benefit rule (which is simply to maximize net benefits with no power weights) that prescribes what should happen. In general, the social-decision rule yields outcomes that are 'efficient' in the conventional cost-benefit sense only in the special case where π_i is the same for everyone.[18]

The social distance between winners and losers affects both types of internalization. As Princen (1997, p. 235) observes, the obscuring of environmental costs and the displacement of these costs to others 'impede ecological and social feedback and create cognitive, institutional, and ethical lags between initial benefits and eventual full costs.' When those who benefit from polluting activities do not have any social ties to those who bear the costs – when they do not know them, or see them, or perhaps even know that they exist – there is little scope for internalization through sympathy. When the winners are very powerful relative to the losers, the scope for internalization through governance is correspondingly limited.

Power Disparities and the Environment: Empirical Evidence

The power-weighted social-decision rule generates two testable hypotheses. The first is that the distribution of environmental burdens is correlated with power-related variables such as income, education, race and ethnicity. Communities whose residents are poorer, less educated or belong to historically marginalized racial and ethnic groups will tend to bear greater burdens than communities whose residents are affluent, well educated or belong to historically dominant racial and ethnic groups. As noted in Chapters 3 and 4, a substantial empirical literature has emerged on this topic. In general, its findings are broadly consistent with this hypothesis. There is room for debate, as always, regarding causal explanations for observed correlations. Some researchers have suggested, for example, that the inverse relation between average incomes and toxic hazards often found by studies in the United States may arise not from disproportionate siting of hazardous facilities near low-income neighborhoods, but rather from market dynamics in which low-income people are drawn to these locations by lower property values.[19] This logic would have to be stretched, however, to explain correlations between hazards and race that persist even after controlling for income.[20]

The second hypothesis is that societies with wider power disparities tend to have more environmental degradation. That is, power disparities affect the magnitude of pollution and resource depletion, as well as their distributional incidence. This hypothesis is based on the assumption that there is a positive correlation between net benefits (b_i) and power (π_i), an assumption that seems reasonable in that both are likely to be correlated with wealth. Empirical studies of this hypothesis remain relatively scarce, but support for it can be drawn from cross-country studies that have investigated the impact of political variables on environmental performance. These studies were sparked by research suggesting that environmental degradation – or at least some types of it – is concave in income, and that high-income countries have passed a turning point beyond which further income gains are associated with environmental improvements. In an early example, the World Bank (1992, p. 41) reported an inverted U-shaped relationship of this type between atmospheric sulfur dioxide and per capita income.

This relationship has been dubbed the 'environmental Kuznets curve' (EKC), owing to its likeness to the original Kuznets curve depicting a relationship between income inequality and per capita income (Figure 9.2). As in the case of its namesake, the EKC sometimes has been taken to imply that problems that accompany economic growth will be resolved, more or less automatically, by growth itself. Thus, Beckerman (1992, p. 482) writes, 'in the end the best – and probably the only – way to attain a decent environment in most countries is to become rich.'

Notwithstanding the allusion to Simon Kuznets's earlier work on income inequality, surprisingly few studies of the EKC have examined the relationship between environmental quality and inequalities of income, wealth or power. Yet combining the two inverted U-curves (and assuming that the income levels at which they reach their turning points are roughly comparable), we can infer a positive correlation between environmental degradation and income inequality, as depicted in Figure 9.2. Such a correlation does not prove causation, of course, but it is intriguing. And because the curves themselves (when found to exist at all) are statistical relationships, rather than iron laws, there are many outliers – for example,

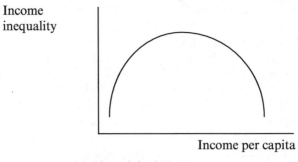

(a) The original Kuznets curve

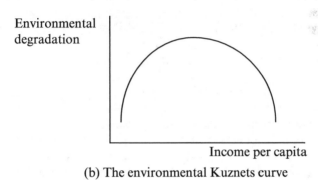

(b) The environmental Kuznets curve

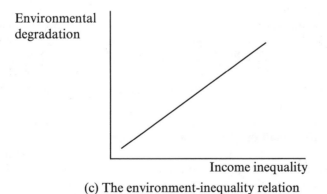

(c) The environment-inequality relation

Figure 9.2   Environmental degradation, income inequality and per capita income

countries with relatively low income inequality and low per capita income – making it possible to attempt to distinguish econometrically between the environmental impacts of income and inequality.

To investigate the impacts of power disparities on environmental quality, Torras and Boyce (1998) analysed cross-country variations in air pollution (ambient concentrations of sulfur dioxide, smoke and heavy particles), water pollution (concentrations of dissolved oxygen and fecal coliform) and the percentages of the population with access to safe water and sanitation facilities. In addition to per capita income and the Gini ratio of income distribution, the analysis included two other explanatory variables – adult literacy and an index of political rights and civil liberties – which can also be considered relevant to the distribution of power. In low-income countries, the estimated coefficients on the rights and literacy variables had the expected signs in all cases: higher literacy and greater rights were associated with better environmental quality, and the coefficients were statistically significant in most cases.[21] They found weaker effects in the high-income countries, suggesting that rights and literacy are most important when average incomes are low.

Other cross-country studies have also suggested that political rights can be an important determinant of environmental outcomes. Scruggs (1998) found greater rights to have a statistically significant favorable effect on sulfur dioxide concentrations, favorable but weaker effects on particulates and fecal coliform pollution and an adverse effect on dissolved oxygen. Barrett and Graddy (2000, p. 440) found air pollution by sulfur dioxide, smoke and particulates to be 'monotonically decreasing in the extent of democratic freedoms.' Harbaugh et al. (2000) also found a strong inverse relationship between an index representing democratic participation in government and atmospheric concentrations of sulfur dioxide, smoke and particulates. Further empirical support for the hypothesis that power disparities have an adverse impact on environmental quality comes from the cross-sectional study of the 50 US states by Boyce et al. (1999), which found that states with more equitable distributions of power had stronger environmental policies, policies that in turn were associated with better environmental quality.

Globalization and Environmental Cost Shifting

As globalization extends the arena for environmental cost shifting, the profound inequalities in the worldwide distribution of power and wealth become more relevant to the political economy of environmental degradation. As Sutcliffe (2003, 2004) observes, income inequality at the global level exceeds that at the national level even in the most unequal of countries, such as Brazil and South Africa (with the possible exception of Namibia). This is hardly surprising, since a global measure of inequality puts the richest strata of the population in the global North in the same universe as the poorest strata of the global South. The 'power equivalents' of this income distribution – a phrase coined by Kuznets (1963, p. 49) – may likewise be more unequal globally than at the national level. If so, the foregoing analysis suggests that globalization may lead both to environmental polarization between North and South and to an increase in the total magnitude of environmental degradation worldwide.

Having widened environmentally relevant disparities by putting the global rich and the global poor into the same basket, globalization eventually may reduce these disparities by promoting faster growth in the incomes of the poor than of the rich. But the evidence for such a trend is mixed at best.[22] More promising, perhaps, is the possibility of social developments – the other side of Polanyi's 'double movement' – that increase the political effectiveness of demand for environmental protection in low-income countries, but here, too, the record to date is not terribly encouraging. While Weidner and Jänicke (2002, p. 440) find some evidence of a global convergence between North and South in environmental policies, they conclude that capacities for policy implementation have become more unequal, resulting in 'convergence of policies but divergence of outcomes.'

But countervailing forces are set in motion by globalization too. Advances in telecommunications can shrink social distances, increasing the scope for internalization through sympathy by giving faces and voices to the people who bear environmental costs, and at the same time giving them greater access to information and the power that comes with it. Alliances across national boundaries, among local communities, NGOs, workers, shareholders and consumers, can alter balances of power. And the phenomenon of global environmental change – environmental impacts where there is little or no scope for cost shifting – may not only give impetus to global environmental governance but also create new opportunities for globally egalitarian politics.

To illustrate these opposing forces, consider the rapid growth of industrial shrimp farming in the coastal areas of tropical countries. This has been accompanied by the widespread and often violent appropriation of land and aquatic resources from local residents, and by adverse environmental impacts on local communities, spurring economic and environmental polarization (Stonich and Vandergeest 2001). At the same time, however, the spread of shrimp farms has sparked international alliances of environmental and peasant-based NGOs that defend and reassert community rights to natural assets (Stonich and Bailey 2000).

Similarly, export markets for beef, timber and minerals have been a major stimulus to Amazonian deforestation. Again, international alliances have emerged to support local people who traditionally have relied on the forest for their livelihoods. These were instrumental in the creation of extractive reserves in Brazil, where local communities secured their right to harvest latex and other forest products while preventing forest clearing (Hall 1997). As such examples suggest, globalization not only poses risks of environmental polarization and increased environmental degradation, but also creates opportunities for countervailing forces to counteract these trends.

GLOBAL ENVIRONMENTAL CHANGE

The phrase 'global environmental change' refers to environmental problems such as climate change, ozone-layer depletion and the loss of biodiversity, whose impacts are global in scope rather than confined to particular localities. This is a counterpart, in the environmental sphere, to global integration in the spheres of the market and governance: in global environmental change, we see integration of the consequences of market and governance failures. Insofar as all countries share in its costs and stand to benefit from remedial actions, global environmental change would seem to be a force for environmental convergence. But in practice, here too, there are some polarizing tendencies, owing to disparate impacts across locations and disparities in the extent of governance responses.

Disparate impacts arise not only from the greater vulnerability of poorer populations, but also, in some cases, from circumstantial factors. In the case of global warming, for example, the Intergovernmental Panel on Climate Change (IPCC) predicts that average surface temperatures on Earth will rise by 1°–4° C in the present century. Even if adverse impacts were distributed equally across humankind, the poor would suffer most by virtue of the fact that they start from a lower economic base. In addition, climate scientists forecast that the hardest-hit places will include parts of Africa, where droughts are expected to worsen in frequency and intensity, and low-lying regions of tropical Asia that are prone to increased flooding and cyclones. 'The effects of climate change,' the IPCC (2001, p. 8) concludes, 'are expected to be greatest in developing countries in terms of loss of life and relative effects on investment and the economy.'

These disparate impacts are compounded by disparities in the extent of remedial actions. Even if international policies to protect the global environment were guided solely by considerations of 'efficiency,' completely insulated from the impacts of political influence, disparities in remedial actions would arise from the application of conventional valuation principles that place equal weight on monetary costs and benefits no matter whether those to whom they accrue are rich or poor. The willingness of the rich to pay for environmental quality, and for goods and services whose production, consumption and disposal cause environmental degradation, generally exceeds that of the poor by virtue of their greater ability to pay. Hence in the shadow markets of benefit-cost analysis, as in real markets, the 'benefits' of emitting carbon dioxide by driving automobiles on American and European highways may outweigh the costs of drought in Africa or inundations in Bangladesh.[23]

In practice, efficiency is not the sole criterion guiding social decisions, including decisions to invest in mitigation and adaptation to global environmental change. Political influences also play a role, prompting action in some cases and inaction in others. Consider the contrast in the international responses to ozone-layer depletion and global warming. The 1987 Montreal Protocol on ozone-depleting substances successfully instituted a worldwide phase-out of the use of CFCs. Although the benefits of CFC use – in refrigeration, air conditioning, fire extinguishers, solvents, foams and aerosols – were concentrated in the industrialized countries, so were the environmental costs. Ozone-layer thinning is most pronounced at the higher latitudes, and light-skinned people are most susceptible to skin cancers and melanomas caused by increased ultraviolet radiation.

This may help to explain why efforts of the scientific community to draw attention to the risks of ozone-layer depletion met with so much success. The United States, along with Canada and the Scandinavian countries, took a leading role in international negotiations to curb CFC emissions. Despite scientific uncertainties over the precise mechanisms of ozone-layer depletion, the US administration under President Ronald Reagan took the position that 'in the real world of imperfect knowledge and uncertainty, we, as policymakers, nevertheless have the responsibility to take prudent actions for the benefits of generations yet to come.'[24] A contrary suggestion by Reagan's Secretary of the Interior, who urged Americans to adopt a 'personal protection campaign' by wearing sunscreen, long-sleeved shirts and dark glasses, met with widespread ridicule (Haas 1992, p. 218).

This experience can be contrasted with the very limited progress of international efforts to curb global warming by limiting emissions of carbon dioxide from burning fossil fuels. The 1997 Kyoto Protocol sought to cap the carbon dioxide emissions of industrialized countries at roughly 94 percent of their 1990 levels – a modest target compared to the CFC phase-out – leaving the emissions of developing countries to be negotiated later. In March 2001 the US administration of President George

W. Bush rejected this accord, maintaining that the scientific evidence on climate change remains 'unsettled' and that the treaty was 'fatally flawed' because it would impose costs on the US economy without setting mandatory emissions ceilings for developing countries. As atmospheric carbon dioxide levels continued to rise, the focus of international negotiations shifted from prevention to adaptation.[25] This increases the likelihood of outcomes that will differ across countries, reflecting differences in their ability to pay for measures to adapt to climate change.

A crucial issue in international climate negotiations is the allocation of property rights to the carbon-absorptive capacity of the Earth's atmosphere. This presents both a stumbling block and an opportunity. The principle of allocations pegged to historic emission levels, which was applied to industrialized countries in the Kyoto agreement, 'grandfathers' rights on the basis of past appropriation. This formula naturally is unacceptable to the developing countries, whose emissions per capita remain an order of magnitude below those in the industrialized countries.[26] An alternative principle would be to allocate rights on the basis of equal per capita entitlements, an idea first proposed by Southern environmentalists (Agarwal and Narain 1991), and subsequently endorsed by Northern scientists on both normative and practical grounds.[27] An egalitarian resolution of this issue would make global environmental governance an instrument for reducing North-South disparities.

WAR AND THE ENVIRONMENT

In the modern era, war has been a major cause of environmental degradation. This differs from 'normal' environmental degradation in that it is often an objective rather than a mere side-effect of the pursuit of other goals. In war, the aim is to make the environment inhospitable or fatal to the enemy. Rather than a cost external to the war maker's calculus, environmental degradation is viewed as an internal benefit.

Examples of deliberate environmental degradation in war include the application of herbicides by the US military to defoliate Vietnam (SIPRI 1976); the Soviet military's systematic destruction of orchards, irrigation infrastructure and agricultural ecosystems in Afghanistan (Swedish Committee for Afghanistan 1988); and, most starkly, the dropping of nuclear bombs on the Japanese cities of Hiroshima and Nagasaki in 1945.

An assessment of globalization's environmental impacts would be incomplete without consideration of impacts related to war. Globalization can affect the extent of war-related environmental degradation in two ways: first, by facilitating or restricting access to environmentally destructive weaponry such as landmines, nuclear devices and other weapons of mass destruction; and second, by exacerbating or easing tensions within and between countries that can precipitate violent conflict. The first affects abilities to degrade the environment for military purposes; the second affects willingness to do so.

The proliferation of landmines illustrates the spread of environmentally destructive weaponry. Today, roughly 60 million landmines are embedded around the world; in the most heavily mined countries, such as Cambodia, there are more than 100 landmines per square mile.[28] Efforts to curtail their production, use and transfer – efforts in which the non-governmental International Campaign to Ban Landmines played a leading role – culminated in the 1997 Mine Ban Treaty.[29] The spread of weapons of mass destruction similarly has been constrained, though not entirely prevented, by the Nuclear Test Ban Treaty of 1962 and the Biological and Toxic Weapons Treaty of 1972, agreements that can be counted among the world's most important international environmental accords. Here again we see a 'double movement' in globalization in the interplay between weapons proliferation and counter-proliferation initiatives.

Globalization can exacerbate the likelihood of violent conflict in several ways: (1) by deepening inequalities of income, wealth and power, including horizontal inequalities across ethnic, regional and religious lines (Stewart 2002); (2) by facilitating the spread of new norms and aspirations that undermine the legitimacy of pre-existing inequalities (Bardhan 1997); (3) by expanding markets for lootable resources, such as diamonds and oil, that can provide both a motive and the means for conflict (Collier and Hoeffler 2004); and (4) by triggering fundamentalist reactions against the values (or perceived lack of them) of mass consumer culture. At the same time, there have been countervailing efforts of the United Nations and other international institutions to prevent and resolve conflicts and to support post-conflict peacebuilding.[30]

The net impact of globalization's effects on the ability and willingness to degrade the environment through war cannot be determined a priori. It will depend on the actions (or inaction) of governments, international institutions and civil society. Possible outcomes include both 'harmonization upward' or a 'race to the bottom' on the war-to-peace spectrum. The dominant trend since the World War II has been polarization rather than convergence: war and its attendant environmental destruction have been concentrated in the global South – especially, in recent times, in sub-Saharan Africa – largely bypassing the North. Once again, this can be attributed to disparities both in the circumstances that lead to war and in the extent of remedial efforts.

PROSPECTS FOR GLOBAL ENVIRONMENTAL GOVERNANCE

In the final analysis, the environmental impact of globalization will hinge, above all, on how our institutions of governance develop as world markets become increasingly integrated. Global environmental governance can develop by both formal and informal means (Haas 2002).

Formal Governance: Three Avenues

In the development of formal institutions for global environmental governance, three broad avenues can be distinguished:

- *Creation of a world environment organization.* One possible avenue would be to establish a new international institution specifically charged with environmental protection, empowered to set and enforce environmental policies. This has been suggested by various authors (see, for example, Esty 1994; Opschoor 2001), based on the same logic that led to the establishment of ministries and agencies for environmental protection at the national level. Arguing that 'environmental externalities should be tackled at their source, which is usually at the point of production, and occasionally at the point of consumption, but rarely at the point of exchange,' Griffin (2003, p. 798) observes that international efforts to protect whales did not proceed by prohibiting trade in whale products, but rather through a ban on whale harvests that is enforced by the International Whaling Commission. However desirable in theory, there appears to be little prospect that an effective world environmental organization will be established anytime soon. Among actually existing institutions, the closest thing to such an entity is the Nairobi-based United Nations Environment Programme (UNEP), whose mandate today is strictly limited to provision of information and assistance.[31]
- *Issue-specific international environmental agreements.* In the absence of a global institution empowered to carry out regulatory functions, the international community has addressed specific environmental threats – from nuclear proliferation to global warming – by means of issue-specific agreements and treaties. While the importance of these agreements is evident, so far they have been confined to two subsets of environmental issues: global environmental change and military-related environmental damage. 'Normal' (national-level and local-level) problems of pollution and natural resource

depletion have been largely ignored, despite the fact that these are often impacted by global economic integration.

- *'Greening' international institutions.* A third avenue lies in efforts to 'green' international institutions that are dedicated to other objectives, so as to bring environmental considerations into their decision-making processes. Environmental impact assessments are now a standard (if at times superficial) element of project appraisal at the multilateral development banks. While skeptics maintain that such efforts 'will never bring environmental interests on a par with economic interests' (Mol 2001, p. 219), it is not evident that the obstacles are any less tractable than those to the creation of a world environment organization or new international treaties. Indeed, the rationale for credit-allocation institutions and policies is precisely to account for externalities and channel financial resources to socially desirable uses. There is no intrinsic reason why international financial institutions should not allocate credit to advance environmental goals (see Chapter 5). Nor is there any inherent reason why trade agreements must rule out consideration of environmental impacts arising from production and process methods. In the end, these are political choices.

Informal Governance: Third-party Certification

As discussed above, informal governance can also have important effects on environmental performance. One example, at the global level, is the advent of third-party certification systems that provide information to consumers and stimulate market-based pressures for improved production and process methods.

Perhaps the best-known case is the timber products certification program of the Forest Stewardship Council (FSC), an NGO founded in Toronto in 1993. Within a decade, 25 million hectares of forests – roughly 5 percent of working forests worldwide (that is, forests not set aside in protected areas) – were certified under FSC environmental and social standards (Conroy 2001). Demand for FSC-certified products has been augmented by campaigns by environmental organizations to persuade large-volume retail firms to purchase only certified timber when it is available.

This informal governance system emerged in the wake of failed efforts to create an officially sponsored certification system through the International Tropical Timber Organization. This created a vacuum into which NGOs moved (Gale 2002). The result has much in common with formal governance:

> Environmental certification programs have most of the same basic organizational elements of legal systems. What they generally lack is a command from a sovereign . . . Firms subscribe to them because they determine that it is in their interest to do so. Yet it is increasingly common to describe environmental certification as a 'de facto requirement' for doing business in many jurisdictions. When interviewed, corporate officials often state that they feel they have 'no real choice' but to become environmentally certified. (Meidinger 2001, p. 10166)

Indeed there are a variety of ways in which informal governance through third-party certification can be incorporated into formal legal systems; for example, by providing incentives via government purchasing or regulatory requirements to firms that meet certification criteria.[32]

Interaction Between Formal and Informal Governance: The Right to Know

Formal and informal governance do not operate in isolation from each other. Formal regulation often emerges in response to pressures from civil society, and the scope for informal governance can be increased (or decreased) by formal regulation. 'Right-to-know' laws – formal regulations that compel private firms to furnish environmental information to the public – are a good illustration of this interaction.

Globalization was the midwife at the birth of the most important environmental right-to-know legislation in the United States: the Emergency Planning and Community Right-to-Know Act of 1986 (EPCRA), which provides the legal basis for the TRI and other disclosure requirements administered by the US EPA (Bouwes et al. 2003). As noted in Chapter 4, the 1984 disaster in Bhopal, India, at a chemical plant owned by the US-based Union Carbide corporation, was the key impetus for the EPCRA's passage. There is evidence that EPCRA-mandated public disclosure of releases of toxic chemicals into the environment has itself led to reductions in these releases.[33] In effect, such right-to-know laws alter the balance of power between polluters and pollutees. As Weidner and Jänicke (2002, p. 432) put it, 'The creation of transparency modifies the power structure in favor of environmental proponents.' Translating this into the terminology of neoclassical economics, such laws can be said to reduce market imperfections, in the form of imperfect information, that impede bargaining solutions to environmental externalities.

The EPCRA's geographical reach is limited to the United States. It does not require US-based corporations to disclose toxic releases elsewhere – in Bhopal, for example. The International Right-to-Know campaign, launched in 2003 by a coalition of US environmental, labor and human rights groups, has attempted to redress this asymmetry by calling for new legislation that would compel US-based corporations to disclose information about their environmental and labor practices overseas. Similarly, the Publish What You Pay campaign launched in 2002 has advocated on behalf of legislation to require corporate disclosure of payments made to governments for access to natural resources.[34] These efforts illustrate how interactions between formal and informal institutions can advance the globalization of environmental governance.

CONCLUSION

This chapter has viewed globalization as a process of economic integration that involves governance as well as markets. In principle, the globalization of governance can counter adverse environmental impacts arising from the globalization of market failure that accompanies the integration of world markets. But there is nothing automatic about this 'double movement' – it rests on human agency, and on balances of power between those who stand to gain and lose from improved environmental governance.

In assessing the effects of globalization, my main focus in this concluding chapter has been its differential impacts on environmental quality in the global North and global South. Closely related to this is a concern with impacts on human well-being. Environmentalists tend to conflate the two, seeing current and future human well-being as dependent on environmental quality. Economists, on the other hand, tend to emphasize the tradeoffs that arise when maintaining environmental quality conflicts with the satisfaction of other human needs and wants. Such tradeoffs pose the positive question of how they are made in practice as well as the normative question of how they ought to be made. A central theme of this book is that both questions are intimately bound up with how we address interpersonal tradeoffs in the well-being of different people.

With respect to the positive question of how societies choose to make tradeoffs in practice, I have suggested that these choices can be understood as being guided by a power-weighted social-decision rule, in which benefits and costs are weighed by the power of those to whom they accrue. This leads to the hypotheses that power disparities affect both the distributional incidence of environmental degradation and its overall magnitude. A growing body of empirical literature has reported findings consistent with these hypotheses.

With respect to the normative question of how societies ought to make tradeoffs, I have noted the stark difference between the wealth-based approach of conventional cost-benefit analysis, in which values are conditioned by ability and willingness to pay, and a rights-based approach, in which all individuals have equal entitlements to a clean and safe environment. These have quite different prescriptive implications. Under the wealth-based approach, if globalization were to promote environmental polarization, so that improvements in the North were coupled with increasing environmental degradation in the South, this might be argued to be welfare-maximizing. Indeed, in the extreme case, pollution that is imposed on people who have no ability to pay to avoid it would be regarded as costless. Under a rights-based approach, in contrast, environmental costs and benefits are not weighed by the purchasing power of those to whom they accrue. The normative stance that ultimately is adopted by formal and informal institutions for environmental governance is likely to have profound implications for how globalization affects both the distribution of power and access to environmental quality.

This chapter has questioned several tenets of conventional thinking on the environmental impacts of globalization. The assumption that production practices in the global North are environmentally superior to those in the global South – shared by many champions and critics of globalization alike – can be quite misleading, and it can lead to the neglect of important environmental issues. It is possible for globalization to promote environmental convergence via harmonization upward, as argued by its proponents, and via a race to the bottom, as argued by its opponents. But neither outcome can be assured on a priori grounds. Instead of convergence, globalization could foster environmental polarization – widening disparities between the global North and the global South. Whether this occurs will depend on the extent to which those who face new environmental burdens are able to take advantage of new opportunities to bridge social distances and narrow power disparities, so as to promote the internalization of environmental costs through sympathy, governance or a combination of the two. Similarly, with respect to global environmental change and war-related environmental degradation, globalization could promote convergence toward better environmental outcomes, convergence toward worse ones, or environmental polarization.

The environmental impacts of globalization not only remain to be seen. They remain to be determined. The outcome will not be dictated by an inexorable logic. Rather, it will depend on how the new opportunities created by the globalization of markets and the globalization of governance alter balances of power, both within countries and among them. As its critics fear, globalization could accelerate worldwide environmental degradation and deepen environmental inequalities. Yet globalization also gives impetus to countervailing forces that could bring about a greener and less divided world. The history of our environmental future has yet to be written.

NOTES

* This chapter is a revised version of an article originally published in the *Oxford Review of Economic Policy* (2004), (1), 105–28.
1. Senator John Chafee, quoted in Behr (1993).
2. 'Sabotage of America's health, food & safety, and environmental laws,' advertisement in the *Washington Post,* 14 December 1992, by the Sierra Club, Greenpeace USA, Friends of the Earth and others; quoted in Commission for Environmental Cooperation (1996, p. 29).
3. There is considerable unevenness within the sphere of global governance too. For example, the World Bank and International Monetary Fund, in concert with other official creditors and private banks, have often made capital flows to developing countries conditional on implementation of various economic reforms. Within the sphere of global governance, environmental policy has lagged behind.
4. For accounts of the European Union regulations, see Becker and Lee (2003) and Breithaupt (2006).
5. See, for example, Jänicke (1990).
6. See, for example, Barrett (2000), who also points out that there may be differences between harmonization of emission standards and harmonization of environmental quality standards.
7. Thus Mol (2001, p. 211) writes that economic mechanisms 'will always fall short in fully articulating environmental interests and pushing environmental reforms, if they are not constantly paralleled and propelled by environmental institutions and environmental movements.'
8. Both community pressure and firm responsiveness may be weaker when foreign firms outsource to unbranded suppliers.
9. There is an obvious analogy with labor standards (see Singh and Zammit 2004). Indeed, environmental protectionism is sometimes depicted by its critics as a smokescreen for other protectionist interests (see, for example, Bhagwati 1993).
10. 'Ecological dumping' need not be intentional. Rauscher (1994, p. 825) proposes a more restrictive definition: 'a scenario in which environmental standards are tighter in the non-tradables than in the tradables sector.' This comes closer to the notion of dumping as a deliberate instrument of trade policy, but most proponents of environmental protectionism are more concerned with the effects of ecological dumping than with the motives behind it.
11. Low and Yeats (1992) found a rising share of pollution-intensive exports from developing countries (particularly in Southeast Asia) in the period 1965–88, albeit from a fairly small base. Extending this analysis to the period 1992–2000, Bouvier (2003) finds that this trend has continued, with some eastern European countries also emerging as major exporters of pollution-intensive goods.
12. If this is accompanied by declining terms of trade for environment-intensive products, the result could be both 'environmental improvement and economic growth in the North and environmental deterioration and economic stagnation in the South' (Muradian and Martinez-Alier 2001, p. 286).
13. Maizels (1992, p. 189, 1995, p. 108) reports that substitution by synthetics reduced the developed market-economy countries' consumption of natural raw materials by 2.9 percent per year from 1963–65 to 1971–73, 0.9 percent per year from 1971–73 to 1978–80 and 1.2 percent per year from 1978–80 to 1984–86.
14. For a more detailed account of these environmental costs, see Boyce (1995).
15. As noted in Chapter 8, several factors contribute to the price advantage of US corn: (1) natural conditions such as better soils, more regular rainfall and a killing frost that limits pest populations; (2) farm subsidies that reduce US market prices; (3) the externalization of environmental costs, such as groundwater contamination by pesticides; and (4) the failure of market prices to internalize the value of sustaining genetic diversity provided by Mexican farmers. For further discussion, see Boyce (1996).

16. See Chapter 8. For accounts of the social impacts in rural Mexico, see Weiner (2002) and Becker (2003).
17. See Chapters 3 and 4. For surveys of the US environmental justice literature, see Bullard (1994), Szasz and Meuser (1997), Bowen (2001) and Pastor (2003).
18. For further discussion of the power-weighted social decision rule, see Boyce (2002, chapters 4–6).
19. See, for example, Been (1994). However, in a longitudinal study in southern California, one of the few to examine empirically the siting versus 'move-in' question, Pastor et al. (2001) found strong evidence of disproportionate siting.
20. See, for example, Bouwes et al. (2003) and Ash and Fetter (2004).
21. Controlling for these other variables, the estimated effects of income inequality were inconsistent. The authors suggest that either rights and literacy capture more important aspects of power disparities, or the quality of the income distribution data is poor (or both). For further discussion of the impacts of income inequality on environmental quality, see Boyce (2007).
22. For reviews of the evidence, see Sutcliffe (2003, 2004).
23. Again, this wealth-based principle for resource allocation can be contrasted to a rights-based approach founded on the premise that all individuals have an equal entitlement to a clean and safe environment (Boyce 2002, chapter 2).
24. Deputy Assistant Secretary of State Richard Benedick, quoted by Haas (1992, p. 191).
25. For an account of this shift, see Revkin (2002).
26. Per capita emissions in the United States exceed 5 tC per year and those of western Europe and Japan are in the 2–5 tC range, whereas more than 50 developing countries have emissions of less than 0.2 tC (Baer et al. 2000).
27. See Baer et al. (2000). A national-level variant of this principle is the 'sky trust' or cap-and-dividend policy that would cap emissions, auction the resulting allowances and rebate the revenues to the public on an equal per capita basis (see Chapters 6 and 7; see also Barnes 2001).
28. UNICEF (1996) reported that Cambodia had ten million landmines, 143 per square mile. At the time, the United Nations put the total number of embedded landmines worldwide at 110 million; more recent estimates are generally closer to 60 million.
29. As of April 2012, 161 countries had ratified or acceded to the treaty. Prominent among the countries that have not done so are the United States, Russia and China. For updated information, see the website of the International Campaign to Ban Landmines at http://www.icbl.org/ (accessed 16 July 2012).
30. See, for example, UN Secretary-General (1992), Carnegie Commission (1997) and World Bank (1998).
31. Strengthening UNEP's mandate to include a larger role in agenda setting, norm development, compliance management, science assessment and capacity building is the first of seven steps toward improving formal 'Earth system governance' recommended by Biermann et al. (2012).
32. In a review of the potential of environmental certification programs to become 'engines of change' in US law, Meidinger (2001, p. 10176) concludes that 'certification programs are natural targets for incorporation by legal systems because they have elements of formality, continuity, and institutionalization.'
33. For discussions of right-to-know legislation and its impact on environmental protection in the United States, see Rich et al. (1993), Konar and Cohen (1995), Khanna et al. (1998) and Tietenberg and Wheeler (2000).
34. See Soros (2002). For more information, see also http://www.publishwhatyoupay.org/ (accessed 16 July 2012).

REFERENCES

Agarwal, Anil and Sunita Narain (1991), *Global Warming in an Unequal World: A Case of Environmental Colonialism,* New Delhi: Centre for Science and the Environment.

Ash, Michael and T. Robert Fetter (2004), 'Who lives on the wrong side of the environmental tracks?' *Social Science Quarterly,* **85**(2), 441–62.

Baer, Paul, John Harte, Barbara Haya et al. (2000), 'Equity and greenhouse gas responsibility,' *Science,* **289**(5488), 2287.

Bardhan, Pranab (1997), 'Method in the madness? A political-economy analysis of the ethnic conflicts in less developed countries,' *World Development,* **25**(9), 1381–98.

Barnes, Peter (2001), *Who Owns the Sky? Our Common Assets and the Future of Capitalism,* Washington, DC: Island Press.

Barrett, Scott (2000), 'Trade and environment: local versus multilateral reforms,' *Environment and Development Economics,* **5**, 349–59.

Barrett, Scott and Kathryn Graddy (2000), 'Freedom, growth, and the environment,' *Environment and Development Economics,* **5**, 433–56.

Becker, Elizabeth (2003), 'US corn subsidies said to damage Mexico,' *New York Times,* 27 August.

Becker, Elizabeth and Jennifer B. Lee (2003), 'New trans-atlantic trade dispute: Washington criticizes Europe's plan to regulate chemicals,' *International Herald Tribune,* 8 May, p. 1.

Beckerman, Wilfred (1992), 'Economic growth and the environment: whose growth? Whose environment?' *World Development,* **20**, 481–96.

Been, Vicki (1994), 'Locally undesirable land uses in minority neighborhoods: disproportionate siting or market dynamics,' *Yale Law Journal,* 103, 1383–422.

Behr, Peter (1993), 'Environmental issues emerge as key to trade pact on hill,' *Washington Post,* 3 March, p. A14.

Bhagwati, Jagdish (1993), 'The case for free trade,' *Scientific American,* November, 41–9.

Biermann, F., K. Abbott, S. Andresen et al. (2012), 'Navigating the anthropocene: improving Earth system governance,' *Science,* **335**(6074), 1306–7.

Bouvier, Rachel (2003), 'Three essays on income, inequality, and environmental degradation,' PhD dissertation, University of Massachusetts, Amherst.

Bouwes, Nicolaas W., Steven M. Hassur and Marc D. Shapiro (2003), 'Information for empowerment: the EPA's Risk-Screening Environmental Indicators Project,' in James K. Boyce and Barry G. Shelley (eds), *Natural Assets: Democratizing Environmental Ownership,* Washington, DC: Island Press, chapter 6.

Bowen, William M. (2001), *Environmental Justice Through Research-based Decision-making,* New York: Garland Publishing.

Boyce, James K. (1995), 'Jute, polypropylene, and the environment: a study in international trade and market failure,' *Bangladesh Development Studies,* **23**(1 and 2), 49–66.

Boyce, James K. (1996), 'Ecological distribution, agricultural trade liberalization, and *in situ* genetic diversity,' *Journal of Income Distribution,* **6**(2), 263–84.

Boyce, James K. (2000), 'Let them eat risk: wealth, rights, and disaster vulnerability,' *Disasters,* **24**(3), 254–61, reprinted in Boyce (2002), chapter 2.

Boyce, James K. (2002), *The Political Economy of the Environment*, Cheltenham, UK and Northampton, MA, USA: Edward Elgar Publishing.

Boyce, James K. (2007), 'Inequality and environmental protection,' in Jean-Marie Baland, Pranab Bardhan and Samuel Bowles (eds), *Inequality, Collective Action, and Environmental Sustainability*, Princeton, NJ: Princeton University Press, pp. 314–48.

Boyce, James K., Andrew R. Klemer, Paul H. Templet and Cleve E. Willis (1999), 'Power distribution, the environment, and public health: a state-level analysis,' *Ecological Economics*, **29**, 127–40, reprinted in Boyce (2002), chapter 6.

Breithaupt, Holgar (2006), 'The costs of REACH,' *EMBO Reports*, **7**, 968–71.

Bullard, Robert D. (ed.) (1994), *Unequal Protection: Environmental Justice and Communities of Color*, San Francisco, CA: Sierra Club Books.

Carnegie Commission on Preventing Deadly Conflict (1997), *Preventing Deadly Conflict: Final Report*, New York: Carnegie Corporation.

Collier, Paul and Anke Hoeffler (2004), 'Greed and grievance in civil wars,' *Oxford Economic Papers*, **56**(4), 563–95.

Commission for Environmental Cooperation (1996), *Potential NAFTA Effects: Claims and Arguments, 1991–9*, Environment and Trade Series No. 2, Montreal, QC: Commission for Environmental Cooperation.

Conroy, Michael (2001), 'Can advocacy-led certification systems transform global corporate practices? Evidence, and some theory,' Political Economy Research Institute working paper no. 21, Amherst, MA.

Conroy, Michael (2007), *Branded! How the Certification Revolution is Transforming Global Corporations*, Gabriola Island, BC: New Society Publishers.

Daly, Herman (1993), 'The perils of free trade,' *Scientific American*, November, 50–57.

Dimitri, Carolyn and Catherine Greene (2002), 'Recent growth patterns in the US organic foods market,' US Department of Agriculture Economic Research Service, Market and Trade Economics Division and Resource Economics Division agriculture information bulletin no. 777, Washington, DC.

Economist, The (1992), 'Let them eat pollution,' 8 February, p. 66.

Esty, Daniel C. (1994), *Greening the GATT: Trade, Environment, and the Future*, Washington, DC: Institute for International Economics.

Gale, Fred (2002), '*Caveat Certificatum*: the case of forest certification,' in T. Princen, M. Maniates and K. Conca (eds), *Confronting Consumption*, Cambridge, MA: MIT Press, pp. 275–99.

Griffin, Keith (2003), 'Economic globalization and institutions of global governance,' *Development and Change*, **34**, 789–807.

Haas, Peter (1992), 'Banning chlorofluorocarbons: epistemic community efforts to protect stratospheric ozone,' *International Organization*, **46**(1), 187–224.

Haas, Peter (2002), 'Environment: pollution,' in P.J. Simmons and C. de J. Oudraat (eds), *Managing Global Issues: Lessons Learned*, Washington, DC: Carnegie Endowment for International Peace, pp. 310–53.

Haas, Peter (2004), 'Addressing the global governance deficit,' *Global Environmental Politics*, **4**(4), 1–19.

Hall, Anthony (1997), *Sustaining Amazonia: Grassroots Action for Productive Conservation*, Manchester: Manchester University Press.

Harbaugh, William, Arik Levinson and David Wilson (2000), 'Reexamining the empirical evidence for an environmental Kuznets curve,' National Bureau of Economic Research working paper no. 7711, May, Cambridge, MA.

Hettige, H., M. Mani and D. Wheeler, D. (2000), 'Industrial pollution in economic development: the environmental Kuznets curve revisited,' *Journal of Development Economics*, **62**, 445–76.

Hogenboom, Barbara (1998), *Mexico and the NAFTA Environment Debate: The Transnational Politics of Economic Integration*, Utrecht, Netherlands: International Books.

Intergovernmental Panel on Climate Change (IPCC) (2001), *Climate Change 2001: Impacts, Adaptation, and Vulnerability: Summary for Policymakers*, approved by IPCC Working Group II in Geneva, 13–16 February.

Jaffe, Adam. B., Steven R. Peterson, Paul R. Portney and Robert N. Stavins (1995), 'Environmental regulation and the competitiveness of US manufacturing: what does the evidence tell us?' *Journal of Environmental Literature*, **33**(1), 132–63.

Jänicke, Martin (1990), *State Failure: The Impotence of Politics in Industrial Society*, College Park, PA: Pennsylvania State University Press.

Keenan, Karyn, Jose de Echave and Ken Traynor (2007), 'Mining rights and community rights: poverty amidst wealth,' in James K. Boyce, Sunita Narain and Elizabeth A. Stanton (eds), *Reclaiming Nature: Environmental Justice and Ecological Restoration*, London and New York: Anthem Press, chapter 7.

Khanna, Madhu, Wilma Rose H. Quimio and Dora Bojilova (1998), 'Toxic release information: a policy tool for environmental protection,' *Journal of Environmental Economics and Management*, **36**, 243–66.

Konar, Shameek and Mark A. Cohen (1995), 'Information as regulation: the effect of community right to know laws on toxic emissions,' *Journal of Environmental Economics and Management*, **32**, 109–24.

Kuznets, Simon (1963), 'Quantitative aspects of the economic growth of nations,' *Economic Development and Cultural Change*, **11**(2/II), 1–80.

Lipschutz, Ronnie D. with Judith Mayer (1996), *Global Civil Society and Global Environmental Governance*, Albany, NY: State University of New York Press.

Low, Patrick and Alexander Yeats (1992), 'Do "dirty" industries migrate?', World Bank discussion paper no. 159, in P. Low (ed.), *International Trade and the Environment*, Washington, DC: World Bank.

Maizels, A. (1992), *Commodities in Crisis: The Commodity Crisis of the 1980s and the Political Economy of International Commodity Prices*, Oxford: Clarendon Press.

Maizels, A. (1995), 'The functioning of international markets for primary commodities: key policy issues for developing countries,' in UNCTAD (ed.), *International Monetary and Financial Issues for the 1990s: Research Papers for the Group of Twenty-Four*, vol. V, New York and Geneva: United Nations.

Meidinger, Errol E. (2001), 'Environmental certification programs and US environmental law: closer than you may think,' *Environmental Law Reporter*, **31**, 10162–79.

Mol, Arthur P.J. (2001), *Globalization and Environmental Reform: The Ecological Modernization of the Global Economy*, Cambridge, MA: MIT Press.

Muradian, Roldan and Joan Martinez-Alier (2001), 'Trade and the environment: from a "Southern" perspective,' *Ecological Economics*, **36**, 281–97.

Myers, Norman (1993), *Ultimate Security: The Environmental Basis of Political Stability*, New York: Norton.

Neumayer, Eric (2002), 'Do democracies exhibit stronger international environmental commitment? A cross-country analysis,' *Journal of Peace Research*, **39**(2), 139–64.

Opschoor, Johannes B. (1992), 'Sustainable development, the economic process and economic analysis,' in J.B. Opschoor (ed.), *Environment, Economy and Sustainable Development*, Amsterdam: Wolters-Noordhoff, pp. 25–52.

Opschoor, Johannes B. (2001), 'Economic development in a neoliberal world: unsustainable globalization?' in M. Munasinghe, O. Sunkel and C. de Miguel (eds), *The Sustainability of Long-term Growth: Socioeconomic and Ecological Perspectives*, Cheltenham, UK and Northampton, MA, USA: Edward Elgar Publishing, pp. 72–92.

Pargal, Sheoli and David Wheeler (1996), 'Informal regulations in developing countries: evidence from Indonesia,' *Journal of Political Economy*, **104**(6), 1314–27.

Pargal, Sheoli, Hemamala Hettige, Manjula Singh and David Wheeler (1997), 'Formal and informal regulation of industrial pollution: comparative evidence from Indonesia and the United States,' *World Bank Economic Review*, **11**(3), 433–50.

Pastor, Manuel (2003), 'Building social capital to protect natural capital: the quest for environmental justice,' in James K. Boyce and Barry G. Shelley (eds), *Natural Assets: Democratizing Environmental Ownership*, Washington, DC: Island Press, chapter 4.

Pastor, Manuel, Jim Sadd and John Hipp (2001), 'Which came first? Toxic facilities, minority move-in, and environmental justice,' *Journal of Urban Affairs*, **23**, 1–21.

Petrini, Carlo (ed.) (2003), *Slow Food*, New York: Columbia University Press.

Pinderhughes, Raquel (2003), 'Poverty and the environment: the urban agriculture connection,' in James K. Boyce and Barry G. Shelley (eds), *Natural Assets: Democratizing Environmental Ownership*, Washington, DC: Island Press, chapter 16.

Polanyi, Karl (1944 [1957]), *The Great Transformation: The Political and Economic Origins of Our Time*, Boston, MA: Beacon Press.

Porter, Gareth (1999), 'Trade competition and pollution standards: "race to the bottom" or "stuck at the bottom"?' *Journal of Environment and Development*, **8**(2), 133–51.

Princen, Thomas (1997), 'The shading and distancing of commerce: when internalization is not enough,' *Ecological Economics*, **20**, 235–53.

Rauscher, Michael (1994), 'On ecological dumping,' *Oxford Economic Papers*, **46**, 822–40.

Revkin, Andrew C. (2002), 'Climate talks shift focus to deal with changes,' *New York Times*, 3 November, p. 10.

Rich, Richard C., W. David Conn and William L. Owens (1993), '"Indirect regulation" of environmental hazards through the provision of information to the public: the case of SARA, Title III,' *Policy Studies Journal*, **1**(1), 16–34.

Sachs, Wolfgang, Reinhard Loske, Manfred Linz et al. (1998), *Greening the North: Post-industrial Blueprint for Ecology and Equity*, London: Zed.

Scruggs, Lyle A. (1998), 'Political and economic inequality and the environment,' *Ecological Economics*, **26**, 259–75.

Sen, Amartya (1975), *Employment, Technology, and Development*, Oxford: Oxford University Press.

Singh, Ajit and Ann Zammit (2004), 'Labour standards and the "race to the bottom": rethinking globalization and workers' rights from developmental and solidaristic perspectives,' *Oxford Review of Economic Policy*, **20**(1), 85–104.

Sonnenfeld, David A. and Arthur P.J. Mol (2002), 'Globalization and the transformation of environmental governance,' *American Behavioral Scientist*, **45**(9), 1318–39.

Soros, George (2002), 'Transparent corruption,' *Financial Times,* 13 June, p. 21.

Spaargaren, Gert and Arthur P.J. Mol (1992), 'Sociology, environment, and modernity: ecological modernisation as a theory of social change,' *Society and Natural Resources*, **5**, 323–44.

Stewart, Frances (2002), 'Horizontal inequalities: a neglected dimension of development,' Queen Elizabeth House working paper no. 81, Oxford.

Stonich, Susan and Conner Bailey (2000), 'Resisting the blue revolution: contending coalitions surrounding industrial shrimp farming,' *Human Organization*, **59**(1), 23–36.

Stockholm International Peace Research Institute (SIPRI) (1976), *Ecological Consequences of the Second Indochina War*, Stockholm: SIPRI.

Stonich, Susan and Peter Vandergeest (2001), 'Violence, environment, and industrial shrimp farming,' in Michael Watts and Nancy Peluso (eds), *Violent Environments*, Ithaca, NY: Cornell University Press, pp. 261–86.

Sutcliffe, Bob (2003), 'A more or less unequal world? World income distribution in the 20th century,' Political Economy Research Institute working paper no. 54, Amherst, MA.

Sutcliffe, Bob (2004), 'World inequality and globalization,' *Oxford Review of Economic Policy*, **20**(1), 15–37.

Swedish Committee for Afghanistan (1988), *The Agricultural Survey of Afghanistan: First Report*, Peshawar, Pakistan: Swedish Committee for Afghanistan.

Szasz, Andrew and Michael Meuser (1997), 'Environmental inequalities: literature review and proposals for new directions in research and theory,' *Current Sociology*, **45**(3), 99–120.

Tietenberg, Tom and David Wheeler (2000), 'Empowering the community: information strategies for pollution control,' in Henk Folmer, H. Landis Gabel, Shelby Gerking and Adam Rose (eds), *Frontiers of Environmental Economics*, Cheltenham, UK and Northampton, MA, USA: Edward Elgar Publishing, pp. 85–120.

Torras, Mariano and James K. Boyce (1998), 'Income, inequality, and pollution: a reassessment of the environmental Kuznets curve,' *Ecological Economics*, **25**, 147–60, reprinted in Boyce (2002), chapter 5.

UN Secretary-General (1992), *An Agenda for Peace*, report of the Secretary-General, 17 June, New York: United Nations,.

UNICEF (1996), *The State of the World's Children 1996*, New York: UNICEF.

Weale, A. (1992), *The New Politics of Pollution*, Manchester: Manchester University Press.

Weidner, Helmut and Martin Jänicke (2002), 'Environmental capacity building in a converging world,' in H. Weidner and M. Jänicke (eds), *Capacity Building in National Environmental Policy: A Comparative Study of 17 Countries*, Berlin: Springer, pp. 409–43.

Weiner, Tim (2002), 'In corn's cradle, US imports bury family farms,' *New York Times,* 26 February, p. A4.

World Bank (1992), *World Development Report 1992: Development and the Environment*, Oxford: Oxford University Press.

World Bank (1998), *Post-conflict Reconstruction: The Role of the World Bank*, Washington, DC: World Bank.

Young, Oran (1994), *International Governance: Protecting the Environment in a Stateless Society*, Ithaca, NY: Cornell University Press.

Zarsky, Lyuba (1999), 'Havens, halos and spaghetti: untangling the evidence about foreign direct investment and the environment,' in Organisation for Economic Co-operation and Development (OECD) (ed.), *Foreign Direct Investment and the Environment*, Paris: OECD.

Zarsky, Lyuba (2002), 'Stuck in the mud? Nation-states, globalization and the environment,' in Kevin P. Gallagher and Jacob Werksman (eds), *The Earthscan Reader on International Trade and Sustainable Development*, London and Sterling, VA: Earthscan Publications, pp. 19–44.

Name index

Subject index